The Loving Struggle

between God and the Soul

The Loving Struggle
between God and the Soul

in which the triumphs and greatness of love are treated and by which is taught the most excellent way for the affections

(Lucha espiritual y amorosa entre Dios y el alma)

by

Fray Juan de los Angeles
(1532-1609)

*Provincial and Difinidor of the Province of St. Joseph of the Friars Minor
Discalced of the Regular Observance
Guardian of the Convent of St. Bernadino of Madrid*

Dedicated to the same Province, his Mother.

Translated by

Eladia Gómez-Posthill

*Introduced by
Father Jerome Bertram of the Oxford Oratory*

The Saint Austin Press
296, Brockley Road, London, SE4 2RA
MMI

The Saint Austin Press
296, Brockley Road
London, SE4 2RA

Telephone: +44 (0)20 8692 6009
Facsimile: +44 (0)20 8469 3609

Electronic mail: books@saintaustin.org
http://www.saintaustin.org

ISBN 1 901157 26 1

First published in Spanish, Madrid, 1600.

Dedication

To my beautiful daughters, Camilla and Natalia Posthill.
This is what I did, my darlings,
that awful year we were kept apart.

A Marita: Siempre creíste en mí.

*The translator acknowledges the valuable assistance of the Taylor
Institution at Oxford University.*

Typeset and printed by Newton Design & Print Ltd, London, UK
www.newtondp.co.uk

Contents

The Loving Struggle

Part One

Part Two

Preface

In presenting this little treatise to the English-speaking public we are breaking new ground, for as far as I know none of the works of Juan de los Angeles have ever been translated into English before. It is not difficult to understand why, for the school of spirituality represented by him and the other, better known, Spanish mystics was never popular among the English clergy, trained as they were almost exclusively on the Jesuit model. Mystical writings of all kinds were looked on for centuries as rather suspect, and ordinary Catholics were warned away from ever aspiring to contemplative prayer. It was generally taught that only a very few select souls were called to contemplation, and naturally it would be dangerously presumptuous to imagine that one was such a soul. The works of St Teresa were indeed translated by Abraham Woodhead in the middle of the seventeenth century, and St John of the Cross was read, for it was difficult to ignore those whom the Church had raised to the altars, but the writings of one who was never proclaimed a saint could be quietly forgotten.

Only at the beginning of the last century was contemplative prayer offered to the ordinary person, largely owing to the influence of Abbot Chapman. His famous Spiritual Letters stress the importance for every soul to "pray as you can and don't try to pray as you can't", and he introduced a wide circle of readers to the mystical writings of the Catholic Reformation period. In the following decades many spiritual writings were translated or re-issued, from a wide variety of traditions, and the wide richness of the authentic spiritual tradition opened up to an increasing readership. The old "Orchard Books" presented many of these in readable form. No doubt Juan de los Angeles would have appeared many years ago, had that movement continued without interruption. But it is not too late—here is his first appearance, but we may hope it will not be his last.

Juan de los Angeles is associated with the sixteenth-century Spanish mystics, with St Teresa and St John of the Cross, although he was not a Carmelite but a Franciscan Observant friar. He was born in the village of Corchuela in Oropesa, near Toledo, in 1532, and studied at the University of Alcalá. He joined the Friars Minor before 1562, and was a member of the Province of San José, based in Madrid. His life and ministry were spent travelling, as a friar should, preaching, writing and hearing confessions. His first published book was the *Triumphs of the Love of God* (1589), followed by the *Dialogues of the Conquest of the Spiritual and Secret Kingdom of God* in 1593. He continued to write, despite a busy active life. *The Loving Struggle* came out in 1600, followed by the *Spiritual Treatise of the Divine Sacrifice of the Mass* (1604) and the *Manual of Perfect Life* (1608). By far the longest of his works is the *Spiritual Considerations upon the Book of the Song of Songs of Solomon* which he published in 1607. While engaged in these works he held various offices in his Order, being Guardian of the Friary of San Antonio in Guadalajara in 1595, and in 1598 of San Bernardino in Madrid. In 1601 he was elected Provincial, a post which involved much more travelling and administration: his health was already poor, and he had to resign the post due to ill-health in 1603. Though most of his work must have lain among the poor, he was able to be spiritual director to a princess, the Infanta who entered religion under the name of Sor Margarita de la Cruz, and he preached on occasion before the imperial court. These contacts with royalty seem to have provoked some resentment among the friars, who also disapproved of his having resigned the Provincialate: this partly accounts for the obscurity into which his writings fell. He died in Madrid in 1609, having remained active in his pastoral ministry until the end.

At the beginning of the last century he was rediscovered by the "*sapiéntisimo* Menandez Pelayo, who reminded Spain of the existence of this unjustly ignored and forgotten mystic", and arranged for his works to be collected and published in the series *Nueva Biblioteca de Autores Españoles*. The work was entrusted to Fray Jaime Sala, of the Franciscan Province of Valencia, who produced the first volume in 1912, leaving the second to be published in 1917 after his death. Footnotes to the text identified as "Editor's note" are translated from his edition. Footnotes identified as "Honeycomb" are new to this translation. Many of Sala's notes are incomprehensible—we have done our best to expand his cryptic references. In his introduction, which I have just quoted, Fray Jaime complains of the way in which the Franciscans of Spain had neglected Fray Juan de los Angeles: "Why did we allow this to happen? Why did we continue to let posterity believe that Fray Angeles was a prodigal son, concerned only with luxury and riches? I have to repeat here what so many times has been said before, that great men, though they captivate and draw admiration from those of noble heart, awake jealousy and envy in lesser minds."

Publication in Spanish did indeed bring our author before a wider audience, and he was appreciated, though not translated, by the well-known English student of Spanish mysticism, E. Allison Peers. In his Studies on the Spanish Mystics (1927), he writes: "Very practical, experienced and active is Juan de los Angeles: the reverse of a dreamer." He draws attention to the wide range of reading demonstrated in the quotations and allusions which fill his writings, not only Scripture and spiritual writers, but also an impressive range of secular authors, both classical and contemporary. Moreover there is, despite this erudition, a tone which indicates the familiar Franciscan preacher, able to quote homely proverbs and give commonplace examples to explain his meaning to a simple audience.

We have selected the *Lucha espiritual y amorosa* for translation, as a work of profound insight into the spiritual life. It is based on an understanding of the Song of Songs, that marvellous poem which has inspired so many great souls. Like St Bernard and St John of the Cross, our author sees the relationship between the human soul and God as an intense loving encounter, with all the pain as well as joy that a loving relationship brings. His title, and theme, is taken from the wrestling match between Jacob and the angel, seen as a parable of the real struggle which so many earnest souls have in drawing close to God.

God so often seems to hide himself, so often we find prayer dry, empty, frustrating: this is not abnormal, and should not be a source of anxiety, but is something which every serious writer on prayer has to deal with. Our author speaks in passing about the easy moments, when we seem to be filled with ecstatic joy, and may express that in extravagant gesture and sound: it is genuine, he tells us, but superficial; it does not last. At some stage in every spiritual life there are times of struggle, when God seems to hide himself. We are familiar now with the phrase "Dark Night of the Soul", and although Fray Juan does not use that phrase, he is describing the same phenomenon.

Where he is strikingly original, however, is in his teaching about the Blessed Sacrament. Often in spiritual writers we get the impression that they have found an alternative way to God without the benefit of the Sacraments; here we find the mystical union with Christ expressed precisely as a Eucharistic union. He cites the Scriptures to show that Our Lord specifically intended the union of his disciples with himself to be as close as that between him and the Father, and that the means to that union is precisely the sharing in the One Body of Christ in Holy Communion. Ordinary food, he points out, loses its identity and what we eat becomes one with us: in the case of Holy Communion it is we who to some extent lose our identity and become one with what we eat, the Body of Christ. In this way the Church is formed by the Sacrament, and the individual soul is caught up into the divinity of Christ, who humbled himself to share in our humanity. I called this teaching "original" but it is of course profoundly orthodox: it draws on the teaching of the Council of Trent, as well as anticipating the ecclesiology of such modern theologians as Cardinal de Lubac. It is startling, perhaps, because we have become accustomed to a rather diminished teaching on the Blessed Sacrament, as if it were a private devotion, something exclusive between myself and my God, whereas the teaching of the Church has always been that it is the whole Church which forms the Mystical Body of Christ, and it is by our partaking of the Sacramental Body that we become members of the Mystical Body.

We are grateful to Eladia Gómez-Posthill for this translation. She tells me that she has tried to present the author as he would have appeared to his contemporaries, with the occasional roughness of language, surprising colloquialisms and simple diction. We remember he is a wandering friar. He does not always have access to his books, and his many allusions and half-quotations from the Fathers and other authors can be difficult to identify. Certainly many of his Scriptural references are quoted from memory, not exactly as they appear on the page. But he is a scholar: he is aware of variant texts of Scripture, and can quote versions other than the familiar Latin Vulgate. We have tried to identify as many of the quotations as possible, but not all can be precisely located. He did not place too much weight on scholarship, after all: the book ends with the charming story of Brother Giles telling the simple little old grandmothers that if they love God they will be holier than St Bonaventure. Holiness has never been reserved for the learned and the clever: it is the property only of those who struggle to love.

Jerome Bertram.

Approbations for
the original Spanish edition

Fray Andrés de Ocaña, Preacher and Difinidor of the Province of San José, by commission of our Brother Fray Juan de Santa María, Minister General of the same Province, I hereby give faith that I have read the book entitled *Lucha espiritual y amorosa entre Dios y el alma,* written by our Brother Fray Juan de los Angeles, Preacher, Difinidor and Guardian of the Convent of San Bernardino in Madrid, and have found nothing contrary to our Holy Catholic Faith. Moreover, it is a most Catholic book, and one which will prove of great benefit to spiritual persons whilst at the same time reveal the great excellence of understanding that its author has of mystical theology, for the rich abundance in his heart makes itself present through his words. Therefore, it is just that this book be published so that all may gain from such holy study and profitable labour. In testimony whereof I hereby sign my own name.

Convent of the Guardian Angel, Alcalá.
21ˢᵗ day of February of the year 1600.

Licence of the Provincial

Fray Juan de Santa María, Master Provincial[1] of the Province of San José of the Discalced Minors of Regular Observance, etc., to Fray Juan de los Angeles, Preacher and Difinidor of the same Province and Guardian of the San Bernardino Convent of Madrid: health and rejoicing in the Lord.

Based on the just and due approval and endorsement of the book (the title of which is *Lucha espiritual y amorosa*) which Your Charity has written and of which the Religious who, having read and examined it under my commission and instruction, has given, and having read and examined it myself, I conclude that religious persons and everyone desirious to love and please God will gain

---

[1] It should read Minister, for such was his title. I would have corrected this had it not been that it is repeated in his signature and kept also in both places in the second edition of the book in Valencia, 1602. (Editor.)

great benefit from it, for the doctrine contained therein is of such high calibre that hardly anyone who has written of it in our language compares while, at the same time, so easily explained and intelligible that even those with no direct guidance from a spiritual teacher will benefit from it greatly.

Therefore, I hereby give Your Charity licence that, when Your Charity has made all other due diligencies as prescribed by the Holy Council of Trent, and having procured the grant and privilege of the Supreme Council of His Majesty the King, that this book may be printed and published.

In testimony whereof I sign my name, etc.

Fray Juan de Santa María, Master Provincial.
On the 23rd day of February, 1600.

Approbation

By Petition of the Supreme Council I have read the present book which is entitled *Lucha espiritual y amorosa entre Dios y el alma*. It is my judgement that this book, in addition to its vast erudition, contains teachings most appropriate for our times and of great benefit for the spiritual life. Therefore, not only should the author be permitted to publish the aforesaid book, but be instructed to do so.

Fray Juan de la Madre de Dios

Convent of San Hermenegildo de Descalzos del Carmen
The 4th day of the month of March in the year 1600.

Tariff

I, Cristóbal Núñez de León, scribe at the court of His Majesty the King, and as one who is member of his Council, give faith that the whole Council having considered a book which by His Majesty's privilege is printed under the title of *Lucha espiritual y amorosa*, written by Fray Juan de los Angeles, Guardian of the Convent of

San Bernardino of the Order of the Discalced Franciscans of Regular Observance, that each of the thirty-five sections the said book contains be levied the sum of three maravedis, which levy must be displayed clearly at the front of each section.

Therefore, by instruction of the aforesaid members of the Council and on request of Fray Juan de Los Angeles, I hereby give faith and sign my name in the village of Madrid on the 23rd day of June 1600.

Grant and Privilege

Father Juan de los Angeles, Guardian of the Convent of San Bernardino of Madrid, shall have, by permission of His Majesty, a ten-year privilege to publish the book *Lucha espiritual y amorosa*, as granted by the Notification of Cristóbal Núñez de León, and signed by the Secretary, Don Luís de Salazar.

Toledo, on the 19th day of the month of March 1600.

Dedication

Fray Juan de los Angeles, Preacher, etc. to his Mother the Province of San José of the Discalced Friars of Regular Observance, wishing them health and perpetual happiness.

I have been wondering to whom to dedicate this book on a most loving spiritual struggle hoping that it would befit and be of benefit to this person, and although I could think of many had its subject matter been different, being what it is, I have hardly found one. Because when I consider the cowardice and effeminate spirit this century of ours has produced (which seems to me to be the one that first came up with that mandate of Pharaoh that males be killed and females spared), I am left not knowing with whom to treat of this divine militia, one which allows only for vigorous and skilful soldiers to be admitted to its ranks. Especially since the Holy Spirit warns us in no unclear terms not to treat of war with the coward.[1] Noteworthy, to be sure, that when Solomon describes in his *Songs* the most chaste love between Christ and his Church, second only to the names of *Spouse* and *Beloved* the words he uses most are those that refer to instruments of war, armies, valiant soldiers, fortresses and all manner of armoury. In chapter 3 he says: *Behold, threescore valiant ones of the most valiant of Israel surrounded the bed of Solomon, all holding swords, and most expert in war.*[2] In chapter 4: *Thy neck is as the tower of David, which is built with bulwarks: a thousand bucklers hang upon it, all the armour of valiant men .*[3] In chapter 1: *To my company of horsemen, in Pharaoh's chariots, have I likened thee, O my love .*[4] In chapter 6: *Thou art beautiful, O my love,*

---

[1] *Treat not with a man without religion concerning holiness, nor with an unjust man concerning justice, not with a woman touching her of whom she is jealous, not with a coward concerning war, nor with a merchant concerning traffic, nor with a buyer of selling, nor with an envious man of giving thanks, nor with the ungodly of piety, nor with the dishonest of honesty, nor with the field labourer of every work, nor with him that worketh by the year of the finishing of the year, nor with the idle servant of much business, give no heed to these in any matter of counsel, but be continuously with a holy man, whomsoever thou shalt know to obseve the fear of God whose soul is according to thy own soul: and who, when thou stumble in the dark will be sorry for thee* (Ecclus. 37:12-15).

[2] *Lectulum Salomonis, sexaginta fortes ambiunt, ex fortissimis Israel, omnes tenentes gladios, et ad bella doctissimi* (Cant. 3:7-8).

[3] *Sicut turris David collum tuum, quae aedificata est, cum propugnaculis, mille clipei pendent ex ea, cum propugnaculis, mille clipei pendent ex ea, omnis armatura fortium* (Cant. 4:4).

[4] *Equitatui meo, in curribus Pharaonis, assimilavi te, amica mea* (Cant. 1:8).

sweet and comely as Jerusalem; terrible as an army set in array.[5] And in chapter 7, the maidens having asked the spouse to turn her countenance towards them that they may rejoice in her beauty, she answers: *What shalt thou see in the Sulamitess but the company of camps?*[6] For such was not the time to treat of matters proper of women and gallants but of arms and men of war. It is not of my beauty that I pride myself but of my bravery; not my look but my sword, and fighting and dying for my Spouse in the challenge that concerns me. And in chapter 8: *If our spouse be a wall, let us mount cannon on it against her enemies.*[7] Ultimately what we have here is a combat, a war of love, in which the delicate and effeminate are cast aside and the only ones welcome are brave, courageous men, robust men, men with hair on their chests, well trained in the art of war. Because if we are to struggle with our passions, if we are to struggle against self-love, against our libertine self-will, against the never-ending lust of this world for prestige and possessions and pleasures, and what concerns me in this book specifically, if we are to struggle with God himself, and wound him in love, and capture him, and suffer his injuries, his chains, his afflictions, his transformations, his inebriations and his deaths, necessary it is that we be brave, that we be like the cavalry or the squadrons of Pharaoh, insurmountable; that we be like the tower of David with its camps, fortifications, shields, and brave soldiers' armoury; that we be terrible as that army of soldiers in array ready for battle, if we are to assist at the couch of our great Solomon and keep watch at his sleep, that we be of the gritty and spirited of Jerusalem, and our sword at the ready be most skilful in warfare, especially that brought about by devils in the night; that we be like a walled and formidable fortress against sin.

And where am I to find one of these valiant soldiers with whom to speak of this war, ruling Pharaoh in the world, and having planned and designed that men die and women live? I have sometimes reflected on that law in Exodus where Moses ordains that all first-born male offspring, of men as well as of beasts, be

---

[5] *Pulchra es et suavis, et decora nimis, terribilis, ut castrorum acies ordinata* (Cant. 6:3). Fray Juan forgot the words *O my love* and *as Jerusalem* and adds *nimis* after *decora* which are not in the Vulgate (Editor).

[6] *Quid videbis in sulamite, nisi choros castrorum?* (Cant. 7:1).

[7] *Si murus est, aedificemus super eam propugnacula argentea* (Cant. 8:9).

offered to God and that which is female be excepted, be they first- or only-born,[8] and it occurs to me that women were excluded, not because of their being women, but because of what *the feminine* signifies: the weak and the flaccid, the fickle, that which lacks valour and distinction, what God dismisses from his house and holy temple. And as punishment for their grave sins Isaiah says that God will take away from the House of Judah and from Jerusalem the brave, the strong, men of war, and give them child-kings and child-princes and effeminate and pampered leaders, those raised amidst fine linens, silks and cotton wool.[9] Of these said Solomon: *Fear casteth down the slothful, and the soul of the effeminate shall be hungry. He that is loose and slack in his work is the brother of him that wasteth his own works.*[10] Not only do the lazy and the licentious not engage in manly works, they are also like those who go around wrecking what has already been built, brothers of the squanderer and the loose. I am saying that the spirit of that Law of Moses was to condemn and exclude from the temple of God and of his service the effeminate, the fond-of-ease, the spoiled, men who can't suffer a sneeze for God. Of these the world is full. Most men these days are dolls, womanish, flaccid and weak, lacking in virtue and lacking in manhood. Like women, they rouge and powder themselves and call to be carried around in litters; they admire and beautify themselves in front of mirrors, and pretty soon they'll be wearing plumicorns and pompadours and bows and sashes at the waist, the sword too heavy for their delicate frames; and Cavalry and Armour and Struggle and Discipline are, to them, villages in France. We are now living in that most unhappy and most dangerous of times of which the Apostle said that men would come to fall in love with themselves, like Narcissus, and of which Plato spoke as being the source of all the

---

[8] *And the Lord spoke to Moses, saying: Sanctify unto me every first-born that openeth the womb among the children of Israel, as well of men as of beasts, for they are all mine… Whatsoever thou shalt have of the male sex thou shalt consecrate to the Lord* (Exodus 13:1, 12).

[9] *For behold, the sovereign, the Lord of hosts, shall take away from Jerusalem and from Juda the valiant and the strong, the whole strength of bread, and the whole strength of water. The strong man and the man of war, the judge and the prophet, and the cunning man and the ancient; the captain over fifty and the honourable in countenance, and the counsellor and the architect, and the skilful in eloquent speech, and I will give children to be their princes, and the effeminate shall rule over them* (Isaiah 3:1-4).

[10] *Animae effeminatorum esurient, et qui mollis, et dissolutus est in opere suo, frater est sua opera dissipantis* (Prov. 18:8-9).

evils that could befall the world. As did Aristotle who said it was the most infamous name that could be applied to men. *Erunt homines se ipsos amantes.* Puffed-up and in love with themselves, concerned only with their comforts, their caprices and delectations; their self-gratification, their own-keeping and self-interest. And the Apostle goes on to give a long litany of the evils that follow from this: *Cupidi, elati, blasphemi, parentibus non obedientes, ingrati, scelesti, sine affectione, sine faedere, sine pace, immites, incontinentes, sine benignitate, proditores, protervi, et voluptatum amatores magis quam Dei.*[11] Look at this sad progeny of wicked children sired by self-love and see what will be needed to take to the field and do battle with them. Not the thirty thousand that Gideon would take with him to fight the Midianites[12] but the three hundred that remained by God's command, excluded and rejected the timid and faint-hearted, the frivolous, those who, to drink, would lay themselves down, the effeminate in spirit. How would Jeremiah cry in his *Lamentations* this lack of valiant men! *The noble sons of Sion and they that were clothed with the best gold: how are they esteemed as earthen vessels, the work of the potter's hand.*[13]

At one time those chosen, those dressed in gold from Ophir, were men who would pass through furnaces of fire and teeth of beasts, and after enduring crosses and swords and racks of iron were left yet more pure and transparent; now we have pots of clay breaking at the slightest jolt. To those who would allow themselves to be sliced and slivered and thrown to the flames for refusing to burn but one single grain of incense to the idols have now succeeded – oh, vessels so fragile – men who for no reason

---

[11] *Know also this, that in the last days shall come dangerous times. Men shall be lovers of themselves, covetous, haughty, proud, blasphemers, disobedient to parents, ungrateful, wicked, without affection, without peace, slanderers, incontinent, unmerciful, without kindness, traitors, stubborn, puffed-up, and lovers of pleasures more than of God* (II Tim. 3:1-4).

[12] *And when the people were come down to the waters, the Lord said to Gedeon: They that shall lap the water with their tongues, as dogs are wont to lap, thou shalt set apart by themselves. But they that shall drink bowing down their knees shall be on the other side. And the number of them that had lapped water, casting it with their hand to their mouth, was three hundred men: and all the rest of the multitude had drunk kneeling. And the Lord said to Gedeon: By the three hundred men that lapped water I will save you and deliver Madian into thy hand* (Judges, 7:5-7). *hat lapped water.* These were preferred that took the water up in their hands, as lapped it, before them who laid themselves quite down to the waters to drink: which argued a more eager and sensual disposition.

[13] *Filii Sion incliti, et amicti auro obrizo, quomodo facti sunt in vasa testa, opus manuum figuli* (Lamen. 4:2).

commit a thousand sins! These are not made for this war of love which demands vigorous, courageous, spirited soldiers willing to put all their passions to the sword, those who have overpowered the world and trampled over its greed and self indulgence, men who have gone through the purgative life for many a year, progressed favourably in the illuminative life and aspire to a most loving union with God. For these I am writing, these I seek for this combat.

And having with great care and diligence pondered over this, I have found none, to whom I should dedicate this work with more reason than to my own Province of Saint Joseph, among all in our Holy Religion a most religious, most penitent and most recollected Province, and well occupied in the exercise of prayer and contemplation. For whom shall I serve but my Mother, she who reared and nurtured me and gave me the life I have? She it was who taught me almost from the beginning; I suckled at her breast, none other's, and though I wish to serve her in greater endeavours, should God will to favour my intention, I would deem this book to be of no small service because her children, desirous as they are of perfection, will have need of no other. It treats of what they treat, not confusedly but imaginatively, and with the light they already have with little toil will become adept in this divine struggle. With it they will learn to love, they will live the effects and gifts of that love, will come to know its power, enjoy its rewards, will walk without stumbling and, as St. Bonaventure says, fly to divine union.

Receive, most dear Mother, my joy and my crown, the small gift that this humble and faithful son offers you. Do not think little of my wish, which is only to add honour to you, my own only in that I am of you (though you have already enough to impart it to all your children), that by this means God be honoured and praised by all. What I fervently ask of the Masters is to keep it in mind, to read and discuss it with the novices that they may profit in the love of God, and also for them to engage in spiritual conversation and understand, when read, the books of Dionysius, St. Bonaventure in his *Mystical Theology*, Blosius and Ruysbroeck, and the other Fathers who have, with great hardship, written on these matters. *Valete et orate pro me, fratre vestro addictissimo.*

Introduction

Declares the Intention of the Author in this Work

Laertius tells us[1] that when an inquiring listener asked Zeno why all philosophers' sayings were too brief, as if disapproving of brevity, he replied: *You speak truly and, if it were possible, so should all utterances be. Because truth is not in need of many words, and we remember better what is concise and to the point.*

Epictetus, as Gellius relates[2] used to sum up and embrace all of philosophy in only two words: *Sustine et abstine,* for a true philosopher accepts all sorrows and abstains from all joys, which offer themselves in equal abundance; neither does he lose heart in adversity nor does he degenerate in prosperity.

The Spartans were great lovers of brevity. When Liturcus was asked the reason for this he said: *Quia silentio finitimum,* meaning that, after silence, the next best thing is abbreviation.

A few years ago I wrote a book entitled *Triumphs of the love of God,* but the difficulty of the subject made me go on and on, adding reasons to reasons and words to more words, and the work grew more than it should have done. Treating, as it does, of an art that teaches the highest path the affections should follow, which Dionysius termed *Mystical Theology,* it is appropriate that a book on this subject should be brief and its precepts few and substantial, even though so-called common people may not understand it. This is because, to speak truly, this doctrine is not for everyone; it is for those who have already been through the exercises of the purgative and illuminative life, for which many long-winded treatises already abound.

Later, with this in mind, and wishing to imitate the Spartans who would not say with words what they could say with silence I determined, having first commended my work to God, and having consulted religious and spiritual leaders, to work for a few days and try to see if I could cut out the superfluous, clarify the obscure, substantiate the uncertain, and to remove passages difficult even for scholars to follow.

---

[1] Diogenes Laertius, *Lives of the Philosophers,* 7, 1.
[2] Aulus Gellius, *Noctes Atticae,* 17, 19.

Because of this, I think I can now say that, although no new chapters have been added, what has emerged is an altogether new book, both in quality and brevity. That is why I changed the title to *The spiritual and loving struggle between God and the soul*, because our spiritual life really is a loving struggle where pure souls come to wrestle with God through the affections: love's holds and throws.

Receive, then, Catholic reader, my good wishes and trust me in this: that no other book will you read that will prove more beneficial or more suitable for reaching the perfect state of the contemplative life. You will find other works that will entertain your weary soul with their elegance, rolling inferences, curiosities, and variety. By the ensuing change in your conduct will we see of how much benefit they have been.

I have seen many people lauding and celebrating these books all the way up to heaven (always the same people, by the way) but all they seem to serve for is recreation, like those elegant, most eloquent sermons people like to hear, after which they come out of church exactly as they went in.

But in this book about the divine art of loving, should you read it with the aim of attaining that love and apply yourself as a student does to the study of grammar, I assure you of its profitability and that, before long, you will find yourself a changed person because, as you will see, you will attain more benefit in one day through this exercise of love than in many months, or perhaps years, in others.

May God grant you the knowledge of the truth of His sacred love, the ointment that, as Jesus says in his Gospel, teaches all things.

Part the First

Chapter 1

Concerning love and its many manifestations, with special emphasis on ecstatic and fruitful love of which we make special mention in this chapter

Of all the passions of the soul, which are many, none is more fervent, none more powerful, none more ecstatic and none more captivating than love. Love has been classified in so many ways one can hardly account for them all, every writer naming each of its manifestations differently.

Some divide love as follows:

Love of Kinship: love that exists between parents and children, or the gratitude we feel towards those who have in some way favoured us.

Love Patriotic: love of a citizen towards his country or community which at times, St. Augustine says,[1] can be so deeply felt as to exceed parental and filial love; as was shown by Marcus Brutus who killed his son because he had broken a law passed in favour of the Republic.

Love Social: we love those we know more than those we have never met.

Love Conjugal: private and most intimate; it can also be greater than that felt for parents.

Love Carnal: which feeds itself upon the delights of the flesh, and this against the counsel of the Apostle who said *walk in the Spirit and do not lower yourselves to do works of carnal love*,[2] for carnal love will induce and provoke man to many a lascivious and mindless deed.

Finally, *Love of Neighbour*, or of any act of creation: a moral obligation by which we are to love all of God's handiwork, for every creature is part of his creation and he is pleased with all, and displeased with none.

Others describe love differently.

---

[1] St. Augustine, *De Civitate Dei*, Book VI.
[2] *Spiritu ambulate et desideria carnis non perficietis* (Gal. 5:16).

Love of Concupiscence: the wish of the lover to be with the beloved. Concupiscent love can also be expressed in a distorted and perverted way, for concupiscence means to desire something only by what one is to gain from it, a love found in brutes, who love their benefactor merely for what they can get out of him.

Love of Benevolence: to want the best for others, genuinely and candidly, be it now or at some future time; to rejoice in their present joy and to wish them well in their future endeavours.

Love of Beneficence: the sharing of one's good fortune with those one loves, for all is shared among good friends.

Love of Harmony: most befitting to those who love each other well, at least as far as daily living is concerned. This need not apply, of course, to relationships of a professional nature, that is to say, to scientific investigation, speculation, or discursive exchanges. There is room for opposing parties to confront one another in the battle of ideas without detriment to friendship, however great that confrontation may be. Indeed, controversy in this context is not altogether undesirable, for knowledge and understanding advance by means of vigorous disagreement and thought-provoking debate.

Still others classify love thus: *Liking, Friendship, Charity*, and *True Love*, or *Loving Passionately* (I do not know which word best defines this impelling force to love one particular person and not another in this way). Each of these four classifications adds its own particularity to what we mean when we say love.

Let us take *Liking* first. To love something, or someone, appeases the sentient, that is, the animal, as well as the intellectual, that is, the rational, appetites. The same word, love, can therefore be applied to both. In animal desire, this impulse to love someone is properly called *attraction* or *instinctual love* and is common to both men and beasts; as for rational desire, on the other hand, the act of loving someone is not impulsive but conscious and selective, exercised by the will and abated only when choosing what one wishes to like, hence more correctly called *liking*. What we have here, then, is that *liking* is superior to *impulse*, or *attraction*, for *liking* proceeds from the will, that is, from man's rational nature, and is, therefore, not found in brutes, who can neither choose nor rationalise. We agree, then, that man can love in both these ways: by *liking,* obviously a conscious act founded on the rational nature of man, as has been said, and also by that passion felt by one person for another brought about by the sentient appetite. Granted, this sensuous appetite may not be altogether sensible (whoever heard of couples madly attracted to one another ever listening to reason!) and, indeed, it may not last long but – can we agree? – it is a *liking* of sorts nevertheless. What is evident is that all *liking* is *to like,* but *to like* is not necessarily *liking.* The lesser can fit into the greater, the contrary cannot be.

The second name that also means love but adds something additional to its meaning is *Friendship.* Friendship means reciprocal, mutual love, and is founded in virtue. As the Philosopher writes: *friendship is to love well;* and to love well is to love uprightly and openly (for true love cannot be disguised), and to love innocently and honestly, and not as a means to an end.

The third name is *Charity.* This love includes everything we have said so far but also brings to the meaning of love an additional, supernatural, quality that makes the one who professes it pleasing to the eyes of God and commends him for eternal life. His other good works, the fruits of other virtues' seeds, become even more excellent now, for this capacity to give of oneself for others is not all of our own making, and we do not possess it solely on account of our own industry. This great virtue is a grace from God.

The fourth name given is *True Love* or *Loving Passionately.* What it brings to love is intensity and ardour, as one can hardly fail to notice in those lovey-dovey sweethearts the world over. It is here, in this last aspect of the word *love* that we find *liking, friendship, and charity.* That is why Aristotle said that friendship is similar to habit, but this impetuous love is similar to passion, as if he had said: the former follows reason, the latter, impulse.

Others divide love into *Good* and *Evil,* a division favoured by St. Augustine when he spoke of two loves building two opposing cities: one divine, the other infernal. The construction of the city of God is built upon one foundation: disdain and disregard of self; the construction of that of the devil upon disdain and disregard for God. *Good* is the prince of all virtues, *evil,* the prince among vices. Or to put it plainly, virtue is love of good and wickedness is

3

love of evil (but I shall speak in detail about this matter on the chapter *On Love of Self*, so let us now move on to yet another classification).

There is a fifth division that distinguishes between *Natural, Animal, Rational* and *Intellectual Love*. I am not going to spend any time explaining this one, reader, because it is all way up there in the stratosphere of metaphysics and, quite frankly, too difficult for most of us to make head or tail of.

But Gerson, in his commentaries on the Song of Songs[3] classifies love into *Free, Optional, Gracious* and *Fruitful* and explains that habitual, or ordinary, love can be observed in rational creatures, first, in three different ways: love *free and co-created*; love *optional and deliberate*, and love *gracious and infused* from above. Of the unity of this trinity of loves, another most perfect and meritorious love flows forth: it is called *living, fruitful love*.

Let us see how this categorization can be applied in the context of love of God.

Love of God is *free* and *natural*. This love cannot be erased from the soul of man because it is imprinted there, it is co-created, it is a love implanted in man who was created in the image of God, an image of consciousness, intelligence, and love. A rational creature is not capable of stripping himself of his own sense of awareness or understanding nor is he able to rid himself of his capacity to love, a faculty by means of which he will come to God and taste him as the greatest good, as the ultimate joy. St. Bonaventure says[4] that this hunger, this thirst for good and for truth is inborn in man, that we are all aware of it in a general sense but lack sufficient depth to discern what this goodness really is with any specificity, nor will we ever be able to do so unless with the help of God. Dionysius, also, came to say that natural love lives in all of us and that the soul, under its weight, leans naturally towards God, even when busy on its way to hell. Hence that worm the holy prophet Isaiah spoke of when he said: *their worm does not die*.[5] And what is that worm, I ask, but remorse, pure and

---

[3] Jean Gerson (1363-1429), *Trilogium animae,* pt. 2, chap. 14.
[4] St. Bonaventure, *Commentary on the Sentences,* II, 28.
[5] Editor's note: From St. Mark's Gospel 9:45. Isaiah's prophecy speaks in the future tense: *non morietur,* 66:24.

simple, a remorse that does not die but stays in the soul because God is there, present in the soul of man whether man wants to accept him or not, remorse for going against the grain of the soul's natural inclination? This is, then, what is meant by love of God being *natural*; natural, not in the sense of force pulling all particles of a stone towards its centre (which might more appropriately be called propensity) but natural in the sense of being autonomous and free, because our rational nature insists on looking up, on aspiring to things higher than ourselves, recognising God as our only goal and ultimate end.

Love of God is *optional* or *deliberate*. It cannot exist unless *natural* love, the root of all other affections, is already active. We are all capable of it, for this intentional love, which originates in our will and capacity to choose, can be found in all: the blessed, the damned and everyone else in between, although in different degrees, of course. In the blessed, this love is established and led by the affective faculty of the soul, while in the wicked, it stoops down to hate and envy of God. For the rest of us, pilgrims, it can go either way because while here in exile, we have been given the freedom to love or to hate God. And when I say 'hate', I am not using the word exclusively and in an absolute sense; I am also including in it all those insulting reasons and offensive excuses for loving him such as, for example, being afraid of punishment or damnation.

Love of God is *gracious, supernatural* and *infused*; by another name we call it *charity*. It is created in the soul, which formally turns the consenting man to God and is acceptable for eternal life.

Love of God is a living love, *fruitful, ecstatic* and *seraphic* and consists in a felt and experienced taste of an inner delight which stems from the intercourse between the soul and the ultimate object of love: God himself. This living, fruitful love is the culmination of the three habitual forms of love already mentioned, a threefold love that, having reached its pinnacle, now moves to a higher plane, more laudable than if it had remained below in any of its three separate forms, for any faculty, when in union with its good and laudable level, is more perfect and more in affinity with its goal than if it had persevered only in the lower, more tepid, sleepy and soporific habit. The Philosopher

5

compared the first, habitual level of love to sleep,[6] and the second, the living love, to wakefulness. This fruitful and seraphic love is not based on our senses, but on the summit, the superior part of our mind to which the spouse in the Song of Songs refers calling it *a kiss from the lips of God*. Trustingly, she will ask of him: *Kiss me with the kiss of your mouth*,[7] as if to say: Grant me, Lord, the taste of your ecstatic, fruitful, seraphic love so that, like a seraph, I may burn in it away from all things of earth.

Hugh of St. Victor calls this love *the life of the soul* and, leaving aside other divisions, such as those made by St. Bonaventure in his *Paths to Eternity*[8], we shall speak later of the characteristics and marvellous effects this love brings with it. That divine book, the Song of Songs, was written expressly for this purpose, to explain by metaphor, simile and images of weddings, betrothed and spouses, the favours with which God will reward the soul and the gifts she receives whilst in amorous conversation with him.

It was as an attempt to explain love such as this, so easily misunderstood by many, that the present book was written.

---

[6] Aristotle, *de Anima*, 2.

[7] Cant. 1:1.

[8] Editor's note: This work, *Septem itineribus eternitatis* is not admitted as authentic by the Quaracchi Fathers who, with Benelli, tend to think it is the work of Fr. Rodulfo de Bibraco, because in the 80 codices which include it, it is either anonymous or under the name of another Religious, save in one case where it is attributed to Enrique Trinacria. See *Discourse 1 of the T.X. Opera Omnia, D. Bonaventurae*, Ad claras Aquas, Prope Florentiam, 1902, pgs. 1-39.

Chapter 2

Concerning the principal quality of love, which is the power to convert itself into the object of its love.

All of the manifold and noble qualities of love to which I shall be referring, all of its accomplishments and all of its triumphs are founded, and spring from, one main and principal quality. This quality is to join, fuse, and transform the lover into the nature of the object of his love.[1] This can be confirmed, if more proof than daily experience be needed, by examining the very nature of love itself which, to all who have written about it, is its main and principal attribute, a gift which is communicable and free. What I am saying is that the intrinsic nature of love, its very reason for being, is to communicate itself to the beloved, not by asserting itself forcibly (for that would not be love) but by the giving of itself voluntarily, lavishly. When love, with free will treading closely on its footsteps, is truly given and imparted in this way, it becomes the personal property of the person to whom it is given; free will, like a lady forever inspiring men in her pursuit, and like the first spark which enkindles all the rest. *My love is my weight*, said St. Augustine. From this it follows that love and free will transform themselves into that which they love: lover and beloved becoming one because of this intrinsic characteristic of love. This transformation is not automatic, nor is this union forced; it is not a burden, but something freely and voluntarily given, innocent and joyous, and so powerful, so direct that no force can bend it: love and free will, voluntarily communicating with each other, undeviating in their nature, unhindered as to their target, subordinating themselves to the jurisdiction of the beloved. St. Paul, despite all he had already done for the love of Christ, was willing to soldier on, to lay himself open to hunger, nakedness, the sword (in terms of allowing himself to be killed), persecution and death, and would disregard all these trials as insignificant. *What can possibly separate us from the charity of God?* he asked. [2] As if he had

---

[1] Plato, *Symposium.*
[2] Rom. 8.

said with Chrysostom: *the impossible will be made possible before the intimate friendship I have with Christ be undone.* St. Augustine said: *Tyrants were able to take the lives of martyrs, but not their love or their will. Those had already been offered to God.*

Briefly, what we have here is that love and will are free, and both will and love, in the act of loving, transform themselves into that which they love: they dress in its garments, call themselves by its name and, by so partaking of its nature, become what they love. Thus said God through the prophet Hosea speaking about his idolatrous people: *They were made abominable, as the things they loved.*[3] And St. Paul said: *He who comes to God through love makes himself one spirit with him,* agreeing with what the philosopher Evantes said of man: *He is an animal of an imprecise nature, he has no figure of his own but many strange and foreign ones because, through the power of love, he becomes that which he loves.* If man loves earth, he becomes *earthly*; if he loves heaven, *divine*; and, ultimately, he will have as much nobleness as the object of his love is noble.

The only thing that our will acknowledges as superior to itself is the supremacy of God. Consequently, since we become what we love, when the chief object of the love of man is not God, he becomes inferior to himself, and loses his dignity. Only by loving God above all else does man ascend above himself, improve himself, and surpass any other creature in as much as his love is excelled. This is the only way in which our love and our will can be well employed, even if we were to get nothing in return; the Book of Wisdom says *He loves the one who loves Him*,[4] and when you love something that cannot requite your love, among other injuries, you will incur these two: first, you will become base and carnal: you will be of this world, and your nature, excellence and dignity will degenerate. This is because, as I have said, you become what you love, and if your first love is for things of the world you will become worldly, in other words, less than you are. Creatures inferior to man have neither will nor generous love to give those who love them, as it is written.[5] To vanity, which is man, every creature is subject, not because man so desires it, but

---

[3] Hosea 7.
[4] Wisdom 8.
[5] Rom. 8; Psalm 38.

because it was the will of God who bestowed this gift to man in the hope of seeing him free from that harsh servitude; for servitude it is, and a most harsh one, to be in the service of vainglorious sinners.

O heart, says St. Bonaventure, heart not of flesh but of iron and stone: how can you not kindle in the love of that Lord who everywhere has so obliged you to his love? Please, God, let my heart be of stone and not of flesh! A stone with heat may become metal, iron becomes malleable when it melts; but this heart made of flesh, amidst so many blazes flaring up in the fire of charity, stubbornly persists against reason in this frozen, hard, and cold self. You, Lord, promised through the prophet that you would take from us these hearts of stone and give us back hearts of flesh instead, to write your law upon them. And if this Word has not been fulfilled in mine because of my sins, I confess I would prefer to have a rock for a heart! A stone can be worked, it can be moulded, it can change, but this rock made of flesh that I have for a heart remains hard and unyielding.

Oh if only God wished, says St. Bonaventure, that hearts were rocks rather than flesh! Because is there anything more astonishing and, equally, more worthy of reproach, than for rational creatures to pride themselves in having hearts more insensitive and more intractable than stones?

O most hardened heart! Why do you not love with all your might Him who loves you so mightily? O most cruel heart! Why don't you abhor yourself for being the cause of His death? O most wicked heart! Why don't you offer yourself to Him who seeks you with such solicitude? Why don't you open yourself to Him who insistently calls you night and day? Why don't you gratefully embrace the one who, being Lord of all heavens, seeks his delectation in you? O heartless stone! Oh Weep, I beseech you, for the callousness of my heart. Because, my dear Lord, you alone are my God, you alone my Protector and my Saviour. Even if you were to despise me I would owe you my unconditional love; and with so much more reason, loving me as you do with such unfailing love. You, the Creator, wanting to die for me, most ungrateful creature; you, God himself, dying for this insignificance, this son of clay, this grandson of nothingness; you,

Father, dying for this son, unworthy of your name. Being Lord you died for me, your run-away servant; being teacher, for me, your undisciplined disciple; being pure, for me, soiled as I am; being holy, for me, sinner and wretched. What more could you have done? what more can I possibly expect you to do? Had the most villainous, uncouth brigand done as much, would I not be obliged to love him forever with all my heart? So why cannot I bring myself to love you, my Lord? Please, don't let me continue on like this, tear this indifference out of my soul, I beg you, loosen this bond I have for things of the world so that I may love only you. May I have no sense or faculty left in me that I may not dedicate to loving you.

Chapter 3

Of how love extends to everything the beloved loves and how the soul benefits in her transformation in God.

Many are the doctrines derived from the perfect union and transformation that love causes between the lover and that which he principally loves. One of them is that neither love, nor will, can go beyond or be greater than the object of one's love, but do reach and extend to everything the beloved loves. And the more common and universal the object of love is, the more common and universal love and will are; and the more narrow and specific, the more narrow and specific will love and will become. And since the thing we love most can only be but one, only one principally loved thing can there be in man, and this will be of the condition and nature of the thing loved because it nourishes itself on it and transforms itself in it. It is the object of one's love that bases and establishes the primary love in our will, and this love is the root and origin of all other loves and affections that are born from it. As a seed begets many seeds, all of the condition and nature of the begetter, so from this primary love many other loves are born, in nothing dissimilar or divergent from it. Because as roots are, so the fruits that grow and sustain themselves from them tend to be.

In this way, if the first and principal love is good, just, and orderly, those that proceeded from it will be just, orderly, and good. Truly, there cannot be in one will more than one love, because that which is most loved cannot but be one. But we speak of many loves because of the diversity of its manifestations, and we speak of one because it is the root, because all other things loved are loved in virtue of this first love, and all of them are connected and subordinated to it. This primary love is so powerful that it obliges and forces us to love everything it touches and everything it loves, and to abhor that which it abhors and is contrary to it.

Since it is the case, then, that all honour, fortitude, virtue and limitation are born in the lover from that which he principally loves (if that be powerful, he will be powerful, if noble, noble; if virtuous, virtuous; if one, one; if universal, universal), it follows that the more powerful, noble, virtuous, one, and universal the object of one love is, so will he be who is joined to and transformed in it. And because God is All-powerful, Almighty, Most Virtuous, Infinitely Good, One only, and Most Simple, if he were the primary object of our love, and our will were joined to him through our first and principal love, of necessity this union would be most powerful, mighty, virtuous, and one. And because this Lord who is the primary object of our love is Most Common and Most Universal to all things, reaching and engulfing all for he is Lord of all, from such love, since it is first and primary, infinite other loves are born with which all creatures are loved, for God loves all.

This is why St. John said, *He is a liar who says, 'I love God' whilst hating his brother.*[1] And St. Gregory gives us the reason, explaining that it cannot be that I love God and do not love what God wants me to love, not because it is mine, but as has been shown, because it is of the primary and principal love. Since it is the will of God, then, that I love my neighbour, even if he is my enemy, if I hate him while saying I love God, I am a liar and truth is not on my lips. Especially since this is an explicit commandment of God, that whosoever considers himself his friend must love his neighbour, enemy though he might be. And it is not possible for God to be what we most love and not to love all that he loves and wants us to love, and to abhor all he abhors and wants us to abhor.

Oh, with what care should a man avoid having an earthly creature as his first and primary love! Because a love based on so flimsy a foundation will have no firmness, nor will it be able to extend itself to its Creator, but only secondarily, through an intermediary, only in relation to this other creature. And the mundane will occupy the place reserved for God, for the true God will be loved only as secondary to it, which is the cause of all misery and evil in the world.

---

[1] *If any man says I love God and hateth his brother, he is a liar. For he that loveth not his brother whom he seeth, how can he love God whom he seeth not?* (I John 4:20).

So that this can be better understood I shall give a rather pedestrian example but very much to the point, I think, that illustrates well the essence and nature of love and that which is principally loved.

I will say, then, that the will of the lover with respect to the thing loved, is like that of a woman with respect to her husband after she has voluntarily joined herself to him in marriage, never to be divided save in death; the wife, I say, is subject to her husband; she obeys him and accepts his governance; and the husband is master and has superiority and dominion over her. And the parallelism between the lover and the wife, and the thing loved and the husband is in such accordance, that just as the wife is exalted or debased according to her husband's standing, so does the will uplift or lower itself in accordance to that which it principally loves.

Let us say that a rustic or peasant had three daughters, all of the same standing, equal in lineage, honour, dignity, and beauty, and that he marries off all three—one to a rustic like himself, another to a king, and the third to an emperor. It is clear that though they were all equal by nature, and none more honourable, more powerful, or richer than the others, after marriage they are very dissimilar indeed, dissimilar according to their husbands' dissimilarity, to whom they are joined. The one who married a rustic remains a rustic; the one who married a king will become queen; the one who married an emperor is made an empress. So we see that woman is altered by man, and it is with regard to him that she is identified, defined, and determined. And so it is with my will and yours, and that of all men; for being, as they are, all equal in honour, as all souls are from their creation and natural existence, they are defined and determined according to the varied things we love. Because the will, as I have said, relates to the position of the female, and the thing loved to that of the male.

I do have the freedom to increase or decrease the carats of the gold I am made of according to the things I principally love, as well as the obligation to give thanks to the Lord who granted such liberty to this vile man, this son of dust, this grandson of nothingness, and enabled him to choose for himself whether from the beastly he wants to become spiritual, from the human, angelic, from the earthly, celestial and divine.[2]

How can we not love you, Lord, if only to attain such honour? Is there a woman who would not want to join with a rich, powerful, prudent, noble, and good husband and share with him riches, power, happiness and comfort? O how much peace, how much certainty, how much joy, how much repose and abundance have the souls whose husband you are! For as you are rich, they do not suffer want; as you are sure, they do not feel uncertainty; as you are most powerful, nothing can tear them down; as you are most faithful, they are free from all worry; and they will never fear losing you because you are infinite and eternal. Truly, you are my God. You are in need of no one, you lack nothing, and the soul who truly loves you can never be in want.

A great good it would be for you, my soul, to have God as your primary love, and an intolerable misery to attach yourself, to join and be transformed into any of the many creatures, because all are afflicted, fickle, needy and poor. Your wretched will has to endure and suffer all their miseries and what is worse, you have to love everything your principal love loves, for without them your loved one cannot remain so. And since they are all short-lived, transient and futile, your will must grow weary and old, and you will waste it, you will lose it, and all you will find is tribulation and anguish. Would not the most beautiful and honourable daughter of a king be unhappy if she had to marry a brute? And much more so, and without comparison, if the soul which is spiritual was to chose as her first love, and marry, earthly and corporal concerns.

Woe is you, says St. Augustine, if you have erred in not following your God's footsteps, pursuing things inferior to yourself, for you were created in his image! If instead of placing Him above all else you place your love on signs, be they in heaven, on earth, plants, animals, or in the whole machinery of the world whose aim is you! Woe is you, I say, if you cannot discern with your intelligence purged and made clean, what this heavenly light is showing you, whose vestiges and signals the beauty and

---

[2] I Cor. 2:14-15.

14

wonder of his creatures you are; if you love the gift more than the giver, love's arrows more than the archer. You are not a spouse, then, you are an adulteress! Take heed of what the Spouse is telling you in the Canticles: If you do not know your dignity and beauty, if you think you are a sign or vestige of God and not his image, leave my house and my presence for you are not worthy of dwelling where I dwell. *Go and follow after the steps of your flock, and feed your kids besides the tents of the shepherds.*[3] As if he had said: If you cannot see the advantage you have over beasts, go and trail after them and live off your senses as they do, and then it will be said of you what is said of the first man, that having been honoured above all creatures, he knew no honour, he followed his animal appetites, and having brought himself down to their level, so one of them he became.

---

[3] Cant. 1:8.

Chapter 4

That only love can triumph over God and wrestle with him, and of the right time and place for this struggle to take place.

Divine Scripture tells us[1] that when the Patriarch Jacob was going to his land carrying along with him much property and riches, fearful of meeting with his brother Esau and having readied himself beforehand to placate and avoid his wrath, he first passed over with his two wives, sons, and servants to the other side of the Jabbok and then in private, and secluded from all, he prayed. And behold, says the sacred passage, a man wrestled with him until daybreak. And when this man saw he could not subdue and overpower Jacob, he gripped his knee dislocating the hip-joint, and the nerve died. But through it all Jacob retained his strength, and so much so, that the man wrestling with him, who was God, or an angel in his name, pleaded with him to set him free, for dawn was breaking and he did not want to be seen by anyone. But Jacob was aware, because of the pinch in his knee, that the man with whom he had been wrestling was of divine virtue, and would not free him until he had received his blessing. The angel asked him his name and he answered that his name was Jacob. And the angel said to him: *Hereafter your name shall not be Jacob* (which means fighter) *but Israel* (which means Prince of God), that you may lose your fear of Esau *for it is with God that you have been wrestling, and he who has prevailed over God shall fear no man.*

The prophet Hosea makes mention of this struggle in Chapter 12 where he says: *With such force did Jacob seize the angel, that the angel wept, and in humility asked him to let him go.*[2]

Admirable contest, to be sure. God grappling with man and man prevailing over God? God weeping and supplicating of man to be given his freedom? God knuckled under and defeated?

---

[1] Gen. 32.

[2] *By his strength he had success with an angel. And he prevailed over the angel and was strengthened: he wept and made supplication to him* (Hosea 12:3-4).

I know that, in its literal sense, this means that God, Almighty
though He is, allowed himself to be out-rivalled by Jacob so as to
give his friend confidence and banish his fear. But in its spiritual
and mystical sense what transpires clearly to me is a struggle of a
different kind, a more admirable struggle wherein man really and
truly prevails over God, and man conquers God.

And what can this struggle be but the struggle of love? For if
not in love, who would dare take God on in an arm-to-arm
contest? Only love can do this, said St. Bernard. And what an
extraordinary thing it is to be able to engage God in open-arm
combat!

If God is angry with me, I will fear him, I will tremble, I will
ask him to forgive me for it is written *who hath resisted him and hath
had peace?* [3] But it is not for me to be angry with God. And should
he argue with me, it is not for me to argue back for my dissension
will only justify him more in his cause. And if he judges me, it is
not for me to judge him but to prostrate myself on the ground,
adore him and say with the prophet: *Hear, O Lord, my prayer: give ear
to my supplication in thy truth. Hear me in thy justice. And enter not into
judgement with thy servant: for in thy sight no man living shall be justified.* [4]

He is Lord, I am servant. He is to command, I am to obey.
For as Job says: *the wrath of God is not for man to resist, nor is there
power in heaven or earth that can overcome him, he before whom angels and
the mighty of the world bow down.* [5]

But because he loves me, and it is this love that wounds and
hurts, should I not repay him in the same coin! Have I not licence
to love God and wound him with my love? Only to Love is it
given to struggle with God, and God in his love wants nothing
more than to be loved in return, and this is the requital he desires
and hopes for.

These are the words of St. Bernard. And elsewhere he says: O
tenderness! O grace! O power of love! The Highest made himself
the lowest of all! And what could have brought this to pass but
love which knows no majesty? Love, rich in deference, mighty in

---

[3] Job 9:4.
[4] Psalm 142:1-2.
[5] *God whose wrath no man can resist and under whom they stoop that bear up the world* (Job 9:13).

17

giving, convincing in persuasion. Is there anything more powerful than this?

When we know that love prevails over God, then we see that it is an act of love for plenitude to overflow, for majesty to acquiesce, for singularity to keep company. Oh Wondrous fight, which Jacob had with the angel; in which God feigned surrender and was finally freed from his grasp.

But we shall not let him feign in our loving struggle with him even if he tries. The patriarch had said: *I will not free you until you bless me*, but a holy soul in love beseechingly says: "Now that I have you I shall not let you go." Not: "Give me your blessing, Lord, and I will set you free", but: "I am holding you and I will go on holding you and I won't let go. It is not your blessing, it's you whom I want. What could I have in heaven, what could I seek on earth that is not you?"

Ultimately, love ignores all that is not of the Beloved for it is only when in possession of this Beloved that we find all riches and bliss. The spouse holds her Beloved and does not let go, and he is happy to be held, and, in order that she might keep holding him, he, with his mighty hand, holds her. *You held me by my right hand,* said the prophet.[6]

I put it in these words so that we see what love is capable of doing and do not marvel at seeing love prevailing over men, since it prevails over God.

What the patriarch did to enter into this open combat is especially worthy of consideration for our own spiritual struggle, as is the time he spent wrestling with God. He took with him, says Divine Scripture, neither sons, wife nor property, but retired alone, and alone he struggled with the angel. Because things external are burdensome and restricting to the spiritual man in his dealings with God, it is pure madness to try to follow Christ, who is barefoot and naked, fully adorned and with sandals on our feet. How can we run after this divine mighty giant, loaded up like beasts of burden?

---

[6] *And I am always with thee. Thou hast held me by my right hand and by thy will thou hast conducted me* (Psalm 72:23-24).

When Moses, by God's command, had to deliver Israel from Egypt, he sent his children, wife, and the father of his wife to Jethro, that he might be free and unconstrained in his journey to the promised land. [7] So did the Apostles, and so do all Apostolic men. At the very least they must unfetter their heart and despise things worldly, as far as they are able, if a meaningful relationship with God is what they seek. For he who desires a close friendship with the Creator and does not leave behind what is of the world is like a bird stuck to the bird-lime. In its desire to fly high it keeps flapping its wings, but never manages to get off the ground.

If runners and wrestlers unclothe themselves to help them win corruptible palms and laurels, said the Apostle, with how much more reason should we divest ourselves of things worldly if we want to win that incorruptible and ever-living crown![8]

But since I an dealing with this shedding of things temporal, with renunciation and abnegation of the will elsewhere in this treatise, it would be well to consider now the time spent in that battle, a battle that took place at night, since the angel said to Jacob: *Let me go for day is dawning.* He wrestled all night but it was upon seeing daylight that he pleaded to be freed.

No time is more propitious for prayer and struggle with God than the night. Because all is quiet. Because we are alone. Night is a time when it befits the heart to be serene and in solitude, collected to itself. As it is said of Josaphat who, seized by fear, betook himself wholly to prayer;[9] and of Solomon it is written that, from the depths of his soul, he begged God for wisdom. The holy prophet David in one of the Psalms says: *Hear me, Lord, I have called you from my heart.*[10] Recollect your heart and all exterior and interior energies unto it, and do not be so imprudent as to think you can start struggling with God carelessly, or in jest.

There is a passage in St. Matthew that exhort us to pray with our doors closed: *And when ye pray ye shall not be as the hypocrites that*

---

[7] Exod. 18.
[8] *Know you not that they that run in a race, all run indeed, but one receiveth the prize? So run that you may obtain. And every one that striveth for the mastery refraineth himself from all things. And they indeed that they may receive a corruptible crown; but we an incorruptible one* (I Cor. 9:24-25).
[9] II Par. 20.
[10] *With my whole heart have I sought after Thee: let me not stry from thy commandments* (Psalm 118:10).

love to stand and pray in the synagogues and corners of the streets, that they may be seen by men. Amen, I say to you, they have received their reward.[11]

I understand this passage to be referring not so much to the vainglory offered us by being seen praying but rather to the need of the heart for solitude and seclusion whilst at prayer, or else it will wander after every puerility and trifle its sets its eyes upon. It is for this reason that all who engage in this high exercise should avoid curiosities and overmuch abundance of images or anything else in their private oratories because sometimes these serve more as a distraction than as a means to devotion. A crucifix, or a portrait of the crucified Christ should suffice, or something similar. Avoid all else if you want to avoid straying and interference from impertinent or idle imaginations. The stillness of the night will help, for it is friendly to spiritual battles and duels with God, and to converse with the Blessed.

The sensual and worldly man fancies that God made the night solely for him to sleep through it, or to go like a night hound hunting for what it is not given him in daylight, and is forbidden by divine law. And I say he deludes himself, for God made it so that we might search for him in it, and remember his grace.

Let us read the lives of the Desert Fathers, many of whom would never lie down to sleep. When they did, the bare earth was their pillow. They slept with such moderation that one of them, Arsenius,[12] came to say that for the servant of God one hour of sleep should be enough. And he would not give to his body the night of the Sabbath: he would begin to pray at sunset and be still at prayer at sunrise. Of the blessed St. Onophrem it is said that he had neither roof over his head nor bed for many a year but the desert itself, and when and where sleep befell him he would only rest a while. St. Jerome, writing to Eustochium, says: *He who allows himself to be easily overcome by sleep will not have the strength to resist the devil.*

All saints were sons of light, and in consequence, sons of God who is Light[13] and not of night and darkness, for they hardly knew what sleep was. During the day we are never exempt of cares that

---

[11] Math. 6:5.
[12] Methaphrastes, in Surius' *De Probatis Sanctorum Viris*, IV, 250.
[13] I Thess. 5:5.

assail us and steal our remembrance of God, but at night, in its silence and quietude, we can raise our hearts to him with ease. *At night*, says Chrysostom, *the soul is purer, finer, lighter, to rise above itself.* The dark, its tranquillity, invites us, summons us, to contrition and tears.

If you look up at the heavens on a fair and serene night you will see that it is full of eyes, twinkling, sparkling, singing, as the prophet says, the glory of God.[14] And if you then turn your eyes and look down below, you will find that those who during the day laughed, played, negotiated and invented all manner of wickedness without end, at night look as if dead in their graves. And then you decry the madness of man: his arrogance, self-deceit, and his idiotic haughtiness. For sleep and darkness are portrayals of death[15] and two of the things that best teach us to ponder about life in a Christian manner.

Prostrate yourself on the ground, says Chrysostom, get down on your knees, cry, at night, pray to your God that he might be benevolent. He is pleased and gratified with prayers in the night, a night that, though delegated by nature to rest and sleep, you can turn into a time for tears. The prophet did well to divide night from day, devoting day to works of service and night to the service of praise. Use the night to occupy yourself praising God, and to talk and get to know him, for during the day he leaves even if you do not want him to, so that you can attend to your duties, to works of charity, to visiting the sick and those confined in all manner of prisons, to managing your family affairs, feeding your children and servants, and other good works. Moses would climb the mountain from time to time to struggle with God, but then he would come down with time to build abodes with the people.[16] Not always should we be Mary, hanging onto God; at times we must all be Martha too, who tends to the gifts of Christ and to his servants.

---

[14] *The heavens shew forth the glory of God; and the firmament declareth the work of his hands* (Psalm 18:1).

[15] *Day to day uttereth speech; and night to night sheweth knowledge. There are no speeches no languages, where their voices are not heard. Their sound hath gone forth into all of the earth; and their words unto the ends of the world* (Psalm 18:2-5).

[16] Exod. 19.

21

Chapter 5

On some of the strategies the soul could use

in her struggle with God

A successful fighter is one who knows how to win fights, and since this book is about a fight, a duel, perhaps, between God and the soul, I thought we might look into some of the tactics experienced fighters use to defeat their opponents, and see how we can make use of them in our spiritual struggle with God.

William of Paris knew of three or four tricks winners always have up their sleeves to overpower their rivals. One was to get hold of your opponent and lift him well off the ground, as it is written of Hercules with the son of earth; the reason for this is obvious: your opponent will lose his bearings and be in no position to fight back. Another trick was to trip him up and make him stumble so that he would lose his balance and fall. Of course, you can always try to exhaust him if you are more agile than he is which is what a lightweight fighter would do to defeat a heavyweight. And if none of this works, go for it and throw yourself at him.

– But can I do this with God?

– Of course you can!

– But how?

– Raise him!

– But how can I raise God?

– By lowering yourself before him in total humility.

Humble yourselves at the powerful hand of God, said St. Peter*, so that you may be exalted and elevated by Him.*[1] This was the strategy used by king Ahab, you remember, who, aware of the wrath of God, surrendered and humbled himself before him, and God was pleased: *Because you humbled yourself in my presence, Ahab, you will not see in your days the sorrows I had thought of sending you.*[2]

---

[1] *Be you humbled therefore under the mighty hand of God, that he may exalt you in the time of visitation* (I Peter, 5:6).

[2] *Hast thou not seen Ahab humbled before me? Therefore, because he hath humbled himself for my sake, I will not bring the evil in his days* (III Kings 21:29).

Amazing, isn't it?, that when we raise ourselves we fall, but it is when we prostrate ourselves that we are elevated. It is only when God helps us to our feet that we can then say we have won our struggle with him. The surest way to bind God to us is to bind ourselves to God, and what that means is absolute obedience to Him. That omnipotent God before whom those who hold the world in their hands are made to bow and beat their breasts, that same almighty God is willing to cede to the weakest and lowliest of all. As the sacred book says of Josua: *The sun and the moon detained themselves and the whole machine of heaven, as God obeyed the voice of Josua, a man like you and me.*[3] And Christ our Lord says: *God will measure you by the same yardstick you use to measure him.*[4] St. Ambrose said that God belongs only to those who want to belong to him. It could not be otherwise. So, you want a tried and true strategy to have God on your side? Humility is the key. Not only does it make God concede victory but it is also an impregnable wall against the devil.

You know the story St. Antoninus[5] tells about the holy father Macarius. The devil appeared to him one day with a sharp scythe ready to harvest him off for himself (as if he would be given the chance!), and mournfully addressed him with these words:

"You do me much violence, Macarius, and you inflict great torments upon me. You are more powerful than I am; you outwit me. I can find no way of winning with you."

"How can I possibly outplay *you*, the devil himself?" asked the saint. "Is it fasts, long vigils, the pains I endure?"

"None of that impresses *me*", said the devil. "I stay up all day and all night, too, and I fast all year long; as for pain, try being in hell."

But Macarius insisted.

"What can this strength of mine be that even the devil himself will admit defeat?"

"It is your humility", the devil replied. "I never win with the humble. Not only do you win God over to your side by being

[3] *So the sun stood still in the midst of heaven and hasted not to go down the space of one day* (Jos. 10:13).
[4] *For with what judgement you judge, you shall be judged, and with the measure you mete it shall be measured to you again* (Matthew 7:2).
[5] St. Antoninus of Florence (1389-1459), *Summa Theologiae Moralis*, part II, xv, 6 and 3.

humble, but you resolutely vanquish me as well. Remember, it is because I cannot bring myself to my knees that I am an enemy of God."

This is why it is written: *The pride of those whom I detest will forever be rising.*[6] Raising God by lowering ourselves, then, is the first strategy.

The second is to make your adversary stumble by making him lose his point of support, his centre, that is to say, the foundation upon his force rests. God's foundation in his struggle with us is our sins. If we take away this wretched base by eradicating them from our soul, he will have no support left. Only then will we find no resistance when we come to him in prayer. This is why it is written: *Nothing can harm us if no sin reigns in us.*[7]

The third strategy is to tire him out and, of course, to attempt to do this with God would be a lost cause and a waste of time. Although, come to think of it, it might not be such a bad idea after all. I know God is tireless and invincible but he might, at times, get a little worn out with all those prayers and pleas! I think he sounded a little exhausted myself when he said to the Canaanite woman: *Let it be as you wish.*[8] And what about holy Moses, forever asking forgiveness for his people?[9] Of the Patriarch Jacob it is written that when he was about to die, one of the many things he did in preparation was to improve in his will what his son Joseph's inheritance was to be. I *give you*, he said, *this well with this land, which I won from the Amorite with my bow and my sword.*[10] To which the Chaldean translator added: *In oratione mea et in prece* (In my prayer and in my plea). This is what the Samaritan woman did too, and she won, and God was hers.

But watch out, my dear friend, and be sure that when you engage God in battle you do not step onto slippery terrain. Do

---

[6] Psalm 37.
[7] Post-Communion Prayer over the people, Friday after Ash Wednesday: "Protect thy people, O Lord, and in thy mercy cleanse them from every sin; for no harm shall hurt them, if no wickedness be found in them." ("Nulla ei nocebit adversitas, si nulla ei dominetur iniquitas.")
[8] *Fiat tibi sicut vis* (Matt. 15:28).
[9] Exodus 32.
[10] *Do tibi portem unam extra fratres tuos, quam tuli de mano Amorrhei, in gladio meo et in arcu* (Gen. 48:22).

24

not trust what you consider your splendid merits to be your point of support for they may prove to be a very weak and flimsy foundation. You will not only be defeated but you might end up pulling your hair out as well. The holy king spoke of this when he said: *Let not the foot of pride come to me*.[11] There you have it. Pride. Arrogance. That was Lucifer's support and you know what happened to him: he fell into the abyss faster than a lightning bolt. Remember the Pharisee? *I thank you, Lord, for I am not like the others: I fast twice a week... etc. etc. etc.* [12] Let your base be God himself, who is strong, firm and safe. For it is written that *those who trust in God will not be moved forever*.[13] And to those who are over-confident in their riches, be they temporal or spiritual, Scripture has something to say in Proverbs 11: *They will go over a cliff and lose themselves*.

There are many fighters known to have achieved victory by boldly hurling themselves against their opponents. We can do that too. Those who abandon themselves in God, not trusting their own worth, are rewarded accordingly in favour and grace. So, go on, abandon yourself in God, throw yourself at his mercy, and don't worry! He is not going to abduct you or cut you up in little pieces, as St. Augustine said. Do not be afraid of God, but do remember that when you start praying you are engaging in a duel, a duel not against another man like yourself, but with the Almighty God. So the first thing you must do is to invoke the help of heaven, for strength and victory can only be yours if it is granted from above. It is because we need his help in prayer that the Church directs all priests, her defenders, to enter into battle with these words: "Help me God, at this time, in this prayer by which I come to struggle with you on behalf of my people, for how can I triumph over you if you do not help me to do so?"

And what is this help we ask of God when we pray? William of Paris says it is the grace of devotion, the device God gives us to win our struggle with him, the shield with which we protect ourselves and those for whom we pray. If a voice without melody

---

[11] Psalm 35:12.
[12] Luke 18.
[13] Psalm 24.

is like the grunting of a pig, as a wise man said, prayer without devotion must sound to God like the bellowing of oxen.

The second Book of Paralipomenon says: *The people offered sacrifices and praises to the Lord with a devout soul.*[14] And in Exodus it is written: *The sons of Israel propitiated God with a prompt mind.*[15] In the *Treatise on the Gifts of the Holy Spirit*, St. Bonaventure says that, if devotion is missing, our deeds will have no life. Hugh of St. Victor, also, speaks of devotion as being the *soul* of our works: once done, he said, the *soul* in them will go on living. It should not be an enigma, therefore, said a Doctor of the Church, that, in Holy Scripture, prayer is always referred to in terms of incense being poured onto burning coals. This is because prayer will have no fragrance unless it is accompanied by the devotion that comes from a heart aflame. That is what the appearance of an angel placing incense in a golden censer full of burning coals meant,[16] with the smoke going up to God. William calls prayer without devotion a messenger without feet, unable to reach his destination, and St. Bernard points out that, if prayer is hesitant, it will lose its way before it can ever set foot in heaven; if it is lukewarm, it will get sick half way there and be unable to proceed; and if doubtful, it was incorrectly launched to begin with, so forget it. It is the humble, faithful and fervent prayer that will go straight to heaven and will not come back empty-handed. If you do not speak to God with your heart you might as well be mute, for God will not hear you however much you howl, said St. Augustine.

Let me conclude this section by emphasising that no sacrifice is agreeable to God unless it has been well basted and saturated in the oil of devotion. So says Scripture: *the entrails and substance will be God's.*[17] A religion that shrinks from drenching itself in this fat is a barren religion. A poorly-hitched construction can never last.

---

[14] *And all the multitude offered victims and holcausts with a devout mind* (II Par. 29:31).

[15] *The children of Israel offered first fruit with a most ready and devout mind* (Exod. 35:21).

[16] *And another angel appeared before the altar having a golden censer; and there was given to him much incense that he should offer the prayers of all saints upon the golden altar which is the throne of God. And the smoke of the incense of the prayers of the saints ascended up before God from the hand of the angel* (Apoc. 8:3).

[17] Levit. 3:3.

So get ready, spiritual son. If they are of help, by all means use these stratagems in prayer, the field where the daily challenge is set, and God will not only surrender and let you wound his heart in love, but volunteer himself to be your captive, happy never to flee. Blessed and happy is the life deserving of this victory. And blessed and happier still he who, having made him captive, refuses to release him come what may, not just content with his blessing, like Jacob, but happy only when in possession of him. Remember that, were he to escape due to your inability to secure him, he would not leave empty-handed; he would take with him your spiritual life as well. He would take away everything worth having.

Chapter 6

On how the soul, in her struggle with God, wounds and bewitches him

You wounded my heart, my dear Sister, my Spouse, you wounded my heart with one eye and a strand of your hair,[1] says the Divine Spouse to his beloved bride, the soul, in the Song of Songs. Succinct words, gentle words, these, filled with divine tenderness from the Word Incarnate; brief in form, not in content. We can all hear them, but only a few, those to whom the grace of apprehending the mysteries of the kingdom of God has been granted, are able to grasp their rich significance.[2] God confesses that he is wounded. This is a matter worthy of serious consideration and profound reflection. God is wounded by one of his creatures. Wounded in the heart, no less. And how? By means of one eye and one strand of hair.

Please be attentive, dear soul. Think about this very carefully. Reflect on how it is possible for God to be wounded. An injury to the heart is not a mere scraping of the knees! A wound to the heart is a dangerous, deadly wound. Deadly because the heart is the innermost, the core, the very being, the source around which life is centred. Meditate on this thought, reader. The invincible, the immortal God of whom the prophet said *there will be no effrontery against you, nor scourge will come near,*[3] that God, wounded. Wounded not by angel or archangel, but by a human soul dwelling in a body of clay. Wounded neither by sword, shaft, or artillery fire, but with one single eye of one's face and one single strand of one's hair.

What can these words mean! They mean the Spouse is in love with his bride, the soul; in love most deeply. The wound is a wound of love, what else could it be? Read the words again: *You wounded me with one of your eyes and a strand of your hair.* God himself,

---

[1] *Thou hast wounded my heart, my sister, my spouse; thou hast wounded my heart with one of thy eyes, and with one hair of thy neck* (Cant. 4:9).

[2] *Because to you it is given to know the mysteries of the kingdom of heaven, but to them it is not given* (Math. 13:11).

[3] *There shall no evil come to thee; nor shall the scourge come near thy dwelling* (Psalm 90:16).

the omnipotent, the impassible God is wounded in his heart by the gentle, blushing, loving gaze of the soul.

I think I should warn you, reader, that we have now reached a point where you might find what follows rather strange, especially if you have never loved, in which case you might just want to close the book and put it aside. Perplexing or enticing you, is not my intention here. It is simply that the art and science of love has its own terminology and ways of expressing itself, understood only by those who have themselves experienced the unconditional surrender of the self that true love requires. All I am saying is that if you have loved much, you will understand much, and if little, little, and if you have never loved you will understand nothing at all.

You will hear and read songs and poems about love, St. Bernard observed, but if you have never loved you will not be able to grasp their true meaning, however much you may think you do, because your heart is not aflame, and a frozen heart is incapable of apprehending fire. How can you be expected to understand Greek if you have never learnt it? To those who have never loved, words of love are unfamiliar, bizarre, a little strange. They are like a bell or a tambourine: the sound is sweet enough—oh, but the music is not there! Treating of love is a laborious task as, indeed, is treating of life itself, but what a sweet labour it is! And what is love but the life of the soul? St. John said: *He who does not love has no life in him.*[4] Love is so ripe, abundant, plentiful and delicious a subject that it will never weary its listeners nor can the speaker ever be short of words. What has been stewed in love will always be delectable to a discerning palate. *Love has no price*, said the sage. All the gold in the world is but a grain of sand in the seashore. All your desires granted cannot compare. Were you to exchange all your property and wealth for someone who would honestly, sincerely, give his life for you, you would soon realise what a good bargain you got out of it; how little, in comparison, you had given up.[5]

---

[4] I John 3:14.
[5] *Neither did I compare unto her any precious stone; for all gold in comparison of her is as a little sand, and silver in respect to her shall be counted as clay* (Wisdom 7:9).

Great, indeed, is the power of love, laudable its qualities, many its degrees and manifestations. But the throne is occupied, and the crown belongs, to that fervent and intense love that warms the heart, inflames the will, and takes over the soul in such a way that, truthfully, one can say with the Spouse: *You wounded me with your look, you entangled me with your hair.* The divine Spouse expresses the nature of love most elegantly when confessing that he is wounded by his bride. Especially so when one is aware that *to wound the heart* in the Hebrew language, like our Spanish *descorazonar,* means *to break one's heart open,* which in itself means *to be captivated, bewitched in love.* Seneca expressed this well: love, he said, is a powerful talisman containing magical spells that make the soul burst out of itself. A magic that frequently is communicated through the eyes, the windows of the soul.

Many are the philosophers who tirelessly studied and investigated love and its conditions and qualities, the Platonists and Pythagoreans being among the best. They all agree that there is no sense or part of the body that better receives and infuses the magic of love than the human eyes. We can express our love to others, or be captivated ourselves, by means of the eyes alone and it was for this reason that some philosophers warned us to safeguard them well, that we might escape the malignant rage and fury of this "disease" called love.

Holy Job said that he had come to an agreement with his eyes, which was not to open them, thus avoiding any thought against chastity.[6] The divine Spouse himself emphasised the meaningfulness of the eyes by the intensity with which he tells his bride in chapter 6 of the Songs: *it is your bashful look that wins me over.* [7]

The importance of the eyes in declaring one's love is evident in human interaction as well. Those in love will often fear the gaze of their beloved and tremble when their eyes meet. The strong, the most valiant, the wisest, will not hesitate to fall at the feet of their beloved, and the mightiest will willingly defer to the weakest should he be the object of his true and fervent love. This is

---

[6] *I made a covenant with my eyes that I would not so much as think upon a virgin* (Job 31:1).
[7] Cant. 6:4.

because what tears them apart, what possesses and makes them tremble is not wholly human, but an image and a gleaming flash of divine beauty which they can instantly recognise. The divine Spouse, like a most chaste lover, now surrenders absolutely to his beloved because her look, he confesses, enraptures him. Later, he will plead that she look away: *Turn away thy eyes from me, for they have made me flee away.*[8]

Ovid, studying the characteristics of worldly love, recommended that love should be avoided at all costs, for a person in love is always either in a state of fear, dread, apprehension, suspicion or worry, adding that once we start loving we start contradicting ourselves, asking for one thing and its opposite at the same time. In the above passage, for instance, the divine Spouse asks his bride to look away for her gaze makes him tremble and then, almost immediately, tells her to *seal him upon her heart and upon her arm,* [9] meaning, do not ignore me, nor for a minute forget me. *Pone me ut in signaculum.* Look at me, gaze at me, never look away. Some doctors of the Church translated *signaculum* as *seal* rather than as the *focal point,* the *bullseye,* because *signaculum* literally means *seal* or *stamp,* as in the quotation from Ezechiel: *Tu signaculum similitudinis. You are the stamp and image of the Creator,*[10] whereat he then goes on to speak of Lucifer's vigour and riches. Based on this interpretation, then, when the Spouse says: *Seal me upon your heart and upon your arm,* he is saying two things. Firstly, that her most intimate wishes, intentions and desires are to be like a closed and sealed book: to be shared with no one but him alone. Secondly that nothing is to be impressed and take root in her but that which carries his seal and living image, internally and externally, in the body and in the soul. In other words, only he is to dwell in her house. All her thoughts and all her deeds, her inner and outer being, are to conform to him only, and she will imitate him in humility, meekness, purity, innocence, peace, patience, and of all the other resplendent virtues of which he is adorned so that, through her, he will be recognised. St. Paul

---

[8] Cant. 6:4.

[9] *Put me as a seal upon thy heart, as a seal upon thy arm, for love is as strong as death, jealousy as hard as hell* (Cant. 8).

[10] *Thou wast the seal of resemblance* (Ezek. 28:12).

would use the same term with the Corinthians who would follow his steps and imitate him in all things: *I am sealed upon you and you are the living image of me.*[11]

Sealed, not *in* but *upon* the heart and the arm. God, omniscient author of creation, having made life emanate and centre around the heart, so determined that its inner palpitation should be expressed outwardly by the pulsation of the artery in the arm, the pulse being a recognisable sign used by practised doctors to determine whether a body is in a state of sickness or of health. In like manner, the divine Spouse, most clement author of perpetual life, by the infusion of the Holy Spirit, and so that testimony may be given that we are indeed the children of God and that, through his grace, we are in good spiritual health if free from sin, implanted his own love and our love for others in our hearts, as a continual internal palpitation according to which the sickness or health of our spiritual life is to be judged. This palpitation, this impulse of the Holy Spirit and of love divine, is represented also by an external pulse according to which spiritual doctors are able to ascertain the state of our spiritual health, if not with absolute certainty, at least with some degree of probability. St. Gregory said it beautifully: *Love*, he said, *if true, is never idle.* True love works great wonders; it is always in motion, its pulsation fast and fervent like that of a high fever. If it does not move, if it does not act, it cannot be true love for one thing is certain: losing one's pulse means that life has ended, or is about to end.

St. Bonaventure sees three different kinds of palpitations in love. He calls them infant, adolescent, and mature love. He agrees with St. Bernard that the thrusts and palpitations of infant love are, primarily, five: contrition for sins committed; a firm resolution not to do them again; delight and pleasure in hearing the word of God and matters of spirituality; readiness to live a virtuous life in accordance to God's commandments; sorrow at our neighbours' spiritual affliction and joy in their recovery.

The palpitations of adolescent spiritual love are, again, five: thorough and frequent examination of conscience, not only of mortal sins but of venial imperfections as well; a diminution of

---

[11] *You are the seal of my apostleship in the Lord* (I Cor. 9).

carnal concupiscence and need of worldly pleasures; rigorous exercise of our inner life because, just as physical activity is a sign of vitality and energy in corporeal life, spiritual rigour and intensity is an indication of vivacity and health in the soul; an assiduous and scrupulous observance of the law of God which cannot be carried out without charity, which surmounts and conquers all; and lastly, a manifestation to us of divine intimacy, for a best friend will always share the secrets of his heart. It is here that we become aware of how very slowly we grow in the love of God and just how little we seem to impress him with our merits, for it is true that many of us will never reach those towering, spiritual heights where the secrets of his House and his Kingdom are unveiled. We will have to depend on his magnanimity towards each of us, not our own worth, to see with what frequency or, indeed, whether or not he will choose to reveal himself.

But let us now look at the palpitations of perfect, or mature, love and see how they are manifested. I am not speaking here of the perfection achieved by those who have already made it Home but of those of us, pilgrims, still journeying there. I shall concentrate on external signs first because I want to continue speaking metaphorically in terms of the pulse of the artery that indicates to medical doctors what goes on inside the body, which is not always evident to the naked eye (I shall speak of internal indicators at length later). We say, then, that perfect love has five orderly palpitations which, together with the others total fifteen, like the fifteen steps to climb in order to arrive at the tabernacle and dwelling of the God of Jacob. These are: a ready disposition to die for the spiritual well-being of others; to love our enemies in the name of Christ and to do them service; to suffer and endure with joy all adversities that come our way and patiently persevere in them until they are over; a readiness and determined will to leave all things of this world for Christ and undeviatingly follow him, however many hurdles we may have to confront, however much we may stumble on the way, brushing aside all that will prove and impediment to his will and to our love. Lastly, to fear no one but God himself for it is written: *perfect charity does away with fear.*

The Spouse, then, says to his beloved: *Seal me upon your heart so that it will be known I am, and that I dwell in it, seal me, also, upon your arm,* so that both inner and outer man will march in tandem, as in Ezechiel's vision.[12] The reasons he gives for this command are the same a lover most deeply in love would give: because *love is as powerful as death.* As if he had said: if you love me as I love you, you will love nothing else, for true love admits of no shared company. Your love for me will be as death is to other men, a death absolute and irrevocable, as if life had never been. My love shall be death to all your other passions; my love shall be a knife to your carnal desires, for I will suffer no other loves in the house where I dwell. I love you and my love for you is jealous, most jealous, and my jealousy is as rigorous and tormenting as hell. I shall tolerate no competition.

He said it even more clearly in his Gospel when he became man: if you are to follow me, you will leave father, mother, children, property, and even life itself; and if you are not willing to do this, dismiss yourself from my discipleship.[13] This is so true, that if he sees you glancing elsewhere and turning your eyes away from him you will be left with neither. If you love husband, son, father, property, to the detriment of his love, he will kill husband, son or brother in you, he will take away your property and health, thus affirming his dauntless and infinite love.

But the contention of the Spouse here is more than an exclusive claim to love. It is a solicitation more mysterious than at first glance appears, and much more mystical than I have been able to explain so far. Because, on the one hand, still addressing the soul as Sister or Spouse, he admits to being wounded with the look of one eye, then he asks her to take her eyes away from him while, at the same time, demanding that she has him sealed upon her heart and arm, meaning, to have him impressed in perpetual memory. What I understand here is that there is one way of looking at him that bewitches and captivates his heart, and another that makes him turn away and flee. And so it is that when he confesses to being wounded, it is always when he is looked at

---

[12] Ezek. 1.
[13] Luke 14:25-27.

with one eye; and when he shows himself displeased, it is when he is looked at with both. It is with the shy look of one eye, reader, that we captivate him. It is with the effrontery of two that we drive him into exile.

Chapter 7

That the place where we wound God is his Heart

Commenting on the passage in Genesis[1] where it is written that God, wounded in his heart, said: *I regret having created man*, St. Augustine[2] then goes on to say: His heart ached when he saw the sins of men for which he had been as if forced to destroy the world with deluge; and sent his heart, his Only-begotten Son, as man, to do penance for them.

In agreement with the spirit of this divine Doctor, we can well attribute the loving quarrel in the Song of Songs to the Eternal Father who, won over by the look of his spouse, tells her: *you have stolen my heart; you have bewitched, you have enamoured my beloved and most precious Son.*

And he calls *theft* that which he so willingly gave us, for love had now slipped in, [3] love, most delicately forcing him to give us the bountiful riches we now have and possess, and can hardly believe we do.

Nicodemus[4] was shocked hearing Christ tell of the mystery of the Incarnation and how, with His Blood, he would redeem the world. And Christ said to him: *Do not wonder at the Eternal Father giving his Sole-begotten Son to the world, because man bewitched him and stole his heart, and for him he will be injured from head to toe, and nailed to a cross.*

Whosoever wishes to see the Father and the Son drink of the magic of love, hear what the Apostle writes of him to the Ephesians: *Due to the exceeding charity with which God loved us, he sent his Son to earth so that, through him, we may live.*[5]

What do you mean, *exceeding charity*, divine Apostle?

---

[1] *And God seeing that the wickedness of men was great on the earth, and that all the thought of their heart was bent upon evil at all times, it repented him that he had made man on earth. And being touched inwardly with sorrow of heart He said: I will destroy man whom I have created, from the face of the earth* (Gen. 6:5-7).

[2] *Substantia Divitatis.*

[3] St. Thomas Aquinas, probably *Quaestiones Quodlibetales.* [Honeycomb.]

[4] John 3.

[5] *But God (who is rich in mercy) for his exceeding charity wherewith he loved us, even when we were dead in sins* (Eph.2:4-5).

Charity without bounds, charity without appraisement, or measure. Exceeding charity, indeed, it was for the Father to give his Son. It had never been done, it had never been seen or heard, nothing close to it had ever been imagined, and when we saw it, with difficulty did we come to believe it.

St. Luke says[6] that when their Master spoke to them one day on how men would sell him, flog him, spit at him, slap him, and put him on a Cross, they did not understand what he was saying, which best declares to me the greatness of what God did for us. Because if, as the Philosopher said, the difference between the eyes of an owl and the sun is equivalent to the distance between the Highest and Most Excellent and the capacity of our understanding, it follows that the greater and more excellent the gifts God gave us, the less our understanding can comprehend them.

We need no further elaboration on the greatness and mystery of the Incarnation of the Son of God than what the Apostle himself says,[7] that for a time some of the angels did not understand it; the gentiles and sages of the worlds treated it as madness; the scribes and Pharisees, themselves versed in divine Scripture, treated it as scandalous; and the Apostles, men who knew so well of the benevolence and mercy of God, did not comprehend it, even when told to them in clear and plain language.

Blessed and praised may you be, my Creator; infinite thanks be given to you by all of the blessed and all of your creatures. You did so much for mankind, my Lord, so much that it far exceeded our expectations and hopes. Our understanding cannot grasp it and we find it hard to believe!

The philosopher does not believe it because what he sees in you is omnipotence, wisdom, providence, and all your other attributes that so shine upon the fabric of the world, but knows little, my Lord, of your goodness and your mercy, that goodness and mercy that put you on the Cross. The Jews were scandalized because the acts of mercy shown to them, your people, Scripture

---

[6] Luke 18.
[7] Eph. 3.

does not specify would be done at the cost of your Blood. Your own apostles did not understand them because they could not reconcile the Son of God and Saviour of the world with the Son of Man. They agreed that thieves had to be flogged, the blasphemous spat at, the witless mocked; but the Only-begotten Son himself, they could not understand that he could suffer such injury and effrontery.

And failing to understand the simplest words, they understood nothing at all.

Such is the magnitude of the favours God did for us that, though we would have no life without them, we have come to judge we are in no need of them and, consequently, that he should not have done them.

If you wish to understand the magnificence of his gift, read the appreciation offered by St. John where the charity of God is enhanced by the gift of the crucified Christ. And read the considerations and philosophies of the Apostles on the subject of the Passion of Christ. Because, to me, the coarseness of the apostles, the ignorance of the Jews, the incredulity of the gentiles, only demonstrates the magnificence and majesty of this sovereign mystery even more.

The reason why we appreciate this benefit so little, and all else that our Lord did for us, is because we see it as something that happened long ago. Things of the past or of the future do not have as much immediacy as things of the present. Go to the Escorial, a magnificent and sumptuous work of art, thought with such planned models, sketches, patterns, and carried out with such detailed execution. However curious you be, however much you would want to study it in its vastness, you will miss the thousand-fold exquisiteness of its architecture, a thousand-fold correlations and adornments of such a work of art because, once the work itself is completed, one cannot fully appreciate what was involved in its making. But had you been there when the work was first being planned, when the patterns began to take shape, there would be nothing you would not be acquainted with and therefore nothing you would be unable to appreciate.

I say it's the same with us Christians. We find the actual deed done and thus barely glance at it, ignoring a thousand-fold exquisiteness of love divine. We do not see the hundred thousand adornments of the charity of Christ and of his eternal wisdom. The holy Apostles, who were there during the actual planning and carrying out of the Passion of Christ, looking at the singularity of this act and watching it closely, could not themselves make a connection between Son of God on the one hand and death on the other; between innocence and flogging; between the wisdom of the Father and the jeers and derision of men; between the Light of eternal light and the spit thrown at him. As they were still novices and coarse men, they could not understand that, although God is an infinite abyss of all virtue and perfection, to our way of thinking he has nothing more glorious and excellent than benevolence and mercy, or in which he himself glories and rejoices more.

And God, aware of being praised in his goodness and mercy, conceded to do something beneficial for mankind, something that man could recognise, and decided to manifest his clemency for all time by concealing his majesty, veiling for a while what we consider most valuable and praiseworthy so as to expose what we consider and deem most excellent and glorious.

If you had a beautiful portrait covered by a beautiful veil in such a way that the only way you could see the portrait was to tear the veil apart, would it be unreasonable to rip the veil open so as to expose the portrait? the beautiful torn so that the exquisite could appear? In like manner, the divine mercy was hidden under the veil of majesty, and for as long as only his majesty was visible, the world could not appreciate the immensity of his mercy. But by dimming the splendour of his majesty solely for our well being, as the most sacred humanity of Christ was torn by his injuries, the heart of divine mercy was then exposed, and seen. Something admirably demonstrated during the Passion of Christ when the veil of the temple with which the richness of the *Sancta Sanctorum* was covered, was torn from top to bottom,[8] and through this tearing of the veil the beauty in the sanctuary was revealed, having up to then been enshrouded. The damaging of one side made it possible to reveal the glory of the other.

---

[8] Matthew 27:51.

Oh, who would have eyes to contemplate with dignity the Crucified Christ! How beautiful inside may be that which to all appearances looks like a leper! Those injuries to his body, what are they but the slashing of cloth that from the inside shows such great beauty! The hiding of majesty was a declaration and manifestation of his benevolence towards us. And God gained such honour with men that Isaiah, speaking of this mystery, could say: *the glory of the Lord will be revealed.*[9] And the Apostles, after the Holy Spirit descended upon them, would refer to the gospel where the Passion was written as the Gospel of the Glory of God, considering it to be the glorious portrait of the wounds of Christ.

Let the wise and prudent of the world judge this act of consummate charity and consider if God was in himself or out of himself when he did this. The Apostle said it well: *exceeding charity.* And Christ meant the same in the words he said to Nicodemus: *Sic Deus dilexit mundum, ut filium suum unigenitum daret.*[10] Yes, to that extent, with such excess he loves us, so differently from the way we ourselves love.

The Saints paint four pictures here: the lover, the loved one, the magnificence of the gift, the reason why it was given to the world. God is the lover; man is the beloved; the gift, or the arrow, is the Word; the aim, so that he may die.

What I am saying is that if you look carefully at what God did for us, he would indeed seem to be more out of himself than in himself. St. Paul says[11] that he exhausted, emptied, abased himself. The love he felt for man was so great, that being God he made himself man, and to such extent hid his magnificence and majesty that, as man, he was judged by men, and found wanting.

Oh, extreme charity of the Father to give us his Son, and of the Son to annihilate himself for us! Who is not stunned and out of himself when hearing of this love! Who does not marvel and tremble, who can contain himself in this joy? Consummate paternal charity, worthy of our love. Dignity of the Son, worthy of all veneration! Benefit of mankind worthy of all estimation!

---

[9] Is. 40:5.
[10] *God so loved the world that He gave His only-begotten Son* (John 3:16).
[11] Phil. 2:7.

Tell me, my soul, if an ordinary rustic had done you a favour you welcomed, would you not be grateful? So if you are willing to return love with love, and if you feel obliged to those who have given you gifts, it follows, not as a blind overall statement but as a prudent and cautious estimation – does it not? – how much more obligation you have to love this God so very in love with you, this God who with such supreme love did you such great favours!

Say it, my Lord, say it again and again for you are right in saying: *You wounded my heart, spouse, you wounded my heart with one of your eyes, and a strand of your hair, you wounded me.*

Truly, no other hook could have opened God's door, the heart that Isaiah cried was closed, but the hook of love. It was love that opened his heart, went in, and stole the Son. It was for us that love wounded him and made him our prisoner, and injured him and put him on the Cross.

And a blunt lance would then open his breast that we may see and contemplate through this window the loving wound in his heart. And the words *you wounded me* that he had spoken as God, he could now speak them again as God and as Man, there, hanging from a Cross, nailed to a piece of wood, killed, for the love of men. *You wounded me, beloved, you wounded me.*

Chapter 8

On the instrument by which God confesses to have been wounded by his spouse.

We have seen how our Lord, chivalrous and true lover that he is, came to be wounded. Let us now consider the tool the spouse and all the souls that proclaim him and comport themselves according to his will used, for the wound is not one but many. *Vulnerasti cor meum, soror mea. Sponsa, vulnerasti cor meum.* Twice he confessed to being wounded by the spouse and many more times can we go on wounding him in love when we look at him with the same eye the spouse did.

In uno oculorum tuorum, et in uno crine collo tui, he said. I have read a number of authors, and I have not found two in agreement as to what this powerful eye may be, this eye that, with a simple look, can so acutely injure God on his throne, enter his kingdom, wound him and steal his heart. Some say it is the eye of faith. Not on the grounds that faith, most laudable virtue that it is, can compare with the grace of redemption (of which we are treating here), but because of the merit God himself placed on the faith of his spouse, at times seeming to be the virtue he most cherished. Look at the promises he made to the patriarchs and saints of the Old Testament of whom St. Paul makes mention,[1] the oracles, the prophesies, the gifts bestowed on individual persons, and you will see that, among all others, it is faith that is endowed with a predominant role. Even St. Elizabeth praising our Sovereign Lady, whilst acknowledging her as the sanctuary of all riches and beauty of heaven, attributed her grace to faith: *Blessed art thou that hast believed because those things shall be accomplished that were spoken to thee by the Lord.*[2]

Some Doctors say it is innocence and purity of heart – as Chrysostom maintains – which baptises our deeds and names them good if they are good, and bad if they are bad. They cite the

---

[1] Hebr. 11.
[2] Luke 1:45.

words of our Saviour: *If your eye,* that is, your motive, *is clear, pure and simple, all your works and deeds will be pure and agreeable to God.*[3]

Abbot Rupert[4] said that this wounding eye is the perseverance and constancy of all our wishes directed to God. Read the First Book of Kings[5] and see how Anna, mother of Samuel, crying incessantly and with anguish of heart, multiplied her pleas to God, went home, and her countenance never again changed. What harmony of countenance is this that will suffer no change, asked this Doctor, but oneness of thought and steadfastness in prayer? Her countenance is our disposition, and it is our perseverance in that countenance towards him that wounds and hurts him and makes him prisoner of our heart.

The hair that entangles him so securely is, to my mind, a total humility of heart, a virtue which, like a single strand of hair, is most tenuous and pliable. Humility is the golden locks that softly and gently model and adorn a maiden's head: locks of hair so delicate that none but the eyes of God can behold. *In altis habitat et humilia respicit in coelo et in terra.*[6] It was with this one hair that the Virgin confessed she brought the divine Word prisoner to take flesh in her most felicitous and blessed womb from the bosom of the Father.[7]

Psalm twenty-eight speaks of the Beloved as the *son of the unicorns.*[8] St. Isidore describes the *unicorn* as an agile, fierce, untamed animal. The ploy that hunters would use to trap him was to place a most beautiful maiden before him, whereupon seeing her, he would lose his ferocity, and wounded in love, appeased and subdued, would abandon himself in her bosom only to be tied up and made the hunters' prey. O Divine Unicorn, the Son of the Eternal Father! For though fierce, untamed and restrained by no one, when this maiden Mary was put before him, wounded by her

---

[3] *The light of thy body is eye. If thy eye be single, they whole body will be lightsome. But if it will be evil, thy body also will be darksome* (Luke 12:34).

[4] Rupert, Abbot of Deutz (Tuitensis), 1075-1129.

[5] *Would to God thy handmaid may have final grace in thy eyes...So the woman went on her way and ate and her countenance was no more changed* (I Kings 18).

[6] *Who dwelleth on high and looketh down on the low things in heaven and in earth* (Psalm 112).

[7] *Thou shalt conceive in thy womb and shall bring forth a son...* (Luke 1:31).

[8] *And shall reduce them to pieces, as a calf of Libanus, and as the beloved son of the unicorn* (Psalm 28:6).

look and chained by her humility he was made tame, and forgetting his majesty and magnificence took flesh in her womb and was made man. He abandoned himself in her bosom, as Samson had done in Delilah's,[9] and his head was shaven and was left ready to be mocked and derided by men. This is why St. Augustine said: *Had he not allowed himself to become man, no one could have captured him, no one could have scorned him, flogged him, or put him on a Cross.* The divine Delilah cut his hair and, dressing him with flesh, concealed the eternity, immensity, wisdom, fortitude and power which, like hair, adorned his head. O sacred and divine Delilah, you who so tied up the strong and weakened the mighty! And with what? With your faith and your humility. I dare say, says St. Bernard, that even if the Virgin had been adorned with all other virtues, had she lacked humility, she would not have pleased God.

You will rejoice in as much love as you are capable of humility. Humility clears and makes ready the path to charity, and is the jewel-case of the House of God because all it keeps and esteems are divine gifts only. Gerrico says that humility overpowers God, and St. Bonaventure that it competes with his omnipotence. Only this meek maiden effortlessly overcomes the invincible God, only she can tie and secure Him who is omnipotent, and from a feared judge turn him into a compassionate father. Humility justifies sinners and lifts and elevates the good to perfection. It does not even see itself as a virtue being so admirable among them; that is why a wise man said that the truly humble have no eyes. We shall never be granted anything we desire, nor our good works be of benefit, if there is no perseverance and humility in prayer. We have two eyes but need only one to hit and wound the prey; the hair may be abundant but only one strand is needed to catch and rein in the celestial unicorn.

The Church has two eyes, it has been said. With the left, the earthly, she tends to temporal matters; with the right, the spiritual, to eternal ones. It is this right eye that steals, wounds and captivates God, the one that the Apostle, writing to the

---

[9] *Then opening the truth of the thing, he said to her: the razor hath never come upon my head, for I am a Nazarite, that is to say, consecrated to God from my mother's womb. If my head be shaven, my strength shall depart from me, and I shall become weak and shall be like other men* (Judges. 16:17).

Philippians, confessed was the only one to have remained in him: *Bethren: I do not count myself to be apprehended. But one thing I do: forgetting the things that are behind and stretching forth myself to those that are before. I press towards the mark, to the prize of the supernal vocation of God in Christ Jesus.*[10] The Apostle knew well that this brief life is a transient one, and therefore considered its concerns to be irrelevant for he was not looking with the left eye at what can easily be observed, but with the right eye to that which cannot. Because all that our corporeal sight is equipped to see is temporal, the eternal it can never grasp.

---

[11] *Unum autem, quae quidem retro sunt obliviscens, ad ea vero quae sunt priora, extendens meipsum, ad destinatum persequor, ad bravium supernae vocationis* (Phil. 3:13-14).

Chapter 9

When it is declared which eye in the soul wounds God.

This doctrine of which I have been speaking so far is of great importance and will be of immense benefit to our disposition in the holy exercise of prayer; but it does not capture the full meaning of the words of the divine Spouse, nor does it reach the depth and mystery contained therein. In order to do this we must first become aware that, to see God, our soul avails herself of two faculties. One is called *intelligence* which, according to St. Augustine, is that quality of the soul that immediately recognises and sustains the idea of God and understands him to be the supreme, true, incommutable good. The other is called *affection*, and is a voluntary, loving and sweet inclination of the soul towards her God.

Contemplatives tell us that the eye of intelligence is the left, the eye of affection, the right. The former knows by reasoning, the latter by loving. Of course, to be logical, one would have to say that we first have to know something before we can love it, for we cannot love that which we do not know. But here we will have to concede, nevertheless, that God never admits to being wounded by both eyes, nor by the left alone, but by the right only. It is of this right eye, the eye of love as the most significant that he is speaking when he says *you wounded me with one of your eyes,* for truthfully, it would benefit us little to investigate, analyse, and get to know great things about God, if love and devotion for him were not to follow close behind. Oh how many theologians choose to travel around each and every investigative and speculative highway and by-way, but how few care to roam along the affectionate and unitive trail! That's why we have so many scholars and so few saints, I suppose.

Each thing, said the Philosopher, *acts according to its own nature: If the being be finite, so will be its qualities and operations.* Since our being is finite and limited by nature, it follows that the more it concentrates in any one thing, the less resources it has to distribute and partake of others.

The mind and the heart of man are like the two sides of a measuring scale, the going up of one means the coming down of the other. If speculation and argumentation go up, love and self-abandonment come down, and contrariwise, the more we love something the less we feel the need to investigate and analyse it *ad infinitum*. This is why the patriarch Jacob was made lame of the one leg when he was blessed in that battle he had with the angel.[1] Because God wishes the soul of the contemplative to limp a little on the left foot, not to let all her efforts go towards analysis and investigation of him but, more leisurely, to leave a little time for the heart to rejoice, for love to savour and feast on these truths, and thus easily and effortlessly slip into that mansion the intellect will never penetrate, wound him and carry him back to us gently, in its arms.

Think of it this way. When a wet-nurse is feeding a child, she will first break down the food in her mouth, crushing it, chewing it well. Only when it is ready will she feed it to the child who is then able to swallow and enjoy it, and the food will then be digested well, and will serve to fatten and nourish him. She will not eat the food herself, for leaving the child with no sustenance would be of great harm to him, endangering his well-being and even causing his death. Reader, the intellect is the wet-nurse of the heart. It is the job of the reasoning faculty to crumble and grind divine truths with attentive and careful consideration, not in order to retain them for its own self, but so that once well masticated, it can feed them to the heart, and the heart will embrace and savour and relish them and thus be enkindled in divine love. Oh how many theologians spend their lives sharpening away their brains without stopping to devote one single hour to the poor old heart! They are intelligent, no doubt, most sharp in scholasticism and speculation, but oh so crude and stiff in mystical theology! They will fail to see God however much time they spend staring at him because they look at him with the wrong eye, the eye that will never enter the bridal chamber, the eye that will never reach the realm of eternal wisdom.

Among classical philosophers, a very difficult and hard-fought question was this: there being two faculties in our soul, one of knowing, the other of desiring, or as we have said, intelligence and

---

[1] *He touched the sinew of his thigh and forthwith it shrunk* (Gen. 32:25).

affection, which one, they asked, was the most appropriate for man to use in order to procure for himself absolute joy and the ultimate good in life? Almost all Greeks agreed that the good life was attained by both *knowing* and *contemplating*. Aristotle, a man of admirable genius, started his books on *Metaphysics, On Science and Knowledge*, by saying *All men, naturally, wish to know*.[2] And in Book X of his *Ethics* he adds that sentence of Simonides: *Man was not born to contemplate human things only*, by which it could be inferred that the principal aim of human life is contemplation and knowledge of divine things. Pythagoras, prince of philosophy among the Greeks, when discussing these questions, as Plato records, distinguished between things human and things divine, and again between finite and infinite good. He advises us to differentiate between the two and not to treat them as if they were the same. Yes, we might have to know finite and transitory goods before we can love them, but I would go further and turn this upside down by saying that we will not really know them unless we are capable of disdaining them. Because the more we are capable of scorning the things of this world and everything that steers us away from virtue, the more, not the less, are we seeing them for what they really are. The reverse, however, is true of things divine and supernatural, of those truths that, because of their dignity and majesty, can only with difficulty be discerned unless our knowledge of them is grounded in love. We study them, in other words, not to know them better but to love them more. That sentence of St. Paul, *The spiritual man knows and scrutinises all things perfectly*,[3] seems to me to allude to this. The reason Pythagoras gave was that love transforms the lover into the object of his love. But since there is no possible comparison between God and ourselves, because no sense of proportion can there exist between him and us, what is missing in proportionality can nevertheless be supplemented by the transforming effect of charity and love for him. Wondrous aspiration, to be sure, and very much in accordance with all worthy philosophy and theology. I understand it in this way: In sacred scripture God is called fire,

[2] Aristotle, *Metaphysics* I:1.
[3] *For the spirit searcheth all things yea, the deep things of God* (I Cor. 2:10).

not because he is formally fire, but metaphorically, or by similitude. For this same reason an angel can be called a luminous and translucent body, and our soul a concrete one for it is, after all, encaged in mortal and corruptible flesh. Consequently, just as diaphanous and transparent bodies such as air and water can instantaneously be observed to be filled and surrounded by light inside and outside, but our solid bodies have first to be heated up, attenuated and thinned down considerably for them to partake of the light and brightness of fire: similarly, divine spirits being clear and diaphanous and thus removed from bodily forms, are immediately recipient of divine knowledge and light, whereas our souls, adjoined to these earthly bodies, are in need of this extenuating and transforming fire of love, so that brought to divine similitude by being thinned down and abated, they might be finally enlightened with the splendour of that sovereign science which is the ultimate knowledge of God. It was from this understanding that Porphyry advanced his celebrated maxim: *to ponder over divine matters with the mind will purify the soul, but to love them will deify it.* And St. Augustine tells us that the more serenely we contemplate God the more affectionately we will love him, and that no supernatural good can be known perfectly if it is not perfectly loved.[4] That is the reason why Ecclesiasticus admonishes us to love much if we want to know much[5] and Plato, in *The Symposium,* calls love master of everything and everyone.

Now reader, so that you may not think I am concentrating too much on *what is not* and not enough on *what is,* let me make clear to those of you who would wish to uplift yourselves to God anagogically, by way of love and mystical experience, that one thing is essential: using your human intellectual capacity for abstraction, you must empty your mind of images, resemblances, similarities and representations of all things created because, as Dionysius declares, he who is not corporeal, he who is neither physically big, small, white, black, yellow or red, nor of any other colour or physical attribute, cannot be compared or represented by any one thing. He cannot, therefore, be apprehended by

[4] Aug. 1.83, q.35.
[5] Cf. Sirach 2:7-9.

similitude through anything that can be perceived by the external senses. Albert the Great agrees when he comments on the words of St. John: *God is spirit and they that adore him must adore him in spirit and truth.*[6] And St. Bonaventure, in his book *Soliloquy,* addressing the affective soul directly, says: *O devout soul! If you aspire to heavenly sweetness, ensure that your understanding is cleared and purgated and your affection well disposed, for the Supreme Good cannot be apprehended but by the purest souls nor can it be tasted but by the best disposed affection.*

The Master of the Sentences speaks of our faculties having to be refined, cleansed and purified.[7] Our understanding is refined when it is cut off and separated from tangible and external things and their forms, likeness or representations because, as we have said, God can neither be seen, or heard, smelled, tasted, or touched. It is cleansed, when it abstracted from the indiscriminate and futile images lodged in the inner senses, because God is neither terminable, or depictable, measurable, circumscribable, commutable or imaginable. It is said to be purified when it disassociates itself from physical and natural syllogisms, discourses, speculations and rationalisations, because God is neither demonstrable, nor definable, deductionable, examinable or intelligible. These same steps of purification apply also to the affective quality of the soul, he says, and these are most important. Our soul will first have to be refined by being clear of all sin, cleansed, by being freed from bad habits which are but the remnants of sin, and purified, not only by being free of sin, but by positively fleeing and running away from the mere possibility of sinning.

The illustrious doctor Gerson explained to us in the *Last Consideration* of his *Theologia Practica* how it is possible for our spirit to separate itself from images and representations in these anagogic exercises. He says there that the contemplative, when thinking and meditating on God, cannot stop at the point of *sensing* him but must endeavour to continue beyond *knowing* to *loving,* hankering in his heart for that wise and luscious taste of the Lord, who being All Good, is infinite Kindness, Gentleness,

---

[6] *Spiritus est Deus, et eos qui adorant eum, in spiritu et veritate oportet eum adorare* (John 4:24).

[7] *Purgated, more purgated,* and *most purgated*—terms used by Peter Lombard.

Delectability itself. During this laborious and painstaking struggle a myriad of images, thoughts, and considerations will make themselves present. Resist them as much as you can, brush them off with the hand of devotion, cast them out. As if you were shaking your head loose, let your spirit free itself from them. Elsewhere he writes: *God is Spirit, and it is as spirit that he wants to be sought and cherished.* But he asks the uninitiated to approach anagogic exercises with great care and caution. Because if all you are doing is concentrating on picturing an incorporeal and imageless God in your mind, a headache is what, most likely, you are going to get.

I expounded on this at length in my *Dialogues* where I tried to explain this doctrine in a way that could be easily understood by ordinary folk, so I will dwell on it no longer here. I shall only repeat what Gerson said when teaching us how to meditate on the Passion of Christ, our Lord. Namely, not to fix our mind for an undue length of time on the images that represent this mystery, but to elevate our thoughts instead from the images to on high – that is, to the spirituality they represent. To show this can be done he reminds us, by way of example, of the Most Sacred Sacrament of the Altar that, as true God and true Man, as the Redeemer of mankind, we worship at the hands of the priest, and says: We do not concentrate our attention on the Host itself as it is seen by the corporeal eyes, that is, its roundness, whiteness, size, and so forth; we force our understanding, which is a faculty that obeys our will, to separate itself from the actual, visible species and enter into the invisible domain the Catholic Faith represents to the spiritual eye. So let us remind our intellect in no unsure terms that God is not simply what the corporeal eyes are looking at, but what the heart is seeing. The same applies to statues of the Virgin or of saints, some people not allowing themselves to go beyond external representations. The Church makes use of artistic images so that, through the external which can clearly be seen, we may uplift ourselves to the intellectual and beyond to the spiritual, which cannot so easily be discerned. But please note: you will never even get to the initial stage of contemplation unless you have first stripped your understanding of imaginations, cleansed yourself of wrong and bad habits and escaped from all occasions to offend

God. You have to be pure inside to look at him with the right eye, or you will not see him, because the eye of blood and bone is not apt to discern the celestial, nor the carnal heart the riches of the spirit. Remember: *Blessed are the clean of heart for they shall see God.*[8]

---

[8] Matt. 5:8.

Chapter 10

Continues on the same doctrine and treats of that most

foolish wisdom that reigns over human intelligence.

The great contemplative Dionysius, deliberating on the wisdom of
the affective faculty of the soul, wrote: This irrational, crazy and
foolish wisdom is worthy of all merit and praise for it is the source
of all understanding, reason, wisdom and judgement.   St
Bonaventure explained this rather pilgrim terminology in this way:
Mystical theology is called irrational wisdom because the intellect
plays no part in its attainment nor is it the way for this wisdom to
be fulfilled.   It is also called *amens*, meaning without mind or
devoid of reason, because the reasoning faculty is not equipped to
learn it, understand it, or acquire it.   Foolish, because it is our
capacity to love, not our intelligence, that is at play here.

Accordingly, and following in Dionysius' footsteps, we say that
mystical theology is an irrational, crazy and foolish wisdom –
foolish, that is, in the sense St. Paul used the term when he said *the
foolishness of God is wiser than all sages of the world*[1] – because all human
deliberation is defective when compared to the purity and
substance of the divine and most absolute intelligences.

We are, moreover, mimicking here those methods of definition
used by speculative theologians who define something, not by
what that something is, but by the contrasting character of its
manifestations, that is, they define by a process of negation. And
so it is that, for example, when engaged in defining the concept of
God, they will call inscrutable, or obscure, He who cannot be
discerned but only because of his abounding brightness; they will
call inexplicable, or incomprehensible, He who is worthy of all
acclamation and can never sufficiently be praised; unobservable,
or unexaminable, He who is present in all things and is there for
all to see.   And those eternal and divine truths that we find
ourselves unable to express and which no ordinary words can
convey, when analysed and examined pragmatically by men of the
world are therefore regarded, quite naturally, as foolish since they

---

[1] *The foolishness of God is wiser than men* (I Cor. 1:25).

obey no logical rationalisation. Consequently, (consistency is, after all, of prime importance to them), this foolish wisdom comes to be considered illogical and irrational although it surpasses all praise and is the source of all reason, understanding, wisdom and judgement, and the mystics who seek it, though most wise in the eyes of the Lord, come to be regarded as silly, absurd, and just plainly idiotic in the eyes of men.

Dionysius, advising his disciple Timothy who was engaged in the pursuit of this wisdom, and so that he would not falter, said to him: *Mind, my dearest Timothy, since you are striving in the study of mystical visions and seem to be gaining such benefit from them that it is essential you endeavour to take leave of yourself, that is, of all your senses and all intellectual activity, of things of the senses and things of the mind, of all that exists and all that does not exist. And then you will be raised, secretly, unknowingly, and as far as it is possible for a rational creature to be raised, to unity with him who is beyond all substance and all understanding. Because by this leaving of yourself, by this breaking loose from all that can encumber your understanding and detain and hamper your will, uncontaminated and purified, you will be elevated to the highest heights, to the luminous ray of the divine darkness. I shall not grant you license to speak of these truths to the gentiles or the sages of this world. I mean, to those who insist on seeing only what is visible, not conceding that there are superior and higher truths that are hidden to the naked eye of the flesh.*[2]

These are the words of Dionysius, and we could just put a full-stop here for there is nothing further to add to these words to become a perfect contemplative. All you need to know is here, encapsulated in these words. They contain all of the nobility to which a perfect soul aspires during its wayfarer state as well as the substance and depth of all that this contemplative ever wrote. With this in mind, let us pause here for a moment and see if, with divine grace and the help of the saints, and to the best of our ability, we can make the meaning of these words a little clearer so as to be more easily understood by everyone.

Let us first point out that this unknowing elevation is attained when the soul instantaneously arises above herself, and this by the fervour of love alone, neither by beholding herself in the mirror

---

[2] Dionysius, *On Mystical Theology.*

and image of her neighbour, nor by any other consideration preceding it or rational movement of intelligence accompanying it. Love alone is touching the soul now, that eye of love with which the Spouse admits to having been wounded. Note, too, the second point being raised here. Of course we can get to know God through the mirror of his creatures, that mirror St. Augustine called *the staircase that enables us to climb to him one step at a time*,[3] as, indeed, we can climb to him by the intellectual exercise of the mind by means of which, by divine enlightenment, we get to know the First Cause through consideration of its wondrous manifestations. But there is another way, a way more excellent than either, and this is the path of unifying love. Because this love will uplift itself by itself to the Beloved with no intermediaries whenever our affective faculty is truly well disposed. This consurrection or elevation is said to be ignorant, or to take place in a state of ignorance, because images, thoughts, motives, or anything else pertaining to the mind have by now been altogether excluded. It is then that the soul, in the fervour of pure love alone, nothing else, senses and experiences at this very moment what rational understanding will never come close to knowing.

This accepted, then, it might now be helpful to re-state the words of Dionysius: *tu autem, Timotheus carissime, circa mysticas visiones…* from which I shall now draw out and try to elucidate the essence of their meaning, as best I can.

So to begin with, what is a mystical vision? A mystical vision is that moment within the soul when the heart takes over. From here onwards it is the mind that will be taught and enlightened by the heart; from this moment love will precede, lead and guide the intellect, not the other way around. Please, reader, do believe what I am telling you here because it really is most true. I assure you it is not an eccentric exaggeration or a dishonourable hoax, and it is far from being a lapse in judgement. The saintly Giles, a mystic friar most experienced in this science, came to say that even faith was absent at this point, so enlightened and inspired by God was the estate of his soul at that moment. *Sensus derelinquat.* All senses and operations of the mind must cease, he said. And

---

[3] St Augustine, D*e Magisterio et vera Religione.*

what he meant was that, in mystical knowledge where the affective faculty reigns supreme, it is essential to cut off and leave all the senses and operations of the mind behind, and by all I mean all of them, root and branch. Allow your heart to open wide now. You need to surrender. You need to abandon yourself completely in God's love. Not a part of you, all of you. Unconditionally. Quit *holding on* to yourself!

The question is, of course, how can this be done? First by leaving aside all of the mind's apprehending faculties, the receptive as well as the perceptive ones; secondly, by dispelling all their manifestations, meaning by this all things sensorial and intelligible, those that are and those that are not, for this science is not like all other sciences which evolve from the pre-existent knowledge we have of sensory things. This science is unique. This science comes from above, from the Father of Lights.[4] It is a most precious gift and, as such, expels all intellectual and sensorial activity and all knowledge derived from their manifestations, human and well as divine. God is not apprehended mystically down below by means of sweet and good intentions, or considerations, or motives. All of these would involve the mind in varying degrees. This wisdom comes from a special place, a place which inner and outer senses cannot penetrate, a place where they will never be allowed in. They would neither see nor understand if they were. Only love is pure enough to enter, and touch.

Timothy is further advised to leave all *things that exist* so as to avoid including in this mystical theology the various other ways of learning about the Divine Nature by means of the mind. *Things existing*, said St. Bonaventure, are eternal *reasons* in the Divine Mind to which his creatures respond by deducing and deriving some meaning of the Divine by means of its manifestations. The words of this holy Doctor are rather abstract and difficult to understand, I know. Abbot Rupert[5] threw some light on them and managed to explain them rather well, I think, by pointing to another translation of that passage in St. John, *life was made in him*, which

---

[4] James 1:17.
[5] Rupertus Tuitensis, *In Johannem*.

reads: *Quod factum est in ipso ludus erat*, i.e. *What was before the Word was play and recreation.* As if to say: all things that had been made in time, before coming to light, were in harmony and consonance with the Divine Word and were as gifts in which the Eternal Father rejoiced. And the Divine Word Himself said that they delighted daily in His presence,[6] and that all creatures made harmonious music in Him. One finds an admirable correlation between His eternal *reasons* and His creatures, equivalent, we might say, to the reciprocity that exists between the musician's art within him and the strings in his guitar. However, when the soul, on the one hand, starts reflecting upon these eternal *reasons*, and on the other, correlating this knowledge to God's creatures as manifestations derived from and consonant with the eternal reasons themselves, for as long as the soul is so engaged I say, the soul will remain here, down below, beneath itself. It cannot rise above because the intellect, though reflecting on things divine, is present, it is in between. Unitive wisdom, on the other hand, moving anagogically, leaves all reflection and deliberation behind, aspiring above itself to the Intelligible One. Thus Timothy is asked to leave *existent things* (admirable contemplation though it is) because wherever correspondence exists, whenever a convergence occurs between a straight line and some other, a deviation, a response to the *other* occurs, which means that this kind of contemplation is not relinquishing all human perception absolutely and unconditionally. Pure divine contemplation, on the other hand, is placed above and beyond all limits.

He is also asked to leave things that *do not exist*. *Things non-existing* are said to be those for which no exemplar can be found in the created world. An example of this would be any deliberation on the Trinity or on the order of Divine Persons, since there is no prototype in anything created with which this sovereign mystery can be compared. It has never been seen that when one begets another, the begotten is the same substance as he who begot him, and that both exist truly and are *in* and *of* the same essence. Even less have we seen love, which interweaves and binds those who love each other to each other, becoming *them*, or of the same

---

[6] Proverbs 8:30.

palpable substance as themselves. But Timothy is asked to leave *things non-existing* behind too, not because this most excellent contemplation is not worthy, but because, I insist, there is a superior apprehending faculty in the human soul by means of which God can directly be touched.

I am well aware, reader, how difficult all this is. I know how laborious it is to explain it and how arduous it is to understand it, and Dionysius, who not only wrote about it but experienced it himself as well, was more aware of it than most. This is probably why his advice to Timothy was such a straightforward and uncomplicated one: *Try as hard as you can, though with great struggle, to abandon the senses and all intellectual activity, leave behind the sensorial and the mental, the existent and the non-existent, and ascend unknowingly, as far as you can. Unknowingly* means, said St. Bonaventure, with no thoughts whatsoever in your mind. Because there is nothing that will hinder this consurrection more than for the intellect to start budging in where it does not belong. In fact, the closer our mind gets to our heart, the more contaminated pure love becomes. Or to put it another way, the blinder the mental eye becomes the higher the affective eye soars. I grant you that this cannot be done without a great deal of effort, but the striving is worthwhile and can gladly be endured on account of Him towards whom the soul is flying. *Ascend,* he said, *unknowingly, to unity with him who is above all essence and understanding.* As if to say: there should be no prior considerations, no ulterior motives, no wish for grace, glory, or forgiveness of sins. Nothing else should be in your heart but the yearning for the taste of God himself. When this path has been trodden over and over and over again with these anagogic desires, and our heart is finally well disposed, all the soul will ever yearn, and long, and sigh for, is unity. What else is there to be desired? And this is Dionysius' advice to us *travellers*: to try, as far as it is possible for us to keep on trying. That is all we can do, because no soul can be recipient of this gift unless it is by infusion, or divine enlightenment, and this comes from above. But what we can do is try, and hope, and strive until we can say with the prophet: *you broke, Lord, my ties and gratefully I shall offer you sacrifice of praise.* And when all those mental considerations, deliberations, speculations and rationalisations, when all those intellectual barricades, those jailers of pure love, collapse through divine grace, then you will see your soul, that sweetest of doves, with nothing but the most ardent yearning of love for its wings, free to enjoy flying high to God any time she wishes. She will pray with such devotion that she will feel the eyes of God on her. Yes, God and you, face to face, gazing into each other's eyes. And sometimes, sometimes, she will soar high, so high, that you will truly believe you are leaving yourself behind.

But remember: if you ever wish to be carried away to that ray of Divine Darkness, you are going to have to learn to abandon yourself first.

Chapter 11

On the Divine Darkness into which the soul enters when journeying along the path of love

Divine Darkness is a subject that should be more appropriately treated in a chapter on ecstatic rapture. I thought it appropriate, however, to say a few words about it here so that I may for a little while longer continue to clarify the words of Dionysius, since his knowledge of the subject and our understanding of his explanation are absolutely necessary if we are to understand this concept of Divine Darkness.

Dionysius would say to his disciple: *Unknowingly, it will raise you to union with Him who is above all essence.* St. Bonaventure said that the eye of the contemplative will fix itself so firmly on God that, while so doing, he will no longer be capable of looking at or considering anything else. But even in this state, he will not be so favoured as to behold all the brilliance of such light all at once, but instead will first go through the darkest of fogs if he is ever to reach it, an *ascending* and a *knowing* that comes to pass only upon rejection and exclusion of all else. This elevation of the soul is called *wise ignorance*, not because wisdom and ignorance can go hand in hand in respect to one and the same subject, but because in this consurrection or rapture, all sensory and mental activity of anything created and non-created that may affect and retract from apprehending God will have to be rejected (at least while it is taking place), or it will obstruct our affective faculty from actual knowledge and love of God. *Wise ignorance,* also, because when a rational spirit is transported by love to this Divine Darkness, by excluding from God all creaturely imperfection, the soul will then, ineffably, know God. Dionysius called it *ignorantly ascending,* as we shall see later with more clarity.

This is a difficult subject and in order to proceed with a reasonable explanation of what it means, I shall emphasise five notable principles that will facilitate understanding on matters regarding affection. These should be kept in mind and committed to memory.

The first point is this: In this consurrection, elevation or rapture, there are two paths for the soul to follow in order to reach and perceive an experiential knowledge of God: one is the path of *privation*, the other the path of *excellence*. By following the path of privation, the soul is eliminating in God all that is imperfect in humans. By the path of excellence, or eminence, all that we consider good in humans, such as power, wisdom, clemency and so forth, are attributed to God eminently and eternally, that is to say, we perceive God not as mighty but Almighty, not as merciful but All-Merciful. To explain the path of privation Dionysius gives us an ordinary but rather admirable example. Just as the sculptor, he says, carving a figure out of wood or stone, chips away all that is not perfect and, whilst adding nothing, unfolds and discloses the secret image he wishes to bring to light, in the same way, by excluding from God all that is imperfect in creatures, we come to the highest knowledge of his magnificence and majesty, Someone in whom no imperfection is possible. It is important to point out here, however, that the path of privation will be insufficient unless accompanied by the other, the path of excellence.

Bear in mind, also, the second point. It is this: although this knowledge of the Creator culminates in fog and darkness, in order to have arrived there, necessarily, we would have had to go through and left behind another fog and darkness, a darkness that consists of all creatures upon which the divine light shines. This darkness, as Dionysius says, is a privation of knowledge and a fading of love for all things because the soul, during rapture, relinquishes all knowledge and love of anything that is not God himself, God who is truly secret, or concealed, and who from his hiding place, surrounds and envelops darkness. Ultimately, it is essential that our mind surrenders, and that all cognitive acts of the intellect and affection of the will for other creatures cease. It is then, quietly, in silence, that the soul dies to all things created, and only the Creator himself lives in her.

The third point to remember is this: during this rapture all sensorial activity is suspended, leaving the enraptured contemplative as if dead. So is all intellectual response, things that are and things that are not, as explained in the previous chapter;

and, finally, the human mind itself. I am not saying that the human mind ceases to exist or is altered in such a way that it does not remain itself in essence. That is a task impossible for any faculty of the mind to perform, unless we start raving deliriously like Almaricus the Heretic, who said that the mind of the contemplative loses its own *sui generis* nature returning to that ideal *state of being* that it had originally enjoyed at the hands of God. This, in my opinion, is equivalent to annihilating the soul. But what I do say is that the soul, while remaining itself essentially, must abandon herself in this darkness and suspend anything pertaining to it or any other creature. For at this moment, love is her only focus, a most ardent love for God, God himself whom she is now adoring.

The fourth point is this: there are two levels of *darkness* for the enraptured contemplative. A *lower* darkness which is the actual knowledge one has of the world, now being left behind, as we have said; and a *sublime* darkness into which the contemplative will enters during rapture, which is an actual ignorance of God insofar as having an open, bare, objective vision of him. It is called Fog, or Cloud, or Divine Darkness because a *traveller* can, in no way, comprehend that ray, or rays, of light, what Job called *the light that God shows to us only through his fingers*.[1] This divine fog is a deficiency in our understanding of the divine majesty, something that not even the Blessed can fully comprehend, for only God can comprehend himself. It would, indeed, be more adequate to speak of the Blessed in this regard in terms of apprehending, rather than comprehending God, for they are in a position to see God clearly, nakedly, instantly, with no shadows or surrounding darkness. But that is not the case for us, *travellers*, when enraptured in contemplation. Our soul is not equipped with eyes that can cope with the splendour of that glory that can see God as a beatific object. That is why Dionysius calls *unlearned* and *foolish* those who say they see God as he is, living as they do, within the bounds of mortal flesh. St. Gregory says that even if the soul were to keep ascending continually in contemplation, it would never arrive to a clear and bare vision of God as he is. Of course,

---

[1] Job 36:32.

I am not talking here of St. Paul's extraordinary rapture[2] nor about our Sovereign Queen. But if others have had the privilege of seeing the Divine Essence bare (as some said they have), free from darkness, it must be understood that this was by special privilege and grace and not by means of ordinary law. Though not lacking in splendour of glory, it was brief and momentary, not permanent as with the Blessed. But I shall say more about this in its proper context.

Note the fifth point. It is in this darkness, this loss of light and privation of knowledge, where the mind of the contemplative, having following the path of abnegation, arrives and culminates. This path of negation, however, has left behind a most excellent trail of affirmation, just as the highest negations contain within themselves the finest affirmations of God. But neither negations nor affirmations are determined in respect to any one thing in particular, but in regard to several, because one negates of God all that is imperfect in creatures who, however perfect they might be, are imperfect in themselves, and God's supreme excellence is his affirmation in relation to whatever perfection they might possess.[3] And this is why, often, when Dionysius speaks of God, he says that he is not existence but beyond existence; not lord but beyond lordship; not good but beyond goodness. And he speaks rightly for God is the most excellent and the most inexhaustible cause of all essence and goodness. As St. Augustine said: *God is all goodness.* Thus it is clear from all we have said so far that God is not good but All-Goodness, and so forth; by which process of negation, knowledge of God concludes in the most august perfection. Negation, after all, though appearing to say little may say a great deal. As if we were to say: God is not a sensorial thing but above the senses; he is not imaginable, intelligible, something that *is*, but above and beyond imagination, intelligibility, being. It is here, at this point, that our soul is enraptured and carried into the fog, and, so uplifted, enters, surpassing all things created, exceeding itself. It is at this moment that all things that can be felt, imagined

---

[2] II Cor. 12.

[3] St. Augustine, *Commentary on Genesis*, Book XII; St. Thomas Aquinas, *Commentary on St. Paul*; St. John Damascene, *Expositio*, IV, 4.

or understood are banished and cast out. It is now, at this moment, that a spirit in love flies to the Divine Darkness.

Eusebius of Vercelli, commenting on this point of Dionysius, said that no human philosophy had up to then understood or apprehended this supra-intellectual, supra-substantial means of perceiving God. It had not searched for it, had not imagined it could happen, nor was it willing to accept that the soul had the power to wound God so forcefully; but the capacity is there, without a doubt, and it transcends understanding as understanding surpasses explanation or fantasy.[4]

Note, too, that what we are here simply calling affection some call *spark of the synderesis* - a thunderbolt. It alone can unite and become one with the divine Spirit, as the Apostle said: *He who comes to Him, becomes spirit with Him*[5]; and nobody can come to God, who is Spirit, if not in spirit, that is, we come to him, not by knowledge but by love, for it is to love alone that this wondrous transcendence and union is granted. And this divine operation is so hidden, so intimate, that only he who experiences it is truly able to understand it because, as St. Bonaventure said, none of the apprehending faculties of the soul is granted access to see and delight in this superior wisdom. All other faculties remain at the edge, at the foot of the mountain, like scoundrels. Only Moses, true love or pure spirit, is allowed to ascend and be there with God, rubbing noses, so to speak, receiving enlightenment in his communication. In this life this means blissfulness, and in the other consummation. How very few understand this language and how fewer still enjoy such bliss!

This way of praying, this predisposition to contemplate is bestowed to us by grace; however, diligence and effort will help us separate ourselves from that which is not of God, and thus detached from things ephemeral, will capacitate us with the resolve for the climb ahead.

The soul that so wholly and absolutely commits herself to this union with God sleeps with great tranquillity; sleeps while keeping watch, as the spouse says;[6] sleeps in regard to the senses and other

---

[4] St Thomas, *Summa Theologiae* Ia, q. 79, art. 8.
[5] I Cor. 6:17.
[6] Cant. 5:2.

faculties, all quietly silent, whilst our affective faculty, ever vigilant, keeps watch. And in this enrapture of the senses, more appropriately called ecstasy, man hears things of which he cannot tell. This is love now, not deliberation or reason. St. Bonaventure says that only that which can be conceived through the understanding can be squirted out in words. This is because language is a sign of concepts and the mind can only interpret what it can conceive.[7] Our understanding cannot communicate or convey transcendence. As St. Brigit said: what is good about prayer can never be translated into mere words.

To bring this chapter to a close, I would like to emphasize that this ecstatic or unitive love to which I have been referring has four noteworthy conditions: first, it keeps us from all adulterous affection, that is, from all other earthly things, because this love is for the Spouse only: I for God and God for me and no more world. [8] Secondly, it brings us the most delicious rest, for it quietens and soothes our senses, our inner as well as outer faculties. Thirdly, it lifts us up high by mystical and anagogical desires; fourthly, it kills in us all carnal impediments because, as we have seen, love is analogous to death, and truly, this love is death to all that is not of God. In this happy state of being, the soul secludes herself into one, for only One inhabits her, and in union with the One, reaches her centre or rises to her apex, which according to St. Augustine's dictum, to the soul is the same thing. And having thus arrived the Spouse now softly says: *Let no-one awaken my beloved. Let my beloved slumber and repose for as long as she desires. Too many vigils did she endure to earn this sleep, and sleep is wholesome to one who so languishes in love.*

---

[7] St. Bonaventure, *De Luminaribus*, II, 10.
[8] Cant. 2:16.

Chapter 12

Two ways of knowing God: as pilgrims and as witnesses

There are two ways of knowing God: one by reflection and enigma, the other face to face, as he is,[1] and each has its opportune season. The first way is for *pilgrims* and *travellers*, the other for the blessed, the *witnesses* and *beholders* themselves. Here, in exile, we get to know God by means of the first way, the reflecting image; the second is to be enjoyed only in the Homeland. Mirroring knowledge is the knowledge through which we come to know God by means of his handiwork, because its composition, harmony, order, beauty and majesty offers to our intellectual eye, in some way, an approximation of things divine, just as a mirror offers and reflects my countenance and appearance back to me when I look at myself in it. St. Paul speaks of this: *Invisibilia Dei a creatura mundi, per ea quae facta sunt intellecta conspiciuntur, sempiterna quoque eius virtus et divinitas.*[2] We call enigmatic knowledge the knowledge we have through faith, because it proposes to us knowledge of things divine with some degree of obscurity, not wholly bare, although with infallible certainty. It is so named because an enigma is an obscure science the true sense of which we can only get to know with some difficulty. As is seen in Samson's pronouncement: *Out of the eater came forth meat, and out of the strong came forth sweetness.*[3] And the prophet says in Psalm 86: *Shall not Sion say: This man and that man is born in her; and the Highest himself hath founded her.*[4]

This mirroring and enigmatic way of knowing the heavenly Spouse can be said to be a transverse, not a rectilinear knowledge, a knowledge with shadows therein, appropriate for us who are still here in this valley of tears. The knowledge that the Blessed have of God in heaven, on the other hand, is clear and direct. They see God face to face and know his mysteries openly, manifestly. They are able to stare at the Divine Sun directly, without blinking or

---

[1] I Cor 13:12.
[2] *For the invisible things of him from the creation of the world are clearly seen, being understood by the things that are made. His eternal power also, and his divinity* (Rom.1:20).
[3] Judges 14:14.
[4] Psalm 86:5.

damaging their eyes. St. John spoke of this in very clear words: *Dearly Beloved, we are now the Sons of God and it has not yet appeared what we shall be. We know that when he shall appear we shall be like him because we shall see him as he is.*[5]

When our Reformer Christ shall appear on his Royal Throne (in the joint resurrection of the dead) we shall be likened to him, that is: clear, light, discriminating, impassible. We shall be like iron which becomes live coal upon entering the forge: iron remains iron in substance but with the qualities and attributes of fire. Likewise, those who reign with Christ are changed, not in regard to substance but in regard to qualities. Like those red-hot coals, being men they will be like gods outshining the sun in radiance many times over. We shall be likened to Christ, St. John says, because we will see God himself, that is, we shall see him perfectly, we shall see him face to face, we shall see him as he is. The Apostle distinguished between our *seeing* from here and *seeing* in the Homeland in this way: *Nunc cognosco ex parte, tunc cognoscam sicut et cognitus sum (Now I see in part; afterwards, I shall know as I am known).*[6] That is to say, God knows me through his essence and I shall know and see him through that very essence. I shall know essence through essence. The *sicut* of St. Paul and *sicuti* of St. John do not mean similarity or reciprocity, that is, they do not mean I shall know God in the same manner, or as well as God knows me, but rather, through the same means. Or let us say that to see God as he is, is seeing him contiguously at one with our understanding, not as we see corporeal things. We see them through the eyes of the body not in themselves, for they are not themselves in our eyes, but through the representations that our eyes make of them, that is, we see them through the medium of our eyes. But God will join our beatific understanding without need of means or intermediaries. And so we will see him in himself, through his handiwork no longer.

I can see light in the air very clearly right now; I can see light in colours. I cannot, however, see light itself. Similarly, whilst in exile we see God not in himself, but through his creatures and

---

[5] I John 3:2, *sicuti.*
[6] I Cor. 3

their attributes; but in the Homeland we shall see him as he is, and the wishes of the saints sighing and clamouring for this blessed vision shall be satisfied.[7] Some try to tamper with this order of seeing and knowing God, but the more they rub the slumber from their eyes to see him better, the less they see, and the Spouse is vexed and distances himself from them. It seems to me that this is what he meant when he said to the spouse: *Averte oculos tuos a me, quia ipse me avolare facerunt*[8] (*Divert your eyes from me for they will make me flee*). As if to say: Do not wish to see me as I am, as those reigning with me in heaven see me, while still in your mortal flesh, for I shall distance myself and walk away. Be glad with the knowledge you can gain of me through my creation, which is a mirror reflecting and revealing me, and be satisfied for now with this humble knowledge which is what faith teaches you. For if you curiously and daringly stare at me directly, questioning, and are wanting to know and see more than your present condition allows, I shall flee and go away. This is why Dionysius said that the mind of the contemplative should have no eyes.

We already know that one eye wounds God, that both seem to exile him. The one eye is what St. Bonaventure calls affection, able to penetrate the depth and mystery of God; the one hair is the uplifting of mental considerations. I would say that the Holy Spirit is not speaking here of one eye, or one strand of hair in particular, but of one of the eyes, and of one of the many strands of hair. And if by the eyes we understand the heart, and by hair we understand the mind (as this passage is understood by most interpreters), he who will only love the One and think of nothing but the One will be able to wound and enchain him: he who would have all desires and all thoughts so at unison in the One will not stray from God. And therefore that *in uno* to me means union, the union of the eyes and of the hair. Blessed be the soul that will not cease assailing and wounding God over and over in this way with the weapons of pure affection, knowing him to be the bullseye of his arrows, for he who so many wounds inflicts will receive them favourably himself.

---

[7] John 14:8.
[8] Cant. 6:4.

Chapter 13

One sole consideration: discussion on whether it is necessary for the understanding to precede or accompany the affections in mystical theology. It is significant. In essence, it is at the centre of what one needs to know to understand this subject.

The seraphic doctor St. Bonaventure discussing the best path to follow when aspiring to unitive and mystical wisdom and its virtues, posed, to my mind, a most significant question. He wanted to emphasise to the contemplative that mastery of this science, ultimately, can only be fulfilled anagogically, that is, by amorous affections and constant desire, and not as a result of our reasoning capacity's process of deliberation and inquiry. The question he posed was this: can the soul, by yearning and desiring alone, and solely by the virtue of its affective quality, come to know God, without the intellect intervening in any way, neither preceding love by understanding nor accompanying it with meditation?

I am aware there are passages in Scripture and some declarations by saints where meditation is put before affection, but I would say this was done with a view to helping simple and devout people, to avoid obfuscation and confusion. In any case, I shall restrict myself here simply to stating the final assessment arrived at on this matter by St. Bonaventure, Dionysius, and other contemplatives, and the reasons they gave for it.

As we have seen in the chapter on Divine Darkness, at the beginning of his *Mystical Theology* Dionysius advises his disciple Timothy to endeavour, as far as possible, to abandon the senses and all intellectual activity, all sensorial and intelligible things, existing and non-existing, to *mysticas visiones*, stating further that it is possible to ascend, unknowingly, to union with him who is all substance and all knowledge. Why is not prior meditation necessary before one so truly in love arises to God, one could ask?

In *Divine Names*, chapter 7, he says: It is important to note that our soul has the capacity to understand, by virtue of which she regards and considers definable and explicable matters that can be understood. But is also necessary to be aware that the soul has a unitive quality that surpasses the understanding of the mind and can join on to things greater than itself. Because of this quality, even though in human and temporal affairs understanding comes before love, in the genuine and experiential knowledge of the divine it is necessary to feel God through love first before coming to think of him via what we have already understood. Whatsoever love loves the understanding will inevitably know.

In the same chapter, this saintly Doctor calls mystical wisdom irrational, foolish, and crazy, as we have seen, urging us not to begin from inquiry and disputation as in other sciences, but solely by means of love and desire. The prophet seems to confirm this when he says: *Savour and see the sweetness of the Lord,*[1] clearly placing the affections before the mind. Others well versed in mystical theology also confirm that in spiritual matters practice is to come before theory, that is, application and devotion in the heart first, knowledge and explanations to the mind later. One commentator also said that mystical wisdom suspends all operations of the imagination, of reasoning and of understanding, practical as well as speculative, that it excludes all understanding, intelligibility and entity, one and true, and transcends all mirroring reflection, all enigma; and, because of its excellence, the Divine Spirit joins it to the apex of principal affection. We can infer from this and other deliberations we shall not go into now, that reasoning and knowledge are not prerequisites in mystical theology. What is necessary is a great willingness to love.

To recapitulate and answer this question, then, I say that this mystical wisdom is not for all but for Catholics only, because its bedrock foundation is the giving of the self, and the only knowledge that is presupposed is the knowledge that comes from faith. No mortal man, however great a philosopher he be, has been able or will ever be able to understand this knowledge by means of investigation and reasoning. It is based and built upon an unrivalled, pure and perfect love within the soul, and transcends all faculties of the human mind. It is reserved for, and

---

[1] Psalm 33:9.

reveals itself only, to those children of God for whom consolation comes only from him. This is why it is called mystical, that is, occult or hidden. It is for the few only.

In order to comprehend fully what has just been said, one should indicate here that our learning is effected in two different ways - in conformity to two natural faculties we possess, and both ways enable us to come close to God. What I mean is this: our soul has the attribute of reason, that is, she can understand; but she is also capable of loving, and this attribute is called affection. With both, reason and affection, our soul comprehends God who is supreme truth and supreme goodness: with the mind we understand truth, with the heart we understand goodness. These two faculties create for us two pathways of excellence to God: one is the path of reflection characterized by Rachel, beautiful to behold; meaning, we are following this path when our mind, illuminated by the heavenly light, gives itself to meditation and to consideration of things divine, yet not enkindling or setting the will of the heart on fire. The other is the path of affection, also called *ardour of love.* We follow this path when our soul, with the fire of the Holy Spirit sent from above, and aspiring to God with heart ablaze, desires him and to be herself tied to him in a most tight knot of love. And this is represented by Mary Magdalen, who as St. John said, *burnt with desire.*[2]

St. Paul declares this is, without doubt, the most perfect way of all. After considering the manifold graces within the Church that her priests must follow, he continues: *Imitate and follow these graces, each one the best and most beneficial.* And at the end of the chapter he adds: *I still have a more excellent way to teach you.*[3] As if to say, these are good ways: teaching, preaching, healing, prophesying, governing, and interpreting Scripture. But there is another, a higher and more excellent way that I wish to teach you. And forthwith he goes on to speak of the value of love.

Having made it clear, then, that this path of love is the most excellent and beneficial, I now have to point out that journeying along this one trail can also take place in two different ways:

---

[2] Cf. St Gregory, *Homily XXV in Joannem.* Mary burnt with desire (*ardebat desiderio*) to see her Master.
[3] I Cor. 12:31.

openly or scholastically, and in secret, or mystically. Along the open path we advance by means of inquiry on and ascent, starting with lesser matters and gradually, and continually, rising to God through the exercise of meditation, although to be of benefit, St. Augustine reminds us, it must ultimately culminate in love. There is another path to ascend to God, nobler still and easier than all others. It is the path of unitive wisdom, already discussed, which Dionysius defined in these words: *Sapientia et divinissima Dei cognitio per ignorantiam cognita, secundum unitionem super mentem...*[4] This wisdom is a most divine knowledge of God, an enlightenment gained not from erudition but from a union that takes place well above the powers of the mind. It happens when this superior part of the soul, detaching itself from all other things created, lets go of herself to join God and become one spirit with him. And so this sovereign operation, this holy wisdom of which I am speaking, without need of meditation or investigation preceding it, is enraptured and brings to God the affection of the mind. It need not think of creatures, angels, or the Holy Trinity, for this belongs to inquiry, which is a faculty of the intellect. True, this applies to the *fulfilled* only. For the rest of us, the *restless*, what is first necessary is to follow the purgative and illuminative way of which St. Bonaventure speaks in his *Mystical Theology,* wherein he then adds that if the flame of affection ignites and rises sufficiently after meditation, reflection and introspection will no longer be needed. All ceases, love alone is. Then the soul ascends gently, anagogically, and in love, yearning, loving at day, night and all times, as effortlessly as we breathe, or continue to be alive. Ultimately love will lead, and thought will freely and unquestionably follow, for as we said before, that which the heart so savours the mind will easily comprehend.

By the scholastic path, then, we ascend to God starting from his creatures; we go from inferior to superior and, having arrived, we pause in love. Along the mystical path, however, the opposite occurs, because that true love which is the Holy Spirit, the third person of the Blessed Trinity, the last of the three, is closer to us and, therefore, it is the first we touch in this consurrection of the

---

[4] Dionysius, *Divinis nominibus*, ch. 7.

soul to God. Hence, this Divine Spirit, through the fire of love, touches and inflames the superior and most eminent part of affection in the soul, free from thought or meditation, enrapturing it ineffably. In this condition, all that is in the soul is like the parts of a stone with respect to its nucleus—there being no impediments in between, they naturally gravitate towards its centre. What a wonderful thing, only within the power and wisdom of God, to see a soul enraptured, the mind well out of the way now, ascending directly to him with no twists or turns, pulled upwards by the sheer force of her love. There, that faculty in our soul called affection alone blends with the Divine Spirit in the dough and batter of love.

This faculty goes unrecognised by most because is the uppermost part of our spirit. Only those know it whose love is instantaneously touched and moved by the fire of the Holy Spirit.

This is what Dionysius says: that this affective part of the soul is moved directly by the Holy Spirit and it is from this that mystical theology proceeds. He adds that because of this grace our knowledge of God, once so moved and touched, is much greater than through any other speculative means. This is because once the zenith and majesty of our consciousness is touched, when our soul, burning, elevates herself to God, from this contact there remains in the soul a real knowledge of this understanding. What one senses of things divine one will truly understand, as one reads at the beginning of *Mystical Theology*. Moreover, from this contact, from this union, the gift to know and discern the highest and most secret matters is marvellously lucid: the whimsical, the illusory disappear; the outer senses adjust and moderate themselves as if fitted with a hand-brake. Even the flesh and sensuality are abated. Because the higher the soul ascends in desiring, the tamer the flesh that so ignites and scalds us becomes.

I say, then, that all manner of objections our opponents might propose can be addressed with this doctrine. Meditation is necessary for *initiates* and *accomplished* but not for the *perfect* who can ascend to God any time they wish solely by the ardour of their own love.

Concluding, then, with this question I say with Dionysius: on ascending to God, the better able we are to dispel and dismiss all intellectual knowledge, the swifter our love, easily floating on the waters of reason, will learn what it seeks and desires. And to those who ask: what am I to do, then, since I am not supposed to think of angels, or lesser matters, even of the Blessed Trinity, I would answer this: walk along the purgative and illuminative paths first; then, aspire to God even when the taste of him is absent. If you persevere in desiring, you will kindle the flame and ardour of love sooner, and from there the sweetness of God, than if you were to meditate on the origin and effluence of divine powers, the creation of angels, or the harmony of all creation.

Chapter 14

On how the soul should continually engage in ejaculatory prayer so as to wound God in love.

Many are the roads, the saints teach us, that lead us to perfect charity and union with God but, although they will all reach the same destination, the shortest cut to get there, according to Dionysius and St. Bonaventure, is for the soul to rise continuously to God with yearning love—what St. Augustine called "ejaculatory prayer". Because these prayers are like burning arrows piercing through everything that stands in between God and the penitent.

There is a verse in the Psalms that says *let my prayer enter into your regard* and then, following on some other memorable words, continues: *Prayer is that wondrous virtue that daringly advances and then penetrates that place where the flesh will never arrive, or can even approach.*

So what kind of prayer is this daring prayer? This is how he defines it: it is an uplifting of the mind to God in supplication, lovingly, from the heart. We pray well when we arise to God continually in loving aspiration, a longing he always receives well. The sage said it: *the prayer of the humble will penetrate the clouds,*[1] by clouds meaning the barrage of distracting thoughts trying to obstruct its journey or, even, the multitude of saints attending before God. This prayer will cut through it all, in the same way that a faithful and diligent messenger breaks through the crowds in order to deliver the message he is carrying to whom it is addressed; as did Eliezer, who would not even pause to eat until he delivered his master's message, and secured a reply.[2]

The posture Elijah adopted of putting his head between his knees when asking God for water is difficult for us to understand. Some say it was the posture expected of a slave about to be scourged, which was probably what the holy prophet wanted: to placate God's wrath by making himself the recipient of all lashes due to his people, and on their behalf. Others say, and better, that he did it in absolute humility and trust in God's friendship, two essential ingredients in prayer. In that strenuous posture the

---

[1] *The prayer of him who humbleth himself shall pierce the clouds* (Sirach 35:17).
[2] Gen 24:33.

prophet would force God's hand, just as we might say to a good friend now: I will wait here for however long it takes until you are ready to hear me. This is how Elijah prayed, bent forward, his head touching his knees, possibly saying: "I shall stay like this, my Lord, until you agree to help me."

I am saying that in ejaculatory and loving prayer to God, great humility and trust are needed. The more pliable the bow is, the more it curves, and the farther the arrow will go. The bird, in preparing to take flight, will lower its breast to the ground; the singer, to reach a high note, will place his key on the last register. Similarly, the greater our humility and trust in God, the higher the soul will soar, and the more we shall wound him in love. If this be our disposition, God will always meet us half-way, bestowing grace, bringing us more gifts from heaven. This is the path the saints called the vehicle – the school – for the attainment of wisdom. You cannot learn it in books, however many you care to read, nor will you acquire it through subtle and sophisticated philosophical argumentation. You only get it by loving God with an ever-deeper devotion.

But be advised, Christian reader, that to attain this wisdom something else is essential, and that is purity of heart. Purity of heart means always striving to deal with God candidly, in good will, and vigilantly keeping our heart free of all sin. It means seeking God in all things with innocence, sincerity and simplicity, seeing him everywhere, having him always present in our eyes; because for as long as we live in this world, if self-love has not died in us, it will prove to be an ever-flowing spring of vices, base thoughts, wayward inclinations and vain desires, which keep us away from God, soil our heart, and perturb our inner peacefulness. So the very moment you notice any of these dire impediments to virtue beginning to show themselves in you, crack them open on that living grindstone that is Christ himself, and deny yourself. I will say this again: whenever you find yourself seeking your own glory, flee, abhor, expel, persecute anything that incites you to put yourself in place of God.

But what exactly does it mean, to deny oneself? It means more than just not hounding after your own appetites; it means trying hard not to have them in the first place. It means dying to all that jumbled and confused love from which God is excluded. If you aspire to purity of heart, take leave of yourself and be vigilant. Don't keep holding on to yourself, hold only to God, and to man in God and, with resignation, accept God's will, in prosperity, in adversity, in whichever way he chooses to make it known to you.

You must also endeavour, as far as it is possible, to clear your heart of ghosts and images of things of the world, of its representations and appearances and above all, as I said before, of all disorderly love. Avoiding gibbering social gatherings will be of much help here, as will, also, cutting down on occasions to speak and chatter, to be entertained, to enjoy oneself looking at beautiful things; to detach yourself from useless affairs and concerns; to mortify the senses, repudiating anything superfluous in food as well as in outward ornamentation and embellishment. And then, to awaken within you that concupiscent power in the soul that will multiply your desire to love God most fervently and virtuously.

You do not need to engage in syllogisms or intellectual speculation to do this, reader. All you need is to be willing to love. All you need is to aspire to God with unflagging passion, to wish for heaven and all else fervently, not resting, not pausing on anything that is not God himself, more and more, forever aiming to please him and to carry out his will. Listen to the Holy Spirit within you and make your own loving arrows. Mine go something like this: O good Jesus! You are my only hope, you are my only refuge! You are my only love! Beautiful Spouse, sweetness of my soul! Essence of my essence, heart of my very heart, delightful calm! My true joy, my hopeful consolation! Brilliant day of eternity, serene light of my heart! Resplendent dwelling, paradise of my soul! You are my beginning, you are all I need! What else could I possibly want on earth or heaven! You are the only truth, you are the only good, my Lord! Seduce me with your fragance so that innocently, joyfully, indefatigably, *I may chase after the odour of your lifegiving ointments!*

It is true that aspiring to God in this way is most efficacious for the effacement of sins, spiritual deformities and disharmony of the soul, for the enlightenment, simplicity, purification and arousal of the heart to God and, ultimately, so that God may engulf us, and swallow us, and join us to him.

But be warned that praying like this can also lead to spiritual gluttony! Sometimes, the result of jumping too high is, simply, a notable bump on the head! Many have gone wrong because they were seeking delights for delights' sake, rather than seeking them in God who gives them to us as gifts. So discretion is called for, and lots of it, as well as continuous vigilance, so that our intention remains pure, chaste and deiform, so that the only thing we seek is the glory of God. In a word, take care not to endanger your health by trying to have too much of a good thing.

Remember, too, that the nobleness of the human heart is so great that, though finite, it can nevertheless desire infinitely. God is infinite and wishes us to love him infinitely, and since there is nothing in finite beings that is infinite but our capacity to wish, God's majesty wants us to wish infinitely. That is why in ejaculatory aspiration and prayer, it is not the impossibility of our wishes becoming a reality that should keep us from wishing, but that our wishes are directed only to the honour and glory of God. For even if human capacity, being finite, prevents us from achieving what we desire, it is the desire itself that will be crowned by God, as the deed would be crowned were we capable of executing it. As our Saviour said: *It is from the heart that everything worthy of honour or reproach flows*.[3] Hence, though our acts cannot satisfy our will, our willingness will receive tribute and commendation.

I shall end this essay by saying that, for man to be aware of his limitations and of the disparity that exists between him and his Creator, nothing is more persuasive than that of aspiring to God when asking for humility, charity, mortification, union, patience and the other virtues. Because each time we ask for a virtue, or for his love, our conscience is suddenly confronted with what we have done, or wished for, that was contrary to what we are asking. Let us repent then before we go on asking. At the very least, while we are praying we should dismiss every thought or wish that comes to us contrary to what we are asking, for our heart cannot hold two opposing wishes at the same time. It follows, then, that while aspiring to God, what is repugnant and vicious in our heart

---

[3] Matt. 15:19.

must cease, or the prayer, sick and feeble, will never reach God because an impure heart cannot generate pure love. Oh with how much care should the servant of God strive not to keep in his heart anything that separates him from his Creator, with how much solicitude should he endeavour to steer his heart only towards him! If this is not done, neither health nor the kingdom of God will ever be ours. When we lose our willingness to do this, we lose more than heaven and earth, because neither heaven nor earth, nor all creation, will be of much use to us if our heart has been otherwise seized and seduced, thus deterring us from transforming, arising, pouring ourselves out on our Creator. This is why we must always struggle to keep our heart pure, so that we may be worthy and well disposed to be recipients of divine grace, to place our love in God, and for our abnegation and submission to prevail. This abnegation, this surrender of the self, by which man abandons himself, takes leaves of himself, disrobes himself absolutely of all that is his, offering it to God with no strings attached, this, I say, is the key that allows man to enter God and God to enter man. And the more man comes out of himself, the more room he leaves for God's grace and for his love to come in.

Chapter 15

On Love of Self: the greatest obstacle in the spiritual life.

It is now time to speak of self-love, the major obstacle we shall encounter on our way to a rich spiritual life.

This is an egotistical, self-serving love aiming towards placing the individual above all else, including God. This "founder of Babylon" is the source of all wrongs and all misfortune. It is an obstacle so great that it will incapacitate any resolve we might have to reform ourselves spiritually and aspire to God.

In order to understand what this love is and how it operates, let us try to understand the following well from the very beginning. There are two enemies, two contending forces within us, each pulling in its own direction, each struggling to gain supremacy over the other and reign supreme in our souls: they are the spiritual and the mundane, love of God and love of the world.

I say they are capital enemies because each struggles to achieve its own aim and objective. They are like two sovereigns each fighting for the establishment of their own crowns. There cannot be two kings in one kingdom ruling jointly, or side by side, or taking turns, there can only be one. And for us this means that there can only be one principal and primary love in our soul, one fountainhead, one source from which and through which everything else we love will be loved.

This struggle is a choice. A choice between the spiritual and the ephemeral; between the eternal and the transitory, between God and the world. If our first choice is not God, then, naturally, it is going to be whatever else our will and heart will choose it to be. And because our own self tends to favour that which it holds nearest to its heart, and being able, as it is, to love itself dearly, the self will choose itself. And so what we are now left with is a struggle, let us remind ourselves, a choice, for primacy in our soul between two contending loves: love of God and love of self. Two opposing sides for whom no agreement, no harmony, no possible compromise can ever be reached.

Love of God is upright, confident, self-assured. It needs no enemies for its own self-enhancement. Self-love on the other hand has a chip on its shoulder, always on the lookout to compete, to be first. It is mundane and mediocre, a bad loser, forever waging war on the spirit. Most unjustly, I may add, because only God can be first and primary, a truth we know instinctively through natural law and the rules of our own understanding.

Love of God cannot be second or third: it is first, or it is not. Even the very nature of any other love demands this exclusiveness, as I said earlier when speaking of love in general.

There is nothing else worthy of being our first love but love of God; He is king of our hearts; our hearts are his kingdom and he reigns over them. Love of God is quiet and orderly: it is just, true and righteous; it is the first just choice of our soul, the first virtuous choice of our will.

But what about self-love? Being against natural and divine law, what can you expect but for it to be messy and false, thwarted, inconsiderate and unjustifiable? It is against God, against truth and against nature; it is the first act of injustice, the first turmoil, injury, and offence to God; the first vice and the first evil; the first slap in God's face. When I take this most sovereign power to myself, I offend His Majesty gravely and do him great injustice; I am, in fact, scorning him, taking away the honour due only to him. I am making myself god in his place. And this is the worst evil deed I can possibly do because, quite unashamedly, I am trying to take away the supremacy that belongs only to him, and destroy it. I am not just disregarding God here. I am treating him as second to myself and, consequently, what I am in fact doing is snatching his crown.

This is the most grievous act of hostility we can do against God. It is the point at which unhappiness begins and from here on, we will hop and hop from vain to fleeting pleasure, all the way down to misery.

But let me say one more word about love. The nature of love is to convert the lover in the beloved. Whatever external object or creature I love, by the mere act of loving it, I transform myself in it, I become one with it. That is what love is. And so, when I love myself over and above everything else including God, I am making myself the object of my own love, in other words, I am making myself my own foundation, my own source and my own goal, my own starting point and my own end point; my own departure and my own destination, outside of God and against God.

I follow myself and love myself as an end in itself, and everything else I happen to love, I love it only because I see myself in it; because it benefits me. I use everything and everybody as a means to satisfy and love myself. I am my own lord and recognise no other. And in all this, what I am really doing is conferring on myself superiority over God. And having made the choice only to follow me and mine, my life will follow on accordingly.

I shall end now but let me just say one more thing: Self-love is the source of our hostility towards anything that is and has to do with God. This is because we see ourselves as gods and each one is a god to himself. And the tragedy of all this is that we end up believing it and wanting to be treated like one, craving God's honour and glory for ourselves. Pride and conceit are something that hurts God deeply and that he punishes most severely.

The major struggle we will face in our spiritual life, and concerning which we will have to remain most vigilant, is in not allowing this self-centred love to enter our souls. It is the seed of all evil, the major impediment to God.

Chapter 16

On how the love of God, when primary in our hearts, is the source of all good, and self-love is the root of all evil.

Ultimately, without love, there is nothing worth having. When love is alive in us, everything else touched by this prince is inheritor to its grace. All we are, and all we do, is affected by it. All our likes and dislikes are related to, and are affected by, the primary love in our hearts. And when this main love is the love of God, everything we do, and everything we love springs from it and is touched by this divine treasure. It is the source of our well being. It is our first justice and light, our rectitude and foundation of all righteousness. It is our first friend, true and good, and origin of all good and trustworthy friendship. It is the primary source of our strength, our first life. Love of God is the only love that makes us divine because of the marvellous virtue love has of converting and transforming our hearts into that which we love. And since it is God we love best, we shall be deified and made one spirit with him, wanting only what he wants, for however long as he wants it.

But, what happens when self-love is the predominant love in our hearts? We have already seen it is the main enemy of spiritual love. I am now going to show you that self-love is the fountain from which all ignorance, blindness, sin, vice and evil originate and hence the source of all injustice and the root of all the pains we suffer.

When Christ, our teacher, was speaking to his disciples as to the best path for them to follow for the improvement and deification of their souls, he gave them renunciation of the self as the first precept on the way to perfection. *If you would come after me,* He told them, *deny yourself, pick up your cross, and follow me.*[1] This is the rule of life and contains three remarkable, intimately harmonised and indivisible affirmations; indivisible, I say, for Christian teaching. They are like three strands of a silken rope leading us, infallibly, to a life of perfection. If one of them breaks,

---

[1] *... for he that will save his life shall lose it; and he that shall lose his life for my sake shall find it* (Matt. 16:24-5).

the remaining two will not be strong enough to enable us to continue on our climb to heaven. It is the three of them, together, that constitute a trinity of precepts, each one being one in itself, different from the others, but all three constituting one essence, the essence of an essentially good and virtuous life. *Deny yourself, pick up your cross, and follow me.* If we ignore one, we will be ignoring them all because we will be denying this essence, and in so doing, stripping our life of spiritual meaning. What I mean is this: if we deny ourselves and pick up our cross, but do not follow Christ, we are not Christians. We might be something else, but we are not Christians. Pagans can deny themselves and carry a cross, too. Alternatively, even if we were to carry a cross (and who is without one!) but not to deny ourselves, we would not be following Christ. Why not? Because Christ and one's own flesh, that is to say, the Cross and a life of worldly pleasures can never be friends. It is impossible to follow Christ if we do not first exile from ourselves the pleasures and passions of both mind and body through mortification and penance. This is, plainly, the first step to a spiritual and religious life: to the perfect life. Deny yourself! he said. A straightforward enough sentence, but if further elaboration were needed, I would simply add this: if you want to follow Christ, and walk in his footsteps, and be his friend and keep him company, give up treading on your own footsteps, or those that the world so seductively puts before you, and cease befriending yourself over and above God.[2] It is only by ceasing to be what you are, that you will become what you are not. Cease being carnal and you will be spiritual: for being a friend of the world and also of God (who is Spirit) is not possible. To live according to the appetites of mind and flesh, the pleasures and delights of the world and, at the same time, trying to please God, cannot go together, according to the New Testament.[3] Saint

---

[2] *And calling the multitude together with his disciples he said to them: If any man will follow me, let him deny himself and take up his cross and follow me. For whosoever will save his life shall lose it and whosoever shall lose his life for my sake and the Gospel shall save it. For what shall it profit a man, if he gain the whole world and suffer the loss of his soul?* (Mark 8:34-36).

[3] *That the justification of the law might be fulfilled in us who walk not according to the flesh, but according to the spirit. For they that are according to the flesh mind the things that are of the flesh; but they that are according to the spirit, mind the things that are of the spirit. For the wisdom of the flesh is death; but the*

Chrysostom says that denying oneself means seeing oneself as one's own enemy and treating oneself as such. And he gives this example by way of illustration:

Suppose you had a friend whom you esteemed and loved greatly, and so pleased were you with his company, that not a moment went by that you would be apart from him, or he from you. When eating, he would be at your table, when sleeping at your bedside, always with you, accompanying you everywhere, one could almost say you were another him and he another you. And suppose that one day you were told, with good reason, to be wary of him, for he was ready, not only to betray you and hand you over to your enemies, but also to take your life. You cannot believe this, of course. "That's not possible", you say, "You are lying to me!" But upon investigation, you find that the account might, after all, be accurate. Astonished and bewildered, you wonder: "How can this be? There must be a mistake!" But more evidence is brought before you, and you have to admit that it is, indeed, true. And you cry: "Is it possible that he was betraying me all along? Could I have been so blind as to believe that the one I thought to be my best friend was, in fact, my worst enemy?" And your like turns to dislike, and your friendship to animosity, your love, even, to hate. And you repudiate and deny him and no longer want anything to do with him. You might not even acknowledge him, or be inclined to help him, were you to see him beaten or persecuted. All you would want to say to him is: "How could you have deceived me so and all the while pretending to be my friend? Do not come near me, I wish for your company no longer!"

My dear brother, you, who continue to read these words, I say to you only this: don't you realise that this body of yours you so delight in pampering and indulging, this friend for whom you seek the most succulent dishes, the dearest wines, the finest silks, the most precious jewels of the Orient, and all those artificial joys and vain pleasures; are you not yet aware that the things of this world you so persist putting all your trust upon, with whom you delight

---

wisdom of the spirit is life and peace. Because the wisdom of the flesh is an enemy to God; for it is not subject to the law of God; nor can it be. And they who are of the flesh cannot please God (Rom. 8:4-8).

in such close company; this master at whose beck and call you serve all day and all night, this lover with whom you so pleasantly cohabit, do you not yet realize that this so-called friend is leading you up the garden path? That, under the guise of friendship, what he is doing is simply taking you along the rosiest road only to hand you over to your enemy, the devil, forever? How wisely and with what experience spoke Solomon when he said: *Do not go after your pleasures and affections, do not follow your will, do not tread on your own footsteps, for you will come to die at the joyful hands of your own enemies.*[4]

A holy monk was once asked what the surest and shortest way to heaven was. His reply was this: Be humble and take leave of yourself wherever you are. How well he expressed in a few, simple, words all that can be said on this matter! For it is in humility and in walking away from one's pleasures, both of body and of mind, that a great part of our ever attaining perfection is based. Because if self-love were to be eradicated from our hearts, there would be nothing left there but love of God.

Let me elucidate this point further. We are made in God's image, so God is the very centre of our souls. He is there in our innermost, there, in the deepest part of our hearts. But between the depths of our being and the *external* us, the *us* as we see ourselves, we have all this *stuffing*, made up of the world and of things of the world. A stuffing that packs the soul and obstructs our being able to touch him, a deafening *padding* that prevents us from hearing and sensing him. And as a result, the more of the world we have in us, the less we can feel our centre, and the more distant we are from God. If we were to rid ourselves of this *buffer* we would reach our depths and get to him easily, and be with him. This is what fleeing from oneself means. Simply put, to ignore any desires and seductions that are contrary to God.

He who truly denies himself and flees from his self at any time, place or circumstance has in his heart the words of Christ: *Not my will, Father, but yours.* These words made all he suffered and was about to suffer, meritorious. Firstly, because he surrendered his will to the will and the approbation of his Father, and for his

---

[4] *Go not after thy lusts: but turn away from thy own will. If thou give to thy soul her desires, she will make thee a joy to thy enemies* (Ecclesiasticus 18:30).

glory. Secondly, because he bound his will to perpetual obedience until death; and thirdly because, one could almost say, he *tied his Father's hands*, and he did this in such a way that the Father could no longer deliver him from drinking the most bitter cup of his Passion.[5] Through Christ's prayer – his act of resignation – and through the abnegation and surrender of his will, the Father was, so to speak, either *forced* to deliver him to that Passion which his will had already assigned and determined, or to disturb the obedience and resignation of the Son through which, above all else, he wished his Father's will to be fulfilled. As a result, the words having been said, it was not possible for Christ to be spared the cup of his Passion, precisely because of these two wills: the will of the Father, efficaciously offered, and the will of the Son, efficaciously accepted.

I hope it is clear how significant self-denial and submission of one's will are to God. There is no sacrifice more agreeable to him or more valuable to the soul than this, because there is nothing man prizes so highly as his freedom to will and to act. And when you give up this freedom, you give all you can give.

But self-denial, submission, and surrender are still not enough for a perfect life. The Divine Master added something else: to pick up our cross and follow him. The life of the Christian is a life crucified, and one cannot take a step forward following Christ without carrying a cross. *Semper mortificationem Iesu in corpore nostro circumferentes, ut et vita Iesu manifestetur in carne nostra mortali.* [6] These are the words of the Apostle and worthy of careful consideration. Weigh them if you want to mortify yourself in the image of Jesus, for there you will see and comprehend how essential it is to eradicate self-love from the soul. You will not find a trace of it in Jesus. All you will find is constant submission and surrender to the wishes of the Father until his death.

I shall end on this note. Self-love, as I have said, is the foundation and root of all evil and, in short, you will not free

---

[5] St. Francisco Ferrer, *De Passione Domine*, p.355: *Tristis est anima mea.*

[6] *We suffer persecution but are not forsaken; we are cast down but we perish not. Always bearing about in our body the mortification of Jesus, that the life also of Jesus may be made first in our bodies. For we who live are always delivered unto death for Jesus' sake, that the life also of Jesus may be made manifest in our mortal flesh* (II Cor. 4:9-11).

yourself from it unless you are ready to destroy it and crucify it in your heart. You must do this, because this self-serving master, once implanted in your soul, is far from sterile. From it two other different loves are born: one pertaining to the mind, representing our worship of status, success, concern for reputation, view of one's own standing and excellence. The other pertaining to the senses, our unquenchable thirst for physical satisfaction of all kinds. Therefore if, in contempt of God, you put yourself above him, you are going to love yourself in either of these two ways: by means of the mind or by means of the flesh, for it is from these two false gods that all others are begotten. If you worship your excellence and reputation, and what others think or say about you, you are going to love everything that leads to flattery, aggrandisement, and adulation. And if it is sensual delights you are after, you will unceasingly search for anything that promotes them, or contributes to them, forever caught in a whirl of increasing them and discarding them and increasing them again. But what is common to both pleasures of body and mind, however, is that we do not love them for themselves. We do not love temporal and external things for what they are but for the satisfaction we get from them. Thus, the more satisfaction they give us, the closer and the more entrenched they become established in our heart. And because the king of all these false gods, to whom they all bow and pay heed and obedience is worldly success, usually represented by the short-cut of money, money tends to be loved above all else.

And so we love degrees, and titles, and appellations and ranks. We love careers, and status, and commissions and positions; and we love dioceses and bishoprics and missions and jurisdictions; all of this we love, but what we are really loving is ourselves. We use them for our satisfaction and aggrandisement. We use them to worship ourselves.

My dear brothers and sisters in the Catholic Faith: I have been saying this all along and I am going to say it one more time. All sins are either founded on this self-centred and self-serving love, or are born from it. Self-love begets arrogance: arrogance being love of the adoring view we have of ourselves; it begets lust and gluttony which is an excessive devotion to carnal joy; it begets avarice: the disorderly yearning for external things, mainly money. And since what we love above all else is our own standing, reputation and the recognition afforded us by others, we are now going to hate everything else that stands in their way. And so now we have rage and anger, which are born out of love of vengeance on those who would frustrate our ambitions, passions, and delights. And we have envy, which is hate of someone else's fortune and love of his misfortune, when it affects us in any way. But it does not stop here. This monster is not content with affecting the mind only. It is eager to spread its tentacles to the body, too, and now we have laziness, lack of discipline, idleness which the body especially loves.

All of these will prevent us from starting or continuing good and virtuous works. St. Bernard was right: if only we could pluck out this poisonous weed from our hearts, there would be no need for hell.

Chapter 17

On how self-love, by destroying brotherly love, brings about division among men, and love of God brings them together and makes mankind one.

I have said many times that the heart of the lover, in loving, is transformed into the one he loves. I shall now add a further consideration: if there was but one primary and principal love shared by all men, and this love was directed towards the same beloved, every individual love would be in consonance and correspondence with the others, and there would be harmony and perfect unity among all. This is a simple and easily reasoned proposition that needs no further clarification. If all mankind would put their love in God, who is One, Most Simple and Common to all men, where would disharmony and division take root? There would be peace, friendship and harmony among men because no one would love their own self and their own will more than the will of the beloved whose love joins us and brings us all together. Each of us would wish what is best for our neighbour and want what God wants. Pity that this divine love reigns within so few of us! No further proof for this is needed than to look around and see how little friendship there is among men. Each man folds himself onto himself, loves his own wants, follows his own will, and so concerns himself primarily with himself, his reputation, his standing, his own tastes and pleasures, his own carnal appetites, his own likes and dislikes! We love ourselves and our own drives and desires; and as these drives and desires vary according to each person, or to speak more accurately, as there are as many desires as there are people, it is not possible for me to love my neighbour's excellence, reputation, tastes and pleasures, his appetites and affections, unless I see some benefit, or he ultimately serves my own ends. It is from here that disagreements, quarrels, hates, animosities, and wars evolve. Because I will detest your good fortune if it in any way diminishes mine, and you will abhor mine if it interferes with yours, and here we are, forever vying with and elbowing each other. Because none of us can ever have enough: enough satiety of the things of this world, enough of our own glory, enough of our good reputation, enough of our own delights; and this is the reason why we are forever hungry, mendicants of riches that will never fill the emptiness in our souls.

It is the love of God that causes unity, harmony, and peace among those who love him. It is self-directed love that causes war, division, and hate. The reason is that I love myself not as "man" but as "this particular man" and be I Peter or Tom, we all go about it in the same way. We turn ourselves into detached units, isolate ourselves from others, concern ourselves with our selves alone and, consequently, since we are all that we love, transform ourselves into the object of our own love and take account of no one else. We love ourselves for the sake of our own selves only, as individuals, not as people in family with others; we love, in short, our singularity, not our humanity. And because love embraces what it loves and nothing beyond, since I am the object of my own love, this singular love of mine concerns itself with me and me alone, and does not relate to any other creature in any way save in what may prove to be ultimately convenient and advantageous to myself over the rest.

Loving God is altogether different. When we make God the primary object of our love, love becomes communal and universal, the root and foundation of all good, because since we emanate from him and we are all preserved and sustained by him, God is communal and universal to all creatures. Common and universal love is good; singular and individualistic love is bad, and it will become better or worse according to how universal or singular the object of our love is.

I wish I could continue on this subject because I have so much more to say about it. I am thinking in particular of the duties and obligations we have towards God, what we owe him as our God and Lord. If you are wise you will have no problem understanding this; remove yourself from that central stage you placed yourself in and put God there instead; by looking at what you wanted, wished and procured for yourself, you will see what you ought to want, wish and procure for God. And that's it. It may seem a simple thing to say (though not as simplistic as you may imagine - it might contain more mystery and theology than it might at first appear) but I shall stop here and move on to talk about how these two seeds, love of God and love of self, finally blossom and what fruits they bear.

First, please note this: Everything that man does, once done, leaves him with either a feeling of joy or a feeling of sadness. These are the fruits that grow from what our conduct plants and cultivates in our hearts. What we all want, of course, is pleasure and happiness, that is the ultimate aim of all our endeavours: to obtain pleasure and joyfulness from them. Indeed, this is how the Italian[1] defined love: "Love is a movement impelled by desire that reposes in delectation." And he spoke well, for when man attains the joy he is after, he is filled, he is contented, he rests.

The opposite of joy is sadness, our natural antagonist, an enemy from which we all want to flee, and as in the case with joy, a wish all men share. True joy emanates from divine love; it blossoms from heavenly roots. True sorrow originates in love of self, from hurtful, devilish, infernal roots.

The fact that true joy can only come from love of God can even be demonstrated philosophically. To begin with, joy can only be derived from love. If there is no love there can be no joy. We feel joy when our will attains what it yearns for. Desiring or loving nothing does not bring about joy. Consequently, when God is the primary object of our love, the joyfulness we derive from this love is a joy that proceeds from loving God, thus, joy everlasting, because God is eternal; he is not going to die, or go missing, or take a holiday. God will always be present to the will and heart that loves him. As St. John says: *God is charity and he that perseveres in charity perseveres in God, and God in him.*[2] And as the will retains what it principally loves and desires, and in loving we become the object of our own love, it follows that if we have God as our first love, since he is immortal, firm and unchangeable, since he lives forever and needs no-one, love for God, then, is immortal, constant and firm, unchanging, and ever abundant. The reason for this is, as I have said, that the lover dons the clothes of his beloved and, since joy is engendered by love, it follows that joy

---

[1] Dante.

[2] *God is charity; and he that abideth in charity abideth in God and God in him* (John 1.4:16).

born of the divine love will be eternal, constant, firm, sound, immortal and persevering in the will, always free, from which nothing can be taken by force. In short, joy assumes the qualities of love and of the object of that love, it is the mirror of our love and the things we love. Can the happiness, the joy, the consolation, the jubilation of the soul so transformed in God by love be ever imagined, always possessing him, always partaking of him with the certainty he will never leave us? No words can describe this. No theories or analysis can explain it. *It can only be had*, said our father St. Augustine, *never appraised or explained.*

The sage said the joy that flows forth from the love of God is the heart of man and the life of the soul, and he spoke rightly. Sadness is either death or a messenger of death. Joy dilates, fortifies, nourishes, and delights the heart. Sadness mortifies, shrinks, weakens, and annihilates it. Of one and the other spoke the sage in his Proverbs: *A heartened spirit prepares us and leads us to health, as a precious medicine; a sad disposition dries the bones.*[3] In another version, it says: *Animus gardens, bonam facit medicinam (A happy patient makes for medicine to be of good use).* The first text is better, I think, and more in agreement with the translation of the Seventy who write: A *happy heart produces a good disposition in man. And its opposite, a sad spirit, dries the bones and eats up all virtue.* Or as Cajetan puts it: *(Joy is) the marrow and medulla by which bones gain strength.* There is a similar passage in Ecclesiasticus: *Life of man is the happiness and joy of the heart, and happiness lengthens the time of life.*[4] Lucretius, the poet, said: *Sickness and anguish bring the wasting away and death of man.* But should we wish, with the Venerable Bede, to move on to the spiritual significance of this, what Solomon is saying is that if in our soul we have the consolation and joyfulness that comes from the love of God, this will externally adorn and beautify us with the flowers of virtues, and we will rejoice in the fruits of heavenly rewards. But he who is tormented and afflicted with the sadness of this age – *daughter of self-love, cause of death*, the Apostle called it – cannot have the stoutness of charity, the medulla and marrow that

---

[3] *A joyful mind maketh age flourishing; a sorrowful spirit dries up the bones* (Prov. 17:22).
[4] *The joyfulness of the heart is the life of man and a never failing treasure of holiness; and the joy of man is the length of life* (Sirach 30:22).

feeds virtues' bones, and will thus perish, enfeebled and desiccated, from his sins. And what is hell but eternal sadness? What, indeed, is heaven but eternal joy? He who has the love of God in his soul has all goodness there is to be had because he has the true joy that derives from the one love that give us a true blessed life. He will not only receive joy in God himself but everywhere God is, for our love extends to all things our heart loves. And what can be more vast, what can be more delicate than the love of God who, having created all creatures, loves all and feels animosity towards none? Then, if I love God, I shall find joy everywhere, and as much joy as diverse are his creatures whom I love, in him and through him, especially man created in his image and for whom all others were created. Let us confess, then, that loving this great Lord God is, in some way, to taste in this mortal and feeble life we live the glory we await, for living in this unceasing state of joy, which nobody can take away but ourselves, is that not living a holy, wonderful, heavenly life?

The good news is that we need neither silver, gold nor any other external riches for us to possess this joy, because when we have in this world God's love, we have in ourselves and within ourselves his riches, which no one can see, no one can touch but he who receives and enjoys them. What could all the riches of the world add to my joy when I am carrying with me a portable heaven, a soul so rich, so overflowing with that true joy that flows forth from divine love? And what could possibly console me if I am hauling around a snarled and twisted conscience which is nothing but a sempiternal hell? The Apostle said it: *Wrath, indignation, tribulations, anguish, is all a man with bad conscience can expect*[5] – not just those already in hell, of whom the Apostle was speaking here, but the living, too, who have offended God, and thus become angry and impatient, full of anguish and heartbreaking tribulations. Oh yes, these are indeed, the signs of man condemned: rage, indignation, tribulation, torment; they can be clearly observed in those who decided to put themselves first, in front of God. They seek honours and pleasures, and they find

---

[5] Cf. Rom.2.8-9:...*but to them... who give merit to iniquity, wrath and indignation, tribulation and anguish upon every soul of man that worketh evil.*

them, and happiness with them too, oh but the strings attached are so embedded in grief and pain by fear of losing them, that this happiness cannot really be called true joy. It is a false joy, a vain joy, ultimately, a deceiving joy.

And if we were to delve a little deeper into whence it comes, we would soon find that it was sired by self-love, and self-love, as we know, is chaotic, unjust, improper, thwarted, false, depraved, corrupt, dirty, against man's nature as human, against the order of the universe, against all creatures; it is vile, lewd and malicious, the first wrong and the source of all wrongs, the first vice, the first poison, the first death; the first darkness and blindness, the first lie and cradle of all lies. Self-love is the first injustice.

So what kind of joy, think you, can be expected from so sad a beginning, from such a bitter root? A joy as confused, false and vicious as the father who begot it: the father outside of God, the son outside God; the father an enemy of God, the son an enemy of God; the father against God, the son without God. As the father so the son. A chip off the old block indeed.

Every time I am pleased and delighted or feel some contentment for loving myself above all else, I am feeling this against God and against the will of God, because such happiness can only come from my contempt, my effrontery, and my lack of respect for him. What I am doing is seizing his crown, putting it on my head, and like the king of Tyre proclaiming: "I am the one God."[6] I am saying to you here that deriving pleasure from this is even more malicious than putting yourself first before God, and therefore a more serious offence. Loving yourself more than God is bad enough, but to derive pleasure and enjoyment from offending his Majesty in this manner is slapping him directly on his face.

To this fatal end had arrived those of whom it is written: *They rejoice when doing wrong, and take pleasure and joy in their abominations.*[7] Among all the visions that Ezechiel saw,[8] when God commanded him to dig in the temple's wall, the one that most provoked God's anger and fury was to see them, not just bringing branches to the

---

[6] Is. 23.
[7] Prov. 2:14.
[8] Ezek. 8.

idols, but delighting in their fragrance as if rejoicing at that kind of idolatry. *And they bring the branches to their nose so as to vex me,* he said, (though some Hebrews translate this passage in a different manner, which results in an appalling insult to God: *Mittunt foetorem in faciem meam*). Such was the insolence, such the debauchery, such the shamelessness they had come to!

It is a grave wrong, and an abominable sin, to love yourself more than God because, in so doing, you are usurping his place, you are making yourself god. But it is worse still, and mind: no amount of tears will wash this away, to be pleased and rejoice and be delighted in showing yourself off as such, a serious offence and a grave insult to the true One.

Holy king David commanded Solomon to take the life of Joab, son of Zeruiah[9] not because, under the guise of friendship, he had killed Abner and Amasa, two courageous captains of his army, but because he had the shameless audacity to smear their blood upon his fastened armour and upon his shoes. As I said, it is sheer malice to add delight and satisfaction to sin, and the sinner is only showing his wickedness when he prides himself on being one.

I could tell you so much more about love of God and love of self, about the joyfulness of one and grief and sadness of the other, but perhaps it is time for me to recount what I have said.

Love of God and love of self, as first loves, are incompatible because of their animosity and continuous struggle with each other. Hence:

Joy from loving God and joy from putting oneself in God's place cannot live together either, because they would necessarily destroy each other.

The first joy derived from love of God is legitimate, comes from truth, and is true. The second joy derived from self-love is sacrilegious, comes from falsehood; it's a liar.

The first is joy based upon justice; the second, joy upon injustice.

The first is born of eternity; the second, of vanity.

The first is of God; the second, against God.

---

[9] III Kings 2:6.

The first multiplies and confirms our friendship with God; the second, our animosity.

The first satiates, fills, fortifies, sweetens and softens the heart; the second, embitters, weakens, drains it; it disturbs and disquiets it; it always leaves it hungry and overcome with thirst.

The first lasts and stays forever; the second is ephemeral and transient

The first never turns into sorrow; the other does indeed, and most certainly: for *pain may be added to that laughter, or laughter to that pain, but the place of joy will be occupied by weeping.*[10]

Nothing bad can come to you from the first joy because it is of good stock, it is healthy; from the second you will have nothing but pain.

The first is life-giving, healthy, kind, glorious, honest, filled with delight, in accordance with nature and reason; the second is deadly, abominable, lewd, gross, rude, against nature and reason.

The first illuminates and clarifies the understanding; the second blinds it and fills the soul with darkness. As St. Augustine said: *the light of truth will abandon and blind the transgressor of divine law.*

The first joy is worthy of eternal prizes in heaven; the second of nothing but grief. It is the cause of all that suffering in hell.

May God – who can – destroy our love and confirm His. Amen.

---

[10] Prov. 14:13.

Part the Second

On the spiritual and loving struggle and the
triumph of God over the rational soul

Chapter 1

On the gaze of the loving eyes of God and the first triumph of love: the wounding of the soul.

Having discussed at length in Part I how the soul wounds God's heart when, filled with faith and charity, she lifts her eyes up to him, we are now going to reflect on how the eyes of God, in turn, wound the soul.

Do not be apprehensive at the wonderful wounds God inflicts on our souls when he visits us, enchanting and stealing our hearts: we do the same to him; and if our love can touch God in this way, what will not the love of God do to us! Great is the power of love and the virtue of charity, said Richard of St. Victor. It grows and deepens in the soul gently, little by little. But how can this ever be explained rationally! Ardent love burns everything it touches: it permeates the heart, it enkindles the will, it so intimately invades the soul, that she can now invoke her beloved with the words he himself had used: *You wounded me, my love; you wounded me with one of your eyes and with a strand of your hair.*[1]

The Philosopher said, and rightly, that whither love goes the eyes will invariably follow. When the soul senses the loving eyes of God gently caressing her with his gaze, she knows that she can then ask, and get, whatever she desires. *I will look on you and make you increase. You shall be multiplied and I will establish my covenant with you.*[2] Abel sensed the eyes of God and he was gratified. Cain did not: his sacrifice was not accepted and he planned his brother's death.[3] God set his eyes on the Virgin and she confessed herself recipient of his grace; he noticed her lowliness and made her the most honoured of all women. *I grew within his gaze*, she said, *and gave such fruit that, through Him, I am blessed through generations.*[4]

There is a verse in one of the Psalms that says *the eyes of God look on the poor* (from the Hebrew *the eyes of God hide in the poor*). [5]

---

[1] Cant. 5.
[2] Lev. 26:9.
[3] Gen. 4.
[4] *Because he regarded the humility of his handmaid; for, behold, from henceforth all generations shall call me blessed* (Luke 1:48).
[5] Psalm 10:4.

The Holy Spirit giving us to understand here that, just as the rays of the sun penetrate the earth pervading all, from precious gems, gold and silver mines and other wonders to the tiniest flower and the littlest bird, vivifying and gratifying all with its warmth, so the eyes of God, permeating the humble and meek of heart, sweetly nurture and nourish them in profuse spiritual abundance. He glanced at Peter and killed his demons, eradicating the poison with which he had been infected. He glanced at Matthew, Mary Magdalene and the Good Thief; and every day he turns his eyes to us, the unworthy, and he justifies and sanctify us. He sweetly and gently gazes at his spouse, our soul, and like a straight arrow, pierces her through the heart.

Richard of St. Victor says: Let us contemplate the magnificence of the love of Christ and how he ennobles our soul with his loving gaze. This uplifting experienced by the soul goes beyond anything love of parents, wife, or children can ever effect. This exquisiteness is so sublime it makes one abhor life itself. O passionate and violent love! It is with this, the majesty and benevolence of God, that we should concern ourselves. Not with defining and speculating as scholars are apt to do, but by humbly acknowledging and professing his glorious and wondrous work, as all saints and holy patriarchs have done.

St. Bonaventure and Richard say this bold and forceful love (forceful, not because it coerces our freedom but because it vigorously raptures the soul to God) consists of four stages, or climbing steps. In the first step there are injuries; in the second, prisons; in the third, enfeeblement and infirmity; in the fourth, languor and death. What they are saying is that divine love wounds, enchains, depletes, empties, and then consumes.

Classical philosophers agreed that love has the power to hurt and wound hearts and souls. They portrayed love as a naked child, blind, with wings, and loaded with arrows, so as to depict the passion and devotion of carnal, but also of pure, love. For this same word, *love,* applies to both human and divine, to the spiritual and that which is not. Although you understand, reader, that when I say *love* here, I am not speaking about human attraction, but referring exclusively to spiritual love, for my intention in this book is to reflect solely on the love that God has for the soul and the soul has for God. I do, however, make use of the tools handed down to us by the poets who sang of human love, and use them to explain love divine, in the same way an architect makes use of frames and scaffolding to erect his building and set up its vaults and foundation. Once construction is over and the building is erected, he simply does away with them because they are no longer needed. The edifice then stands, and it is seen, for what it is.

So love is a child, we say, either because those in love tend to mirror as much discretion and prudence as children do in their behaviour, or because they become as uncomplicated and transparent as they are. This transparency is most evident in spiritual love, which restores man to a state of innocence such that they can actually walk that winding path and enter through that most narrow of doors into the kingdom of God.

It has wings because it is with great fleetness that lovers make themselves visible to their beloved. As Euripides said, they live not in themselves but in the object of their love. Also because, as we all know, true love is never reluctant or dilatory to get going. As it is written of those animals Ezechiel saw[6] that they would go and come back like rays, glowing with a fire that could neither be seen or heard. Meaning that the saints who burn in the love of God are like fire itself: they go to God rapt by his sweetness and they are forced back to us in charity to alleviate our needs. St. John speaks in his Apocalypse of four animals covered with eyes and wings who would encircle the throne of God, resting not day or night, chanting: Holy, holy, holy.[7] The divine Dionysius when explaining the qualities of seraphim, who are nearest to God, said that they are forever loving, fervently loving, loving without end; they pervade all that of God can be pervaded and, for him, descend like beams to touch the love of his creatures.

---

[6] *And as for the likeness of the living creatures: their appearance was like that of burning coals of fire, and like the appearance of lamps. This was the vision running to and fro in the midst of the living creatures, a bright fire and lightning going forth from the fire. And the living creatures ran and returned like flashes of lightning* (Ezek. 1:13-14).

[7] *...and in the midst of the throne and roundabout the throne were living creatures, full of eyes before and behind...and the four living creatures had each of them six wings, and roundabout and within they are full of eyes. And they rested not day and night, saying: Holy, holy, holy, Lord Almighty, who was, and who is, and who is to come* (Apoc. 4:6-8).

But why did they depict love blind? Because although it has a mind of its own to begin with, it does not depend on reason for its nourishment and growth. St. Bernard spoke most elegantly about this when referring to that section in the Song of Songs when the spouse pleads to her beloved: *Kiss me with the kiss of your mouth.* And let no-one misconstrue this prayer now, or go about attaching some coarse or vulgar meaning to the words the soul says to her God in an exuberance of love, for both in spiritual as in mundane love the cry of the lover is the same: I know I am given what I merit but, oh, so much less than I desire! It is the heart that encourages the lover, not the mind. Do not reprimand him, then, for being too bold and intrepid. The intensity of love induces such pain and anguish in the soul that the lover can in no way hide or dissimulate his passion. Perhaps this was what the sage had in mind when he said: *Can a man hide fire in his bosom and not burn his garments?*[8] And what is love, I ask, but a fire that, by its very nature, has to reveal itself? A fire that no amount of reasoning or discretion can conceal? Plato admitted that it was impossible to hide something the effects of which were so obvious to the naked eye: he mentioned the eyes, voice, colour, tongue, countenance, and many other external signs.

To these, Richard and St. Bonaventure added five more intimate and secret signals by which, in their estimation, love can truly, with absolute certainty, be discerned: deep and heart-burning sighs, day-dreaming reveries, languishing thoughts, vexing hopes and an ecstasy-inducing elation. Each of these manifestations will need to be explained and commented upon in detail, and I intend to do so at some length in the section on forceful and violent love. But let us now move on and look at those mighty arrows love brings in his quiver: those sharp, piercing arrows so eager to wound men and gods alike.

---

[8] Prov. 6:27.

Chapter 2

On the arrows of love

Why did the poets depict love carrying bow and arrows? First, because it shoots from afar and straight into the heart; secondly, because like that of an arrow, love's piercing is clean and direct, the pain it produces deep and intense. Lastly, because though the puncture itself may hardly be noticeable, the injury takes long to heal, much longer to cure.

It should be of no surprise to anyone to hear that love causes anguish and pain. It is clear in the words of the Beloved when he acknowledges that the spouse has wounded him with her gaze, as it is in the confession of St. Augustine to the crucified Christ: *My heart has been wounded in your charity*; also, in what is written of our holy father St. Francis who, sensing God looking lovingly at him, was left wounded in his hands, his feet, his heart. Personally, what assures me absolutely is the way in which this most chaste love between God and his spouse, the soul, is treated in the Song of Songs. In this holy book, the delicacy of love is often alluded to in terms of battles, clashes, bucklers and shields, garrisons, castles, armies. In chapter 6 we read: *Thou art beautiful, O my love, sweet and comely as Jerusalem; terrible as an army set in array* [1] or, as the Seventy interpret it, *all to my taste.* Indeed, it is as soft and sweet as kindness itself, but also terrible, that is, powerful and commanding as a well-disciplined army ready for war. I confess that, to me, this is one of the most beautiful passages in the whole of Scripture, a passage that, in my opinion at least, best proclaims the energy, the vigour, and the power of love. Because here we have the Beloved himself confessing to being subjugated to the beauty of his spouse as unconditionally as if an armed force had defeated him in battle; as if he were saying: "your eyes drew me as powerfully as if an artillery of brave soldiers had engaged me in combat. Let my surrender pay tribute to your loveliness and be it known how pleased and gratified I am with you." The line that follows: *Turn thy eyes from me for they have made me flee away*[2] confirms,

---

[1] *Pulchra est amica mea, et suavis, et decora nimis, terribilis, ut castrorum acies ordinata* (Cant. 6:3,9).
[2] Cant. 6:4.

I think, this interpretation. Theocritus,[3] St. Ambrose,[4] and Plotinus[5] all spoke of love in the same way. Plato in the Symposium speaks extensively of the power of love, how it conquers and subdues every other passion making itself lord of all hearts, men's as well as gods. There is no straight lance that love cannot bend. It reveals itself through the eyes, those fortresses whence spears are charged directly into the heart, wounding it, stealing it, captivating it. As the poet so beautifully sang of Helen: *How beautiful, O Helena, are thou for whose eyes all hearts expire!* As Tibullus praised Sulpicia: *Her eyes, desiring to scorch the gods, became two magnificent lamps of fire.* Richard of St. Victor says that God intimately moves us, and with such frequency, that we are not even aware of when his arrows are shot. The soul only feels the wound; a wound so deep that the heart itself can come to feel physically injured. Though invisible, this pain is evident and real, and could not be ignored if one tried. God wounds, and upon wounding he leaves, hides, and the soul becomes confounded and distraught at his absence, the wound gets bigger, and so desire grows. And now it burns, now it scorches, and she hungers and desires and at the top of her voice cries:

> No more jollity, mirth, joys
> I seek only God who has me wounded
> For his I am, my Innermost his own.

Only in him who caused the pain can the cure be found.

The quality of God's arrows and this bellicose pageantry of Christ, King of Heaven, is beautifully described by the prophet: *Your arrows are sharp and under thee shall people fall into the hearts of the king's enemies.*[6] He first girt Christ with his sword in the manner of a most gallant gentleman always accompanied by his three most faithful pages, truth, justice and meekness of heart, and then put arrows in his hand. For God engages the soul not only with his

---

[3] Theocritus, *Bucolics*, 2.
[4] St. Ambrose, *On Cain and Abel*, chap. 4
[5] Plotinus, Enneads, III, 5.
[6] Psalm 44:6.

sword, a face-to-face weapon, but with sling and arrows as well, which injure from afar.

In Psalm 126 it is written: *The sons of the shaken*, that is, the "brushed-off", the rejected (in the Hebrew, the sons of the act of shaking itself, i.e. of rejection) *are like arrows in the hands of a good archer who, accurately and unequivocally, shoots from afar wounding his enemies.*[7] By "Sons of Rejection", some understand the Apostolic Fathers, who rejecting, or brushing aside, the mendacity of the world, became like arrows themselves, arrows shot by the arm of a skilled archer which hit the enemy with such accuracy and speed that no obstacle can obstruct or thwart their way. Others interpret these arrows to be the uplifting and affection with which we are favoured when God touches our soul, inspiring it to faith, hope and charity, not stopping until they have reached their target. And how sharply they hit sometimes! But how quickly, too, one succumbs to being touched by God with one of those arrows shot with his omnipotent arm! The mightiest of the earth bite the dust and with St. Paul plead: *Lord what wilt thou have me do?*[8] Submitting to God the weapons with which she had been offending him, as St. Paul did, is a most telling sign of a wounded soul. *It was with my will, O Lord, that I made war on you. Here it is, take it. I leave it in your hands.*

Mother Teresa of Jesus, a holy Religious,[9] wrote of the ecstasies of love she had experienced. In one passage she says: *I can't explain it very well because I don't think I even understand it myself. I mean, how it is that God hurts the soul in this way, and the pain and the sorrow that one feels inside. You can end up losing all consciousness of yourself, that's how intense it is. But together with this pain and this sadness, I mean, at the same time, there comes such gentle, such tender but such overwhelming joy! Oh, the joy inside is so immense, there is nothing in the whole world like it. I didn't want it to fade, I just wanted to stay like that forever and ever if only I could.*

But this pain and this joy and this anguish and this everything-altogether-at the same time would leave me so anxious...so confused... For a time I

---

[7] Cf. Ps. 126:3-5.
[8] Acts 22:10.
[9] St. Teresa of Avila.

really thought I was losing my mind. I couldn't understand what was happening with me.

Further on, she describes one the visions she had:

I saw an angel. He was standing next to me, physically, right there! He was small, he wasn't very big, oh, but he was so beautiful…his face was absolutely glowing, he was so radiant! I thought he was one of the higher-up angels, you know, the ones that are always burning? Cherubim, I think. I know there are differences between angels and angels, these angels are different from those, and those from some other ones, but I don't think I really know which ones are which, and they are not going to come and present themselves to me! This one was holding an arrow in his hand. It was a long arrow, made of gold, I think, and the end tip of it was on fire, it was burning. And then he just turned and plunged it into my heart! And I could feel its piercing right down to the very essence of my being. The pain was so intense…I think I ended up screaming out loud! And then when he removed it, it felt as if the whole of me was coming out of me with it. So there I was, burning to a crisp! The love of God was scorching me inside. But there was such tenderness with this pain… Such sublime joy! Oh, it's such a beautiful thing, this, that goes on between God and the soul! The pain itself is not a physical pain as such, it's something that goes on in the soul, but the body knows it too, you know, and plenty! Now I know. I know the difference. I know that I will never be whole with anything that is less than God. And I pray and pray to the good Lord to let others go through these experiences as well. Then they'll know for themselves I am not telling any lies![10]

I believe Mother Teresa. Our Father St. Francis, too, had a vision in the Mountain of Alvernia where, being favoured with Christ's physical and spiritual wounds, he humbly sensed within himself the image of the Crucified. But still, even though the pain was so intense that his body could hardly endure it, this seraphic gentleman would not wish for the vision to fade away.

Those words in the Song of Songs by which the spouse confesses herself languishing in love: *Stay me up with flowers, compass me about with apples: because I languish with love,*[11] according to an older translation, instead of *amore langueo* – I languish with love – it is written *Vulnerata charitate ego sum* (I am wounded with charity).

---

[10] St. Teresa, *Life*, XXIX, 16-17.
[11] Cant. 2:5.

So, you see, reader, spiritual love hurts too. It can hurt deeply. It has a death and it has a life of its own. It has been said that the pain derived from divine love comes about when the yearning of the soul is unfulfilled. Others say that it is self-induced by its own ardour and intensity, burning and ailing the body as it does, and this is because when the beloved is absent from the one who loves, sadness, sometimes referred to in literature as "illness", sometimes as "wounds" will always, inevitably, follow.

In the *Tusculine Disputations*, Cicero[12] says that the sadness caused by the intense desire to win what one loves is a wound in the heart and an illness of the soul. And he says so rightly, because hope and desire for some good, by themselves, afford delectation. But it is the recognition of its actual absence that awakes sorrow and sadness in the self, as it is written: *Hope that is deferred afflicteth the soul: desire when it cometh is a tree of life.*[13]

Dionysius says that spiritual love is intimately, intentionally, actively and reducibly acute. [14] Intimately acute because just as a sharpened sword divides one thing into two halves, so this tender love, by wounding the heart, cuts off the lover from himself to unite him to the Beloved.

It is intentionally acute in regard to both the cognitive and affective faculties. In regard to the mind, because, when God is the first and principal object of love, the lover, totally immersed in love and oblivious to himself, is brought to understand only God; in regard to the heart, because, when one loves God intimately, he cannot possibly be content with mere company or friendship. This lover wants God to come in and take over. This lover wants God to penetrate and pervade all of him and be submerged in him. He would even want to become one with God, if that were possible.

It is actively and reducibly acute as fire is, introducing its form to all it touches, excluding what is alien. This is what happens when the Beloved looks lovingly at our souls: he moves us, he draws us to him with such intensity that all we can do is sigh: *I am wounded with your love.*

---

[12] Cicero, *Tusculan Disputations.*
[13] Prov. 13:12.
[14] Dionysius, *On the Celestial Hierarchies*, bk. 7.

This pain, this anguish for the Beloved is not continuous, however; at least not during this first step up the staircase to spiritual union. There will be landings in between and, with them, some relief. Spiritual lovers can, and do, tend to other things. The ardour is not at high-fever pitch yet, it is more like hot flashes which come and go, sometimes with more frequency, sometimes with less, sometimes disappearing altogether, only to return. But always after a short interval they reappear with increased intensity, seizing the already weary nerves and abated spirit and kindling them with greater fire.

Such is the staircase of growth in divine love. Continual absences and visitations, more painful and more joyful each time but always with increased intensity, for there is less resistance each time, there are fewer barriers to break down, less impediments in its way. A high fever that lasts several days may sometimes weaken the body to the point where serious illness can occur and the patient might have to be confined to bed. Divine love will take over the soul, subdue and bond her in such a wonderful way that it will eventually speak, think, and occupy herself with nothing but the love of God.

Origen said there is no perfect love without wounds. In the Scythian tradition, when two of them wanted to consecrate and perpetuate their friendship, it was customary that they would injure themselves by having their fingers slit open. The blood gushing forth would then be collected in a vessel in which both of them would dip the tip of their swords first and then drink the rest. What this ritual meant to them was that, from that moment onwards, they were no longer two but one. In other words, one could not hurt the other without injuring himself.

The first step to union with God, then, is being wounded in love.

Chapter 3

On the second triumph: the chains of love.

I did warn you at the beginning, reader, that at some stage you might feel inclined to close this book and lay it aside. I said this because I am aware that what I have been saying might seem rather strange, especially if you have never loved. But you are still here with me, and since what I am going to do now is to talk about bonds, prisons, and chains, I am going to ask you to pray before you continue reading if you feel yourself enslaved to any sin or vice, so that those chains with which the devil captured and jailed you be forever broken, and you may be ready for a captivity of another kind: a bondage that takes place in prisons of bliss and freedom, there where spiritual love dwells.

I shall speak about these rescuing chains of liberty now, these chains of which God spoke through the prophet Hosea: *I shall draw them with the cords of Adam, with the bonds of love.*[1] Saint Jerome and the Seventy interpreters replaced the word *Adam* for that of *men: In the chains of men and in the bonds of charity I shall bring my subjects to me.* As if God had said: I do not want to force men to me by threats, lashes or fear. I want to bring them to me by the same means they use to attract one another: by way of love. You see what he is saying here, reader. He is saying: I do not want you to come to me because you fear me. I do not want you to come to me because you think you may be punished if you do not. I want you to come to me because you love me. It is the love I have for you that will pull you to me. The Latin word *traham* expresses this passion well. *I shall captivate them and they will come to me, for my love and compassion for them is greater than all the attractions the world can offer them.* The Chaldean paraphraser puts it this way: *I shall cajole and entice souls to me with the over-indulgent love reserved for one's beloved and spoiled children, and they will be bound and chained to me with the power of love,* for love is the most powerful tool there is to sway and conquer the hearts of men, be they harder than rocks.

Do not go looking for love in conjurers and magic spells, said Seneca to one of his friends. I'll hand over to you freely love's

---

[1] Hosea 11:4.

most powerful talisman: *Love and you will be loved,* meaning, if you want to be loved, be a loving person yourself first, you will not attract love to yourself otherwise. Brilliant reasoning, this, by Seneca! The philosopher's dictum is based on this: when individuals have a particular characteristic in common, it is through this shared distinctiveness, or likeness, that they are able to recognise each other. Plato had already explained that love is a resemblance which, first, we become aware of and, then, we communicate to the other; so that if both you and I possess this mutual bond, it will urge you to love me and it will compel me to love you. And more. The one who loves, the lover, has this likeness of the beloved carved in his soul, thus becoming a most lucid mirror upon which the beloved is reflected; and the beloved, seeing himself in the other, is then compelled to love back for he is instinctively drawn to loving that wherein he dwells.

This is the glorious device of which our Lord availed himself to draw men to him. He took our likeness and came into the world as we are. He walked among us willing to serve, approachable. He ministered to us, helped us, endured humiliation, suffered; he opened his heart to us. He loved us. He was hungry and thirsty, tired, weary and hurt; and then he died crucified. What did *he* get out of it, you ask! I'll tell you. He got exactly what he wanted to get. He captivated and bound us to him with the chains of his love. Saint Ambrose, speaking on that passage of Saint Paul to the Phillippians: *He humbled Himself being obedient unto death* [2] said: All the grace and favours that God had bestowed upon me had done nothing to move me. But it was when I saw him there, nailed to a wood, humiliated in that manner, that I prostrated myself, acknowledged him as Lord, and adored him.

What would you say the most triumphant victory in the history of the world has been? It has been Christ. Christ incarnate and killed for mankind. *They surrounded me like bees and they burned like fire among the thorns, and in the name of the Lord I was revenged of them.*[3] And St. Augustine remarks: *Hearts that were of thorns before then*

---

[2] *Humiliavit semetipsum usque ad mortem* (Phil. 2:8).
[3] Psalm 117:2.

burned with the Spirit of God, and like bees to the comb they came to Christ and in the name of the Lord he avenged them.

How did he avenge us? By destroying iniquity and awakening faith. And so it was that soon after his death men would willingly die for him, some crucified, some burnt to cinders, others pelted down with stones, many skinned and excoriated, others with their bodies severed in pieces with iron racks, and even those who had been blasphemers would later come to suffer the gravest torments in his name with patience, perseverance, and still greater delight. *Et in nomine Domini quia ultus sum in eos.* O magnificent revenge and sublime victory of the Lord! *In the name of the Lord he avenged them.* I tell you honestly, reader, that nothing shows more clearly to me God's immense benevolence and love towards us – and, personally, nothing binds me more securely to him – than to see him there, hanging on a piece of wood like a common criminal, and all because of his love for me and for you and so that we may love him and come to him.

How magnificent you were, Lord, said Saint Bernard, in your glory of old, and how magnificent yet when, for me, you laid it all aside. Because, Lord, by exhausting, depleting, by emptying yourself for us, your forgiveness glowed and your love blazed. Everywhere you are beautiful, my Lord, to the soul that loves you: you are beautiful in heaven, beautiful on Calvary, beautiful among angels; you are beautiful between two thieves and beautiful seated at the right hand of the Father. Beautiful, dear Lord, nailed to that Cross. From the throne of David did the Son of God battle for the hearts of men; and he rapt and stole them to himself and they were enraptured. *And I, if I be lifted up from the earth, will draw all things to myself.*[4] The Cross is Solomon's luxurious and lavish litter by which hearts were won and souls bewitched. The Cross is the place wherein love for the daughters of Jerusalem truly dwells.[5]

There are some human qualities, so powerful, that they attract us like magnets: love and kindness, of course, but also wisdom, riches, power, achievement, originality, magnanimity, and many

---

[4] *Et ego si exaltatus fuero a terra, omnia traham ad me ipsum* (John 12:32).
[5] Cant. 5.

others besides. They are all evident on the Cross if we care to look. No one who looks candidly at the crucified Christ can come away unmoved, not finding something, a bait that attracts him, a hook that grabs and clinches us to him and won't let go. Can what he did for us ever be measured? His infinite love, the kindness and compassion shown by his death? The wisdom and riches embosomed in his presence? The power with which he freed and liberated us? The victory that he procured against the devil, prince of the world, while nailed by his hands and feet? The originality with which he redeemed us? An extraordinary work of God, a prophet called it. The magnanimity with which he forgave us and shared his treasures with us until he was himself left bare? You have to be made of stone not to be moved and forever enchained.

Seneca regarded freely-imparted privileges and favours as chains; quite rightly, I think, because they are like fortresses that confine those who receive them to their benefactor. How can a soul, when aware of what she has received, remain distant from God? The Psalmist himself was chained: *Flight hath failed me.*[6]

Captured and in chains is the soul that can neither forget the Beloved whom she so passionately loves nor live for anything that is not of him. Captured and in bondage when in all she does, says, and thinks while in the world, has eyes for him only. Day and night he stirs inside her. She is with him when she awakes, with him when she retires; in vigil and in sleep, forever dreaming of and musing on him.

This second triumph of love has a stronger hold than the first in that here, because of her constant yearning for the Beloved, not even for a brief moment does the soul enjoy serenity. That is why I say that, even though it is not a general rule, in this particular case as well as in some ordinary affairs, a chain is more effectual than a wound, for it is certainly preferable to come out of a battle wounded but with one's freedom than to be wounded and in chains besides. Wounds heal and the pain is gone. But what degree of pain is caused by being wounded and imprisoned besides? Freedom is priceless. What I mean to say is that there

---

[6] Psalm 141:5.

are some redeeming qualities in being wounded and free, there are none in being wounded and captive. The unrelenting ardour of the soul's desire in this second stage keeps inflaming her without repose, never yielding, continually burning, keeping the soul aflame. One possessed by this violent love is like a patient with a high fever who is confined to bed and tied to a post with a heavy chain, able only to move as far as the chain's length will allow. It is the same for the one possessed by this tyrant love. Whatever he does, wherever he turns, he knows himself to be irremediably tied and bound. When the beloved is truly implanted in one's heart, there are no means of escape.

Chapter 4

On the third triumph: the illness of love

Diotima, in Plato's Symposium, said many notable things about love, one of them being that love induced illness. She painted the lover as haggard, sapless, unsociable, and blundering, because those in love will lack the necessary bodily humours and warmth of which animal life consists and sustains itself. In consequence, they become thin, they sicken and wither, because nature cannot go in two directions at once, and physical complexion will reflect the intent of the lover's soul, which is always away from himself and towards the beloved, and it is to the beloved that the lover incessantly attends.

When our stomach lacks the necessary warmth to do the work of baking our ingested food properly, even the most exquisite delicacy, being only slack-baked, turns with the majority of the food into excrement and superfluities, the remainder going to the liver, again underdone. The result is that very little blood, and that raw, makes it to the veins and consequently all body limbs, lacking in good blood because of its crudity, thin down and emaciate thereby losing their freshness, colour, and vigour, and the person sickens and fades.

Now what Plato said of human love in general can also be said of spiritual love in particular.

It is the soul that will be made ill but, as we shall see, physical illness will also befall those who have achieved perfect love, or those longing to get there, because this love in its intensity and ardour, rapts the intent of the soul towards God only and, since bodily humours will inevitably follow, the stomach now lacks its indispensable warmth and generates only crudities, oppilations, amanorreahs and a host of other similar agonies.

But let us leave all this aside and talk about this third stage of violent charity; although it might be good to examine first if there can be a stage of love higher than the second stage we have just considered in the last chapter.

We saw there that no other affection has mastery over love in this second stage. Therefore, is this love not the most excellent love? And if it does not admit of any other interpolation, is this not a love that has no end?

But Richard of St. Victor answers that there is a great deal of difference between being Most and being the One, as indeed there is between being in the beloved's presence and admitting of no other company in that presence. Experience shows that the beloved can be present to us and yet others can also partake of our love even if the one most loved has priority over all others and occupies the principal place in our hearts. This distinction makes it clear that, although the object of our love is that which we love most, as occurs in the second stage, the one we love most is not necessarily the only one we love.

It is when spiritual love excludes all other loves for any other creature or all of them together; when it does not admit or allow us to love anything else but God, when this love has become the one and only love, only then can we say we have reached the third stage of this violent charity. And nothing else will satisfy the soul now, nothing will delight her but this love alone. There is only one she loves, only one she wants, only one for which she thirsts, one that she desires, one she yearns and sighs for, a love with a fire that scorches. It is in one love alone she rests, one love that fills and satiates her hunger. Nothing else tastes sweet, nothing that has not been stewed in this love is pleasant to the palate, and should something else be offered she will push it away, kick it aside, unconditionally reject it, for it does not set her desire sizzling or gratify her affection.

There are no words that suffice to describe the tyranny of love at this stage. It is so great it will enfold all desire, exclude all care, oppress and do violence to all that will not satisfy its will and appetite. Everything else to do or think of she will judge useless and intolerable when it is not directed and guided to the one and only end she so longs for.

When she rejoices in this love and in peace possesses it, our soul feels the mistress of all, for all else comes with it. Without it, however, all else causes horror, mortifies her, hits her in the face. The vitality of her body takes leave now, her heart gnaws and corrodes; she does not welcome advice or listens to reason, and she heeds no warning. She cries out for help now clamouring:

Sustain me with flowers and nourish me with apples for I am injured and ill with love, and like all those whose health fails them, she who so speaks craves for flowers and fruits.

These words from the spouse are so mysterious that I hardly dare touch upon them, and I shall treat of them with care in my *Commentaries on the Song of Songs.* But I will say a few words now for they pertain to what we are discussing here.

Two great favours did the King grant this soul we have here so ill in love. One was to take her down to the cellar in which he keeps his wine, as she herself confesses, and there unhitch all the wine barrels. The other was to ordain her to charity. The first gift is immense and exclusive to best friends only. Because if we look at the argument in this Book of Songs which is pastoral and rural, among ploughmen and farm-hands the cellar is where all the wealth and jewels of the house are kept, and no one enters there except blood relatives, and close blood relatives at that. And when the soul says she entered the cellar of God she is manifesting to us that he showed her the richness of his glory and gave her his most delicate wine to taste; which for the Hebrews signified all manner of gifts and delights.

What can possibly come after these two gifts but contempt for everything that one finds outside the cellar of God? Is there anyone who, having tasted this fine wine of divine consolation, does not flee and value as vinegar the gifts and delights offered by the world? Who, having contemplated the riches and treasures of the house of God, as Paul who had been taken to this cellar himself did, would not treat as manure the riches, honours, dignities, offices and prelatures of the world? St. Augustine explained this very well. All flesh is insipid once the spirit has been tasted.

But the favour of the King went further still for he ordained her to charity. The Hebrews read this differently from us, because where we say: *Ordinavit in me charitatem,* they say: *Vexillum eius super me dilectio* ("He put the sign of his love upon me").[1]

Of St. Inez, virgin and martyr, we read that being continually importuned by the tyrant's son with offers of marriage, she said

---

[1] Cant. 2:4.

she could not. And the reason? *My Spouse put a sign on my face,* she said, *that I might admit of no other lover but Him.*

The sign the Spouse put on his beloved nobody knows. We know only it was a sign of love, that she may not accept love from any other source. And either because of the awe of the manifold riches she saw in the cellar, or the robustness of the wine she drank, or the sign the Spouse placed on her, she confesses herself ill and implores remedy for her illness, and the remedy she asks for is flowers and fruit.

Pliny, in Book 7 of his *Natural History,* among other things tells of the astomous monster-men who had no mouths. They dressed in the leaves of the trees, neither ate nor drank, but kept alive on the fragrance of apples and flowers. And truly the aroma of some things can be of sustenance, just as a satisfied craving for fruit can alleviate a patient's illness.

What I think, personally, is that the spouse is here pleading for holy wishes and perfect conduct in her fellow men, understood by apples and flowers. Because there is nothing that lightens and gladdens the enamoured soul of God more than to see her brothers advancing in the service of his Majesty.

And if anyone should ask what love sickness is, I would say it is an affection, a desire, a yearning that consumes the soul in the absence of her Beloved causing, at the same time, physical pain; a yearning that benumbs and does away with carnal love, lascivious sentiments, and sensual appetites.

Oh, forceful passion of love if it is not tempered or satisfied! Forceful, I say, because, once this amorous passion is kindled in the soul, the impetus that possesses her renders her impotent and in nothing mistress of herself; it will encompass everything from beginning to end, it will heighten and grow, and will not end until it makes our soul faint.

Sometimes, especially when at prayer, these amorous desires are magnified even more and it is now that the lover is made ill because the intensity of this passion, though only passing by, will make her faint in her frailty. The soul is ill at the start of this happiest of hours, but by the end it will faint, and melt, as wax before fire. But mind that when at prayer you take great care not to have your spirit sagging and wandering, for, should God ordain that you be touched by this passion, you may not detect it and make ready in time to be filled and consumed: for it is not in the habit of turning away or taking its leave until it has drunk all the spirit of man – as it was seen of Daniel, a man of desire, who in that celestial vision was made ill and fainted, forsaken of all energy.[2]

This is the third stage of violent love, very different from the second. In the latter there is room for men to occupy themselves in matters of the world, although their thoughts will not break loose from God to whom they are so forcibly bound. In this third stage, however, the soul is left ill and as if consumed by its own overabundance. She can think or meditate on nothing but on whom she loves, neither can she attend to external affairs. In the second stage the hands and feet are still free to move, we can still occupy and exercise our free will in virtuous works, taking some, leaving others, at our discretion. But in this one, the force of love, as a grave illness, debilitates our hands and feet so that we can neither move them nor assist ourselves with them when we need to, and the soul remains as if immutable, for it will not move or think of anything else but where her desire takes her. Which is what Ezekiel said of those divine animals: where the impetus of the spirit took them was where, without resistance, they went.[3]

---

[2] Dan. 8.
[3] Ezek. 1:20.

Chapter 5

On the Insatiability of Spiritual Love and how it does not

content itself with the possible

And so, where can love go from here? Can it continue to grow? We saw that, in the first stage, love wounded us; in the second, it chained us; in the third, it incapacitated us for all but the Beloved, making itself master of our will.

So, now, what else can love do? The impossible, says Richard of St. Victor. The unthinkable, because if it is within reach it will not satisfy spiritual love.

The first degree of this love is impassible: it cannot nourish itself through any other source. The second is indivisible: it allows for no discontinuity or neglect. The third is singular: it admits of no shared company. This fourth degree of spiritual love is insatiable: it will never be filled, be it by what is or by what is not. Its heart is wounded, its mind is in chains, it is in abject surrender to the Beloved but still it is not satiated. Nothing is ever enough.

On reaching this happy and blessed state, there is nothing the soul can do or have done for her that will fill her. She is thirsty and drinks, but her thirst is never quenched, nay, she is left more thirsty still, as if she were suffering from spiritual dropsy! Her eyes see the Beloved when he is present but that is no longer enough; her ears hear him when he is absent, but that, too, is not sufficient. Like a miser with his money, like hell swallowing up souls, she is now possessed of an insatiable hunger for God, always crying: More!

St. Augustine said of burning passion such as this that those who experience love in this violent manner will never accept the possibility that their yearning may never be fulfilled. This will bring them no relief or consolation but neither will it deter them. What did he mean? He meant that love such as this is different from all others; that this burning passion is different from the zeal with which we seek things of this world: love of riches, for instance, love of praise, success, pleasures of the flesh. It is different because in worldly pleasures once the mind, in time, comes to acknowledge, accept, and reconcile itself with the impossibility of ever reaching its goal, reason will begin to attenuate passion, and desire will wane. Not so with this love divine. Spiritual ardour judges the impossible to be possible; for this celestial ostrich there are no hurdles. It may not be a judgement made in heaven, perhaps, but it is what the soul desires and longs for, and in this yearning, she languishes away.

How plain and how true it is that our soul, constrained in her bodily fortress, chained to the senses, can never entirely rejoice in that eternal happiness for which she was created! But being so in love with her God as we see her here, does the soul ever find relief or consolation? Does her desire fade with the impossibility of ever attaining fulfilment? Does the yearning ever stop? Is the flame of her desire to see and enjoy that which she so perfectly loves ever extinguished, certain, as she is, that it cannot be fulfilled in this world? It is not, but do not hold this against her! God is not offended by her yearning. On the contrary. His Majesty seems to have left the door well open for it. But before entering, the soul must pass through that tortuous and narrow passageway, that rigorous commandment on love that says: *Thou shalt love the Lord thy God with thy whole heart, and with thy whole soul and with thy whole strength.*[1] We know none of us can fulfil this commandment perfectly in this valley of tears, in this miserable exile, as we will be able to in heaven, yet it is right that we may long for it. Scripture says of the yearning soul: *Blessed is the man that feareth the Lord: he shall delight exceedingly in His commandments.*[2]

And what does it mean *to delight exceedingly* - asks Richard - if not to exceed in desire our human potential, our human strength? It is in this same sense that the spouse speaks to her beloved: *The righteous have loved thee.*[3]

God is infinite and therefore, the soul that loves him must strive to emulate and commune with this immensity. The soul cannot love by weight, or number, or measure; lovers don't love by the yard. The soul in love loves as deeply as she can but not as far as she wants to. Love in and of itself can be measured, but the desire to love cannot. The soul loves only as a human creature

---

[1] Deut. 6:5.
[2] Psalm 111:1.
[3] Cant. 1:3.

can love, but desires to love above and beyond what is humanly possible, and if she could gather the love of all creatures inside her heart and give it all to her Maker, she would most certainly do so. And still not be satisfied.

It was with this in mind that the glorious father St. Augustine came up with that little riddle of his when referring to perfect and insatiable love: *If Augustine were God and God were Augustine, God would gladly become Augustine so that Augustine could be God.* In other words, if it were possible for him to possess all that God possesses, he would gladly give it all, and keep nothing, to the one he accepts as God. He felt that a lowly soul offering God all the honour and love she is capable of, still comes far short of what God deserves, and so he would gladly become God just so as to love God as only God can love. This is what all righteous men have felt, of whom it is written: *Tell the just man that it is well: for he shall eat the fruit of his doings.*[4]

When it comes to pleasing God, it is the holy who always end up tying themselves up in knots. When Scripture says: *My soul desires to desire you at all times,* would it not it be better to just say: *My soul desired you* than *My soul desired to desire you?* Not at all, says Richard. *Desiring* belongs to one of those stages of love we have previously mentioned; perhaps to all three. But *desiring to desire*: that is what insatiable love is. He who desires to continue desiring will not be satiated.

Desire is the hunger of the soul, and the soul can never be filled because God is love, and he who loves God loves love. And to love love makes an infinite circle where love has no beginning and no end.

Love is insurmountable because it conquers all and is defeated by none. It is insatiable because it engulfs everything but is never replete; only here can plenitude beget a need for more. *They that eat me shall hunger: and they that drink me shall yet thirst.*[5] God is food and God is love. He who loves God eats God, and he who eats God eats love. And what can love beget but love? And if love so eaten is infinite, will it not beget infinite love in the soul? O my

---

[4] Isaiah 3:10.
[5] Sirach 24:29.

Lord, my good Lord, my love and my food, how you regale those who love you, and by loving you they eat, and are still left so hungry! He who has never tasted you does not know what hunger is; for you alone can so delight our souls that in an superabundance of life and satiety, you leave us hungry for more. It is the food you promised the righteous.

Our Sovereign Lady Mary, visiting Elizabeth, filled with God and with His Spirit, said: *He hath filled the hungry with good things.*[6] She is not referring here to the poor suffering physical hunger, for God does not always alleviate them, not if their time is not yet due. The rich are hungry, too, vain and empty, as the prophet had said: *The rich have wanted, and have suffered hunger; but they that seek the Lord shall not be deprived of any good.*[7] The soul that feeds on God is filled with goods. Filled, not satiated, because in charity, the fuller one gets the less satisfied one becomes.

But what goods are those received? The Apostle named them: peace, patience, magnanimity, humility and meekness of spirit, chastity, continence, joy in the Holy Spirit; in sum, all tenderness, gentleness, mildness, sweetness. And it is written: *When thou shalt do wonderful things, we shall not bear them. Thou didst come down, and at thy presence, the mountains melted away. From the beginning of the world they have not heard, nor perceived with their eyes; the eye hath not seen, O God, besides Thee, what things thou hast prepared for them that wait for thee.*[8] In other words, what you, O Lord, have in store for those who love you, only you can tell, for our eye cannot see it, our ear has not heard it, nor can such fullness be contained in the heart of man. We can own these goods, says St. Augustine, but never fully apprehend them for they exceed, they surpass, the powers of our affection.

How much hunger for God the child Jesus must have felt when he went up to Jerusalem: with the eight days of the feast over, he stayed for another three. Later, he would sometimes spend all night in prayer: *And it came to pass, in those days, that he went*

---

[6] Luke 1:53.
[7] Psalm 33:11.
[8] Isaiah 64:4.

out into the mountain to pray; and He spent the whole night in prayer to God.[9]

St. Gregory, having been elected Supreme Pontiff, wrote epistles full of grief and regret at no longer being able to retreat in solitude to his cell, his own private corner where, in quietness and calm, he could enjoy God by himself for as long as he wanted, which speaks to me not only of the magnitude of his love but also of the resolve of his hunger for God. Mary Magdalene clings to the feet of Christ, eating delicacies that would leave her hungrier still, and however hard you may try you will not get Anna, the prophetess, out of the temple, accustomed, as she was, to being there from childhood.

Saintly souls have always searched for ways to have more of God, and God fills them, and in so doing, leaves them hungrier still.

---

[9] Luke 6:12.

Chapter 6

On pure and mixed delight

One of the most admirable manifestations of the spirit of God in our life are those moments when we are able to feel God alive in our soul: when we sense him wanting us, when we know he is there; when we feel his caress. But then, suddenly, he seems to disappear. He is gone.

God has not gone away, he is only hiding. But the soul doesn't know this and feels disconcerted, helpless, and abandoned. And then, just as suddenly, he comes back and fills the soul with such an overabundance of cheer and consolation, and envelopes her and pours such light on her that she begins to think that earth is heaven itself. An enigma, indeed, but one of the most ingenious ways God has of showing us his power and his wisdom.

I thought that, if only he would guide me, I would try, as best I can, to say a few words about this.

There are two kinds of spiritual delight: the first is most sweet and transforming. It is delight itself. It sizzles with the joy the Blessed rejoice with in heaven. It is pure. The second is somewhat of a mixture, one could say: a mixed delight derived from the soul enjoying the benefits of a clear conscience but, at the same time, agonising over the absence of God.

When the presence of God is felt, the soul rejoices in the first, the purest of delights, and with such assurance and abandonment that she forgets everything and concerns herself with nothing else. We see this in St. Peter who, seeing God transfigured in Mount Tabor, as if the world no longer existed, said: *Lord, it is good for us to be here.*[1] The spouse in the Canticles gives us to understand this sweetness and taste of heaven with words of great meaning: *My soul melted when He spoke* (in the Hebrew: *My soul came out of myself).*[2]

Dionysius, before attempting to write on seraphic love, decided first to research the etymology of the word seraphim which in Hebrew is the same as that for incendiaries, *sive calescentes*. He concluded that seraphim have five faculties, as difficult to

---

[1] Matthew 17:4.
[2] Cant. 5:6.

understand as they are startling once they are understood. In the name seraphim, which means fire, it is implied infinite mobility, heat, intensity and ardour, meaning by this that they are like fire itself, continuously burning for as long as there is something left unburned; and if what is being burned were infinite, infinite would be their burning. Forever loving, endlessly loving, their ardent love penetrating, permeating, melting, transforming.

But what is infinite mobility, this moving without pause, asks Hugh of St. Victor? What does this perpetual motion, this hot, piercing and fervent moving of the seraphim mean? If we say it means love itself, we will not be saying much to those who don't know what love is, and nobody really knows what true love is but those who experience the love of God, so let me see if I can explain this a little better.

Within the nature of spiritual love there is an inner movement, a *móbile*, because in love there is life therein; there is unceasing continuity, because this love is eternal; there is heat because love is fire: love cannot exist without warmth; there is sharp accuracy within it, because it penetrates and goes right into the innermost core of the object of one's love, and all of this just so that it can unite and be in the beloved. Now, you have observed that water over a slow fire will simmer, but if the heat is increased, it no longer simmers, it boils, and when the boiling is incessant, the water gushes forth and spills over and, you could say, comes out of itself. This is what happens in spiritual love. And so it is that seraphic love reaches such a *superfervidum* state, ebullience of such a high degree that in boiling, love swells, and in swelling, overflows.

In the first phase of love we look for reasons so that we may continue to love; that is why it is called *móbile,* because it is restless. It will not come to a halt, it cannot even remain idle, because love is never inactive. If it pauses, if it wanes, it cannot be said to be perfect love.

The second phase will tell us more than the first, for here love is not only *móbile* and *continuous* but also *persevering* and *eternal.* Spiritual love feeds off infinity so it has no end.

In the third phase we see an *expansion*, a spreading over of this spiritual love. Just as in cold weather objects shrink, harden, and freeze, in the heat they expand, soften, and liquefy; they thaw out and melt. The holy prophet provides testimony of this when, faced with such bereavement and desolation, he cried out he was like a wineskin left out in the frost to shrink, harden, and shrivel.[3] Also, in our Vulgate, we read what the spouse says about her Beloved warming her, melting, filling her.[4] For a soul melts in the presence of her God as wax dilates before the sun, or fire. In one of the Psalms it is written that the mountains melted and ran like wax in obedience to God, and the whole earth thawed out and was made liquid. Origen, explaining the words of the spouse, wrote: The soul melting is, to me, a most felicitous sign of the divine consolation. The soul melts when, by means of great devotion, it softens, it mollifies in a way that the Beloved can now tenderly lean and repose in her with no harshness, no resistance to his divine counsel. It melts because the soul overflows out of itself with love, and in so doing surrenders to the beloved; and he now has complete mastery of her to the point where all movement, all faculty, all impulse rests only with him.

St. Bonaventure says that, once the thick skin left on the soul by our sins is shed, the soul becomes soft and pliant; and this softening moulds her in readiness to love God and receive his inspiration. As one liquid mixed with another becomes a unity of both, so by the spirit of God inspiring the spirit of man with grace, the soul is made spirit.

I am not talking here about the unity that results from the identity of real existence, that identity of which Christ spoke through St. John saying: *That they all may be one, as Thou, Father, art in me and I in Thee*,[5] that is, my Father and I are One: one substance, one essence; for a created thing cannot be its own creator. Nor am I speaking in this instance of the union that the soul, when assenting and conforming to the will of God, has with him, for that is shared by all endowed with spiritual grace: of the first Christians, for example, of whom it is written that, though

---

[3] *My eyes have failed for thy word, saying: When will thou comfort me? For I have become like a bottle in the frost* (Psalm 118:83, Caph).

[4] *My soul melted when he spoke* (Cant. 5:6).

[5] John 17:21.

many, they were all of one soul and one heart.[6]   What I am discussing here, is a union of a different kind, a loftier union, one which occurs when the soul, melting, is made spirit with God through the fusion, the intense love of ecstatic contemplation, where a magnitude of overflowing gentleness and intense love dissolves and steals into God; and God, in turn, pours himself out on the soul and becomes her, stirring her, vivifying her.

To understand this union better, one really ought to listen to those who have experienced it and do know what they are saying, not to those like me who just talk about it. Because not everyone is able to reach this state: only those who are able to apprehend it through experience or revelation. It is most intimate, mysterious, intense, and profound.   It has to be tasted to be loved. And it cannot be loved unless it is apprehended.

We can surmise, however, that this liquefying, this melting of the soul is like that of ice or wax when exposed to the rays of the sun. First, there is a separation of the heterogeneous from the homogeneous, or vice versa. We call homogeneous, those things the components of which are of the same nature as the whole, such as the elements: any one part of water is water, any one part of fire is fire.   Heterogeneous are said to be those particles composed of diverse natures, such as the bodies of animals, for example, which consist of bones, nerves, and flesh. In this *running* and melting, we see that the altered substance cannot be contained by itself within its own boundaries: if it is to be held back it needs an external agent to do so.   For example, melting wax cannot retain its own form by itself but depends for its rest on a mould made of solid matter; its own nature would be to run and melt away, and it would continue to do so until it comes across an object, foreign to itself, that would restrain it. This assumed, then, what needs to be understood here is that love has the nature of heat, that is to say, the nature of assembling and uniting homogeneous elements and separating heterogeneous ones.

Spiritual matters have homogeneity and similitude with other spiritual matters and their nature, so to speak, is greatly dissimilar to those of corporeal or earthly matters. And so, what is spiritual

---

[6] Acts 4:32.

or divine in man, in a certain way, by the power of this vivifying love, sets itself apart from all that is temporal and corporeal, and so a separation is made between soul and spirit: between physicality or sensuality and spirituality. When the precious is separated from the base, what remains is the feculent or impure, which belongs to the lower faculties. Because God is spirit, and enables this union to take place, it is clear that the rational spirit, once filtered and purified, leaving behind the sediment and pulp of earthly concerns, will join the divine spirit, because of its similitude with it. And so a division is made between soul and spirit, that is, between sensuality and animality on the one hand (which includes soul and body), and spirituality, on the other, which is lifted from the superior faculties of the soul itself to join the purely spiritual substances in unity with God. Of this division St. Paul wrote to the Hebrews: *For the Word of God is more living and more piercing than any two-edged sword and reaches into the division of the soul and spirit, of the joints also and the marrow; and is a discerner of the thoughts and intents of the heart.*[7]

To my mind there is one more thing of still greater consideration here and it is this: that the spirit, assimilated to God, and so adapted and disposed towards love by such copiousness of divine virtue, proceeds consequently to adapt and dispose the body to itself, and is able to clothe it now with spiritual faculties and properties, helpless, as it was before of ever attaining them. That is why Aristotle said that in the virtuous man, external and internal matters are in harmony with reason. And so, indeed, it is; for our spirit, being attracted to God first, then proceeds to attract all things of the flesh to itself. And so two most wondrous unions take place: a union of the spirit to God and a union of the body to the spirit.

I said earlier when speaking of melting that certain substances have no capacity to come to a complete rest by themselves but require outside assistance to enable them to do so. I say the same of spiritual love and spiritual melting, for our soul finds rest only in God, the only goal there is. It is after his image that the soul is modelled; in his image it is sealed and transformed, simplified and

---

[7] Heb.4:12.

unified. All things rest once they arrive at their destination, all halt upon reaching their own perfection point, only then are they able to become at one with it: matter rests when it reaches its form; a stone rests within its centre; all things rest having reached their purpose. In the same way, our spirit, joined by perfect love to its Supreme Perfection – God – can rest only in him. Only in him will it find quiet and calm. Only in God can our soul make its nest.

And with melting, of course, comes permeation. Because what melts, yields and spreads and permeates, as does wax or a hot balsam. I am belabouring the point here with this example but all I really mean to say is that nothing stands in the way of love. It spreads, it engulfs, it fills every nook and cranny. Among the Evangelists, even St. John, already so favoured in love, with amazing precision entered into the bosom of Christ, taking out the great riches of the Gospel, as St. Augustine declares and the Church proclaims. But how did he enter his heart so piercingly when the blunt lance had not even penetrated him yet? In a word, by loving. By means of contemplative love. Because love always finds a way. Love is a trailblazer. It paves the way and does not rest until it reaches the most intimate, the innermost of the beloved. And spiritual love penetrates into the deepest and most mysterious of God. There is no secret that an enamoured spirit cannot scent, no mystery it cannot unravel. There are no locked doors for love: it is the most artful picklock there is.

Penetrating, then, and probing the enamoured spirit into the secrets and mysteries of the Beloved, with the freshness and liveliness with which she is contemplating, and with the softness, the sweetness, and the beauty with which she is rejoicing, it takes leave of herself and comes to a mental ecstasy. This is a most mystical and intimate matter, as I said before, and one that nobody really knows much about save those who receive this grace, and no one receives it save those who long for it, and one does not long for it unless such desire is inflamed by the Holy Spirit. This is why the Apostle says that this science is a science revealed. It has little to do with one's disposition, diligence, inquiry, knowledge, works or wisdom. If anyone should ask, says St. Bonaventure, how spiritual ecstasy comes about, tell him: ask for grace, not doctrine; ask for desire and yearning, not speculation; ask for devotion in prayer, not the study of lessons; ask for the Beloved, not the master theologian; ask for God, not man; ask for fog and darkness, not clarity; ask for the ardour of fire to transform the mind into the beloved, not light. To reach such good and such delight, death to all worldly attachment that lives within man must have preceded it, for it is written that *men will not see God if alive.*[8]

---

[8] *Thou canst not see my face; for man shall not see me and live* (Exod. 33:20).

Chapter 7

On the second delight: joy at the presence of God and anguish at his absence.

Tauler, a man of considerable wisdom in contemplative prayer and spiritual perception, tells us that when we first start out on our spiritual journey, the Lord courts us and woos our soul, charming us with favours, pouring grace on us with such abundance, softness and sweetness, that an indigent and fragile body can hardly hold it all. This could well be the case with those oh so lavishly regaled! They wave their hands, they jump, they bleed, they faint! All those gestures, all that physicality, methinks were they to be restrained they would somehow crack or burst and place their health in peril! They speak daring words, they scream, they shout (some bellow!). Such is their delight, it seems, in God's hugs and kisses.

But it does not last, of course. Even if it were a sign from heaven, it would only be coarse bread at a wedding feast; milk for babes, sweets for toddlers, necessary, perhaps, at a first stage of initiation. For once the soul abundantly vivified and leaving all childishness aside embarks upon a higher road to perfection, she will then eat nothing but humble pie. God now proposes an arduous, narrow, bleak, disconsolate and sorrowful road ahead, and she will have to wheel and deal, and feed off crumbs, and live on her wits. He leads the soul to the gate, leaves her there, and goes away, and the soul feels alone and stranded. He will take and hide all gifts and grace once so generously bestowed, and then disappear, leaving no trail. And with no news or trace of him she will ask with anxiety and dismay *have you seen Him whom my soul loveth?*[1] And she will examine her conscience to see if her faults are the cause of this absence, and finding little in word, deed or thought that could have offended her Spouse so gravely, she cheers up, reassured. But the desolation persists and the soul is not abated. And finding no tranquillity, it quits searching for him whom she has lost. But the Beloved is very much present. It is

---

[1] Cant. 3:3.

he who intentionally causes this disquiet and heartbreak in the soul. It is he inciting her to search for more, to dig deeper. He, awakening and whetting her appetite. It is God who ignites this fire and holy yearning. But throughout it all he is neither seen nor heard.

Oh, how the soul wanders, and stumbles, and falls during these times! She begins to fade, lose colour, tone, zest and strength. Her health deteriorates. She no longer wants to speak, just to sigh with the spouse: *I adjure you, O daughters of Jerusalem, if you find my beloved, that you tell Him that I languish with love.*[2] It was languishing, wounded and hurt, that Mary Magdalene would wander in the absence of her beloved; and having him present, would not recognize him, so disguised was he.[3] He feigns and dissimulates that being there, he is not, so that our love and longing for him may grow, that he may with more eagerness be sought, with more tenderness be found.

Sometimes he hides so exclusively that, keen foxhounds though we might be, we are left with no trace as to where or how to perceive his scent. When someone does not want to be noticed, he will not move. He will not dare blink or breathe. And if you were to spot him and move him from one place to another he would not even stir. This is how God behaves with the soul at this time: secretly and silently, that the soul might believe herself abandoned and forgotten.

When Elisha bade Elijah farewell, he kept the mantle with which the prophet had divided the waters of the river Jordan. Elisha wanted to cross the river without getting wet, too, so he spread the mantle, as Elijah had done. But the waters did not part: *Ubi est Deus Elie?*, he then cried, *Where is now the God of Elijah?*[4] God had not deserted him: He pretended not to hear at first to incite Elisha to call him with more fervour and zeal. The spouse knows this of her Beloved: that he hides when he pleases and reappears when he deems it beneficial, and says to him: *Flee away, O my Beloved, and be like to the roe, and to the young hart upon the*

---

[2] Cant. 5:8.
[3] John 20:14.
[4] IV Kings 2:14.

mountains of aromatical spices.[5] A roe or a young hart, you notice, not a rabbit or a hare. Why not? Because these animals never turn their head in flight. Rather, with their ears pricked and altogether crestfallen, they run away, only to hide. The roe and the young hart run, jump, leap, flee with great swiftness, only from time to time they turn their heads to see if they are being followed. As if the spouse had said: *Flee, make off, beloved. Flee in good stead, but do turn your gaze upon me now and then, that I might console myself in your absence.*

Holy Job said that God conceals the eternal light in his hands[6] allowing us a glimpse of it every now and then. Not all, of course, for not even the angelic spirits could withstand it all at once, but a little, through his fingers. As it is read of the saintly Ephrem who being abundantly regaled of God would say: *Withhold, O Lord, the abundance of your glory upon me, for I cannot suffer it, nor is there within me a large enough cup to receive it.*

In between fingers, then, does God reveal to us a few tiny rays of that eternal light we long for. He gives us these intense joys suddenly, but only when he chooses, to assure us that he will manifest his glory to us if we persevere in his friendship.

It is during these desolate times that torturous temptations arise in our soul, agitating and perturbing our inner peace, clouding the serene sky of our conscience. It feels as if someone was punching us squarely on the face: the face of a holy life. They vex and offend us and tire us out of works of penance and exercises in virtue. And we are forced to want what we know we should not want, and wish what we know we should not wish, and entertain thoughts we know we should not entertain, and judge as sweet things we know only too well taste most bitter. We cannot even hold a holy thought for more than a second, so great is our instability and misery.

We turn to God with the desire to want only him, but these horrors, confusedly and contemptuously, throw us off his presence. We pray, but the gates of heaven seem to have turned to impenetrable bronze. God seems deaf now and the Guardian

---

[5] Cant. 8:14.
[6] *In his hands he hideth the light, and commandeth it to come again* (Job 36:32).

Angel is nowhere to be seen. We turn to Holy Scripture and get as much inspiration from it as if we were reading a stone. The horrors of hell no longer frighten us, the consideration of heaven does nothing to awake us, the multitude of favours so far received does not, in the least, inspire us.

God had covetously wooed our souls at first. He had baited us, as hunters and fishermen do to catch their prey. He regaled us with favours, soothed us, visited us; he gave us the nourishing milk of consolation, the joys of his divine spirit. But once grabbed and caught in his net, he treats us with such rigorous severity, and in such way he deserts us, that the flesh rebels against the spirit and embarrass it into such plight that we doubt we will ever be God's friends again.

The soul does not feel God during this time. She does not know him. But neither does the world delight her entirely for she is well aware of what she is missing. So there she is: left high and dry, one foot in each world and standing on none. It seems to me that if hell could be experienced here on earth, it could not be more rigorous or tormenting than what a soul goes thorough during these lonely times, loving God so intensely and wishing for him everywhere. And what can I say about those annoying, trying thoughts charging against her like an artillery battery ready for battle? And those seductive images that revive the passions of the flesh, continuously assailing her, shamelessly harassing her, gathering strength, attacking her with more force than when she was living subject to all vice and sin? It so often comes to pass that the more the soul wishes to equip herself and make ready to serve God, the more tempted, dry, spiritless and without devotion she finds herself! The calamities go so far (and God allows this to happen!), that we may even lose our good name or the respect and regard others hold for us and that, in time, even those who undoubtedly radiate sanctity come to judge us as useless and of poor consequence.

In these occasions, St. Bernard used to say: *Ecce in pace amaritudo mea amarissima: Being in God in sweet peace, he has me now like bile.* And holy king David, wrestling with himself, said: *Quare tristis es, anima mea, et quare conturbas me? - Why are Thou sad, O my soul, and why dost thou trouble me?*[7]   It was these temptations, right there inside of him, making him doubt and lose faith and confidence in God, urging him to stop praying.   As did Job's wife telling her husband to stop all that humility and go ahead and die:

So Satan went forth from the presence of the Lord, and struck Job with a very grievous ulcer from the sole of the foot even to the top of his head. And he took a potsherd and scraped the corrupt matter, sitting on a dunghill. And his wife said to him: Dost thou still continue in thy simplicity? Bless God and die. And he said to her: Thou hast spoken like one of the foolish women. If we received good things at the hands of God, why should not receive evil? In all these things Job did not sin with his lips. [8]

And Tobias' wife, also, telling him that since faith had done nothing for him he would from then on have to live and depend on alms.

Now it happened one day that, being wearied with burying, he came to his house and cast himself down by the wall and slept. And as he was sleeping, hot dung out of a swallow's nest fell upon his eyes, and he was made blind. Now this trial the Lord therefore permitted to happen to him, that an example might be given to posterity of his patience, as also of Holy Job. For whereas he had feared God from his infancy, and kept his commandments, he repined not against God because the evil of blindness had befallen him: but continued in the fear of God, giving thanks to God all the days of his life. For as the kings insulted holy Job, so his relations and kinsmen mocked at his life, saying: Where is thy hope, for which thou gavest alms, and buriedst the dead? But Tobias rebuked them, saying: Speak not so. For we are all children of saints, and look for that life which God will give to those that never change their faith from him.   Now Anna, his wife, went daily to weaving work; and she brought home what she could get for their living by the labour of her hands.   Whereby it came to pass that she received a young kid and brought it home.   And when her husband heard it bleating, he said: Take heed, lest perhaps it be stolen: restore ye it to its owners, for it is not lawful for either of us to eat or to touch anything that cometh by theft.   At these words his wife became angry and answered: It is evident thy hope has come to naught, and thy alms now appear.[9]

---

[7] Psalm 41:6. (And again: *Why are thou cast down, O my soul and why dost thou disquiet me?* Psalm 41:12.)

[8] Job 2:7-10.

[9] Tobias 2:10-22 (Vulgate).

Such harsh words spat at a blind, grief-stricken old man!

But holy king David did not give in to temptation and responded instead: *Spera in Deo, quoniam adhuc confitebor illi, salutare vultus mei, et Deus meus: Hope in God (for amidst these storms) I shall proclaim Him and comply with His will.* And that is precisely what God suggests that we do when he tells us: *Hope in God, behave manfully, comfort your heart, and keep and suffer in God.* [10]

Sometimes God makes himself so heavy in our souls that he feels to us as if made of lead, and our shoulders can no longer carry him. At this time, the prophet counsels us to endure and sustain him valiantly and not to descend into sugary consolations or vain sentimentalities which would only make matters worse and add to more errors and desperation. On the Cross, Christ, forsaken by the Father, was surrounded and tormented by enemies. And when the Jews dared him climb down he would not do so until the will of the Father, who had put him there, had been fulfilled. *He saved others; himself he cannot save. If he be the king of Israel, let him now come down from the cross; and we will believe him.*[11] And again: *And Jesus said: Father, forgive them, for they know not what they do. But they, dividing his garments, cast lots. And the people stood beholding. And the rulers with them derided him saying: He saved others; let him save himself if he be the Christ, the elect of God. And the soldiers also mocked him, coming to him and offering him vinegar.*[12]

Amidst labour, anguish and pain is God to be found. There, in the midst of our suffering; right there, at the bottom of the well. He is there, at the very heart of those enduring trials and tribulations that so hurt and prick the soul. That is where God is. Do not despair, my soul, do not despair! Do not give up now! Do not go searching for him in greener pastures, you will not find him there. Amidst brambles and thorns: that's where you will find him. That is where Moses saw him, according to Scripture.[13] He wanted to come and speak to God, wearing sandals on his feet, and God commanded him to remove them and leave them

---

[10] *Expect the Lord; do manfully, and let thy heart take courage; and wait thou for the Lord* (Psalm 26:14).
[11] Mathew 27:42.
[12] Luke 23:34.
[13] Exodus 3:2.

aside. But how, Lord, can you want Moses to walk barefoot into thorns? Why, Moses, it is not much that your blood flow because of thorns. Look at me, here, in the midst of them!

The holy text says that when Moses and the elders, by order of God, climbed to the top of the mountain to speak to His Majesty, they found him on an ark of glory, the same ark the Israelites had built during their affliction in Egypt, giving us to understand by this that he has his throne and glory in all our works, however painful they may be, and that he never truly abandons us. May the soul have patience and not lose hope during this suffering, for all will be well, and with greater benefit and glory to the Beloved. Let the soul humble and subject herself to the divine will during these difficult times, resigned and ready to accept and endure these miseries for as long a time as God wishes. And with this assurance: that God is present in her now with more certainty than during those former times when she was recipient to all manner of consolations and joys, however great and extraordinary they might have been. This surrender to the will of God is of immense benefit to the soul and an exercise in virtue more meritorious than any other. Happy is the soul that, afflicted in this way, does not search for doors or ways of escape, but perseveres in these afflictions until the will of God has been fulfilled, for however long it takes, and for however many years these sorrows and torments might go on.

Leaving a thousand worlds for Christ does not compare with the benefit we get from this resignation and surrender to God's will. What the martyrs suffered does not seem severe compared with what a soul goes through during these arduous times — unable to feel God while having him so intimately within her, and, in some way, the soul is more of a martyr. I say this only because when the martyrs suffered, it was with such an overabundance and outpouring of divine grace that they even had the inner strength to mock their being tortured! But what can a miserable soul do, left to herself! What possible torture can equal that of a soul so filled with God but so in need of Him?

I could tell you many stories about many souls having to endure these absences of God, and how they coped and were made whole again. But so as not to exceed the brevity I promised

137

you at the beginning, let me just tell you what is written about our father St. Francis; that our Lord wanting to probe and test his patience, and thereby increase his merits, let him be tempted by the Devil in a grave spiritual matter, as with Job. And God so tightened his reins this time that St. Francis lost all external and internal joy to the point where he would distance himself from all the other friars. He would not speak to them, as he always had done, not only to concentrate on prayer, but because he could no longer communicate with them joyfully. He would afflict himself with long fasts, flagellation, discipline and silence, but would find no relief. He would go alone to the mountain, shed tears in great abundance, sigh densely and profusely from the bottom of his heart. He would show the Beloved the anguish in his soul and with patience and perseverance ask Him to help him in this malady, repeating the verse of David: *Please God restore unto me the joy of thy salvation: and strengthen me with a perfect spirit.*[14] At last it came to pass that, after two years of this temptation, being at prayer at St. Mary of the Angels, his spirit heard the voice of the Beloved saying: *Francis, if you would have as much faith as a mustard seed, you would command that mountain to move, and it would.* And the saint, understanding that that mountain referred to the temptation that so afflicted him, replied: *Let it be, Lord, in conformity and accordance with your Word.* And he was freed.

---

[14] Psalm 50:14.

Chapter 8

On the wondrous effect that the absence of God causes in the soul, and on fainting in love

Enamoured spirits, still confined and encumbered in the straits of corruptible flesh, says Richard of St. Victor, will often have the joy of the presence and visitations of God though not with the satisfying frequency and abundance they would wish. For these visitations are never lengthy, they do not last their time, it seems: they are not carried through to their fulfilling end. As if, let us say, God were engaging them in that lovely game of Blind Man's Buff that children play, all the while pretending to escape yet hoping, and trying, to get caught.

God wishes us to catch him. Yes, he feigns disappearing, that with more tears and cries he may be sought. This is why Job said that God would come by, and be with him, and he would not see him.[1]

God delights us with his presence and disquiets and afflicts us with his absence. How startled, with what horror and shock is the soul left when God takes away the sweetness of his presence in which she had enjoyed the greatest liberty, and leaves her captive again in the fetters of her senses and the fortress of her flesh. As if she had been snatched from glory itself and brought back to this valley of misery, where true charity is in a state of chronic pneumonia, perhaps even dying, where physical indulgence reigns supreme, where the eyes of spiritual discernment are blurred and blinded and the bodily senses in full vigour and force. She languishes now and with deep and heart-felt sighs confesses her wretchedness for one who was once so blessed. Because the greater the gifts God gave her during his visits the more she is now aware of their loss.

To deprive someone of what he loves most is to increase his desire. And the soul now, yet with ever increasing fervour and zeal, will seek and yearn for that which she no longer possesses. This is, to my mind, what *love sickness* is, a fatigue caused by love

---

[1] *If He come to me I shall not see him; if he depart, I shall not understand* (Job 9: 11).

impatient whereby the lover is compelled to endure the absence of her beloved.

Oh, present absence and absent presence of him whom one loses and at the same times possesses! In vain one tries to alleviate the pain of those so stricken in love, or to soothe the sadness and affliction in their heart, when the wound of love is so deep that it can only be cured by he who put it there. It is not possible to mitigate the bitter taste of that secret pain because the privation of inner delight can neither be redeemed, nor remedied, by external comforts. Rather, the soul that has arrived at this stage of love will only be more burdened and weighed down by outside consolations, as Job said.[2] Had not the Psalmist reached this state when he said: *my soul has done away with human comforts. I remembered God, and received gifts and delights aplenty, and my spirit languished.*[3]

Happy sadness, blessed bitterness brought to pass, not by creatures, but by the absence of the Creator himself! Vile, indeed, to crave for the consolation of another creature, or of all creatures put together rather than that of God, for he who has unlearnt to love everything but God will find consolation in nothing else. Keep ye the vast array of your vain comforts of which the wisdom of the Father said, *Woe is you who seek your comfort here,*[4] for the soul in love will seek solace only in him who dwells inside her, he who never fails the righteous. He will, however, absent himself that he might console her the more: the sweetness will be taken away and she will be flooded with nutriment. God's gentleness is always present, but since he is not touching her heart, she cannot feel his caress. It is because his tenderness is hidden that she thinks he is no longer there.

Let us remember that when the soul feels the absence of the Beloved she does not sleep or slumber. Instead, shaken by her weeping and awakened by her cries, she cannot dissimulate her sorrow or hide the fire scorching her heart but, as the Prophet says, her eyes languish awaiting to see and touch the

---

[2] *I have often heard such things as these: you are all troublesome comforters* (Job 16:2).

[3] *My soul refused to be comforted. I remembered God, and was delighted, and was exercised, and my spirit swooned away* (Psalm 76:3-4).

[4] Luke 6:24-5.

wholesomeness of God whose arrival is prompt and swift but she always judges tardy and long-coming. Troublesome, to be sure, neither to be able to divert one's thirst whilst combating it nor to refresh oneself with drink. Wondrous hunger that no medicine can expel or food can pacify. Irremediable illness for which, though sought, no remedy can be found, but rather what once was procuring our health is now instead increasing our fever.

It is at this stage of love that the soul begins to faint. She is like a patient who, deserted and abandoned by doctors, and seeing herself deprived of the freedom of movement afforded her by her limbs, wanting no more of earth, agonizes, awaiting death. Here was the Psalmist when he said, *My soul had fainted waiting for your health*,[5] of which words St. Ambrose warned: Let us not misinterpret the words of the prophet, so often used in worldly affairs, that we may not judge this fainting as the outcome of one who is exhausted after much physical work. Because the Psalmist does not say *my soul fainted*; he said *my soul fainted for your health,* that is to say, for loving and yearning for your Son, who is my well being. Fainting in love, then, does not mean the end of love, as the fainting of one whose physical strength leaves him after strenuous work; it means growth and perfection in love.

Experience tells us that when we want something with all our heart and are hoping to get our hands on it soon, though the wait may be short in fact, it may seem to us long in coming, and the waiting tire us and vex us and, ever hoping, we fade.

In the end, all that is much desired causes he who desires it to faint in this desire and, in a way, even die if it is not received when wanted. But this fainting and this death do not mean the end of love, as I have said, but its nourishing and growth. And the farther away she regards her beloved, the more her love grows, and the more she faints.

It is upon this that she broods; it occupies her thoughts and considerations; and broken and melting, she is transformed and faints, and the more she languishes the more love swells; and the longer the possession she longs for evades her, the more lovesick she becomes.

---

[5] *My soul hath fainted after thy salvation and in thy Word I had very much hoped* (Psalm 118:81).

Liconense,[6] a grave author, points to that fastidious and wary hope as a sign of love most perfect, and agrees that there is nothing in the world that is swifter, more piercing, more delicate, or more penetrating than that love that steers and pulls her towards the object of her love because love, naturally, does not rest, does not quieten, until it has substantially penetrated the beloved in all his depth, until it has transcended his totality as far as it is able; and when this lover is hindered or delayed by whatever means, in whatever way, the soul feels anxious, sorrowful, and distraught at the delay and hope yet unfulfilled because, as Richard says, for lovers all tardiness seems lengthy, all waiting troublesome and weary, and with Job they cry: *O Lord, I am tired and weary!*[7]

Concerning these words, St. Gregory explains that everyday living will then *hit us in the face*. We begin to see life for what it really is. We will value it less, as love divine starts tasting sweet and appetizing. And so it is that those who love perfectly abhor anything that proves to be an impediment and holds them back from their getting to what they love.

Spiritual love, says Gilbert, becomes most impatient with the world. It feels drained by its preoccupations; rejoices only in repose, nourishes in quietude, and wanting free time for inner delectation, confesses that it is difficult for those who love Christ to divide their soul between him and the world and for love to admit of pilgrim cares and allow celestial secrets to be perturbed by secular noise, because all that love wants to do is to love. From this we can gather what the prophet meant when he said: *my soul fainted in your salvation*. Not that he was tired of loving, or that he had no more love to give, but that he was wishing for nothing else but Christ, who is the health and wholesomeness of the soul. And the yearning was so great that in the intensity of love, and thinking it would never come, he would faint.

---

[6] I cannot identify this author [Ed.].
[7] Cf. Job 14; not an exact quotation.

Chapter 9

On perfect mortification: the *hanging* of the soul in God.

Why is light given to him that is in misery and life to them that are in bitterness of soul? that look for death, and it cometh not, as they that dig for a treasure: and that rejoice exceedingly when they have found the grave?[1]

"The Just wish for death", said, in an exceptional remark among many, the divine Gregory, deliberating on these words of Job.[2] He understands Job to be speaking in spiritual terms, to mean that the just and righteous wish for death to all things temporal because it is only upon fulfilment of this mystical death that one comes to see and contemplate the face of God. And when this death finally comes, those who have been eagerly awaiting it are like treasure hunters rummaging for gold who at last are able to experience the exhilarating joy of finding the burying ground where the gold is hidden.

But the fulfilment of this most perfect mortification is often slow in coming. Not because of insufficiency of merit but because hope, which expands the heart, deepens desire, and therefore devotion. Gold diggers who know where the treasure is hidden do not relent in their pursuit or succumb to impediments in their journey, but gain heart and resolve the closer they get, and with greater zeal if, every now and then, they find traces of its riches along the way.

The Apostle St. Paul upheld this thought of St. Gregory when he wrote to the Hebrews:

Let us draw near with a true heart, in fullness of faith, having our hearts sprinkled from an evil conscience, and our bodies washed with clean water, let us hold fast the confession of our hope without wavering (for he is faithful that hath promised). And let us consider one another, to provoke unto charity and to good works; not forsaking our assembly, as some are accustomed; but comforting one another, and so much more as you see the day approaching.[3]

---

[1] Job 3:20-23.
[2] St. Gregory the Great, *Morals on Job* I:5.
[3] Heb. 10:22-25.

Blessed is the soul that, absolutely dead to the world, finds a well-hidden sepulchre, as St. Gregory calls the contemplative life, in which to shelter herself.

Finding a grave was a sign of good luck in the ancient world, for it was in graves that treasures were hidden, and so it is for the soul to cloister herself in the sepulchre of contemplation, a tomb painstakingly made ready during the purgative and illuminative stages of initiation in the spiritual life. As the body conceals itself in a grave not be noticed, so this hungering soul hides where it can neither see nor be seen by the world.

But why make contemplation the sepulchre? I would ask. Why not God himself? He is, after all, the aim of contemplation, its ultimate object. He is the place where the soul, absolutely dead to the world, truly comes to sojourn. The Apostle had said that his life, having been retrieved from the world, was now hidden.[4] How truthfully he spoke! Because only by entrusting it to God is our life safe and out of danger. We shall lose it if we place this trust anywhere else. The prophet agrees, saying that God will hide those dead to the world from the contradictions and perturbations of men: *Thou shall hide them in the secret of thy face from the disturbance of men. Thou shall protect them in thy tabernacle from the contradiction of tongues*[5]

What does this mean, to be hidden from the boisterousness and restlessness of the world? It means witnessing God in contemplation, that spiritual hiding place where the anxiety and disquiet of men can never intrude. Happy is the life that empties itself in Christ, for that is where corruptibility turns to purity, and the transient and mortal are transformed into the eternal and divine. It is written: *Amen, Amen, I say to you, unless the grain of wheat falling into the ground die, itself remaineth alone. But if it die, it bringeth forth much fruit. He that loveth his life shalt lose it; and he that hateth his life in this world keepeth it unto life eternal.*[6]

Only when we are willing to disentangle our life from all mundane gratification can we then go on to safeguard it in God. Only by laying aside the world will we ever attain life ever-lasting.

---

[4] *For you are dead; and your life is hid in Christ the Lord* (Col. 3:3).
[5] Psalm 30:21.
[6] John 23:25.

Holy Job, disgruntled with living in this animal world, would cry out in anguish: *My soul rather chooseth hanging: and my bones, death.*[7] These words have been interpreted by some as a sign of despair: as if Job were wishing for a violent death like those who die hanging above ground. And, if unexamined, it would appear, indeed, as if he was praying to be delivered from this life suddenly and swiftly, so much was his affliction and desolation. But St. Gregory, again, offers a spiritual interpretation. By bones, or body, he understands physical life, that is, the world and its lure; by soul he means the spirit. In other words, he understands that when Job wishes to hang his soul and do away with his bones, he is longing for death to the world and repose of his spirit in God. And this interpretation should in no way surprise us. The Book of Wisdom is full of references to this "hanging of the soul". It tells us that our dependence on our animal life, the life of the flesh, and all temporal concerns that accompany it do, indeed, vex and hinder this hanging, preventing us from entering into God's serene and tranquil dwelling. Peace and rest cannot be found in noise and disorder. The just long to *hang* in God because calm and repose is not of this world. They cannot find joy in worldly consolations and wish only for their soul to ascend and hang in spiritual and eternal riches. They want to be left to themselves, unencumbered, in Christ. They want freedom from the world: death to their bones. Not all of us are capable of this death and of this hanging, but only those few exceedingly favoured in love. It is reserved for those whose yearning and longing for God have so mortified their flesh that not a drop of Adam's old blood is to be found inside them.

I have done with hope. I shall now live no longer.[8] Many raise their thoughts to God, says St. Gregory but, unable to rid themselves entirely of the flesh, they are like birds with their wings stuck to the lime: the more they thrust themselves forward to fly, the more fastened they remain. And this, too, might well be what the prophet had in mind when he said that his soul yearned for the palaces and mansions of the Lord and fainted with longing: *How*

---

[7] Job 7:15.
[8] *Desperavi, nequaquam ultra iam vivam* (Job 7:16).

lovely are thy tabernacles, O Lord of hosts! My soul longeth and fainteth for the courts of the Lord.[9]

Many are they who hope, long, and aspire, but do not faint. They wish for eternal life but cannot bring themselves to let go entirely of the transient one. They are easily tempted by its pleasures, too readily enticed by its delights; the allurement of the world proves too powerful for them. Their souls do not grow weary, their disdain for the flesh is indecisive, their surrender to God never complete. The soul that faints, on the other hand, is one that will forego all the world has to offer for the riches of heaven. Captive of the spirit now, of the flesh no more, she will loosen all shackles and break all bonds to the world, and clasped and clinging to God, she will plead to be carried away: *Draw me: we will run after thee to the odour of thy ointments.*[10] As if the spouse had said to her Beloved: "Break these chains that bind me and carry me in union with you."

The spouse of Christ hungers for this absolute and undivided union and, aware that the flesh is but a veil standing between them, she wants it forever torn and cast away. She would passionately do that herself with her own hands were it not iniquitous to do so.

Woe is me, says St. Paul, when will my body be freed from this death?[11] He knew where the treasure was in that glorious sepulchre. He was like a falcon fastened to a perch who, upon espying a heron, cannot stand still until it breaks loose ready for the chase. And like a hooded bird, this blessed contemplative would wrestle to strip off the cause of this unrest, he would struggle to break the chains that confined him to this world so that nothing would stand between him and Christ. As the prophet Habakuk said: *I have heard and my bowels were troubled: my lips trembled at the voice. Let rottenness enter into my bones, and swarm under me, that I may rest in the day of tribulation, that I may go up to our people*

---

[9] Psalm 83:22.

[10] *Trahe me post te, in ordorem curremus unguentorum tuorum* (Cant. 1:3).

[11] *For me to live in Christ and to die is gain. And if to live in the flesh, this is to me the fruit of labour* (Phil. 1:21-25).

that are girded[12]. This is a soul hungering for union with her beloved.

Reader: my intention in writing this book was to try to show you how to earn that first kiss the spouse so avidly asks for at the beginning of the Song of Songs. With this in mind, I am now going to tell you what I personally have come to understand about this blessed union, and the necessary steps you should take if you want to climb and to arrive at such a good.

---

[12] Habakuk 3:16.

Chapter 10

Of the blessed union that, by means of ecstatic love, exists between God and the soul

It is of the condition and nature of good to be by all things desired, said Aristotle. And the same can be said of Unity, because that which desires the good, will also desire to partake of its unity and become one with it.

Boethius said[1] that a part has as much of goodness as it is in union with the whole; and all that is, perseveres and continues to be only inasmuch as it is of the whole, and upon ceasing to be of the whole, it necessarily ends and ceases to be altogether.

If we abstract unity from the body, for example, that is to say, if we disjoin the parts from that which constitutes the whole, the body will inevitably perish. If body and soul are divided, death follows as a result. And if the principles of the soul, which are matter and form, were to be separated, undoubtedly neither one would continue to be.

This is wonderful reasoning by Boethius. All things, he says, wish to be and perpetuate themselves in being, and retreat, as far as they are able, from non-being and extinction. And if being is not possible save in unity with others, by necessity there will be attraction and desire amongst the parts themselves as well as towards the whole.

If union is of such significance, and natural attraction to it common to all creatures in order to preserve their being, how much greater will the desire be for the enamoured soul to engage through love in union with God who is infinite Goodness! Because it is the nature of love, as we have been saying throughout, for the lover to wish to join and convert himself in the object of his love.

Aristotle in his *Ethics*,[2] treating of union through love said: *My friend is another I.* It follows, then, that when our spirit draws to God in tender and intimate love, by a conformity of wills, it becomes one with him. For an understanding of these lofty

---

[1] Boethius, *de Consolatione Philosophiae*, section 1.

[2] Aristotle, *Nichomachean Ethics,* IX.

considerations, understood by few and experienced by fewer still, the following has to be noted:

First, that for a rational and intelligent creature to join to God, both here in this present life and in our heavenly Fatherland, this union cannot be effected by the transformation of the divine essence in the intelligent created nature, but by a union of a different kind, a union that is *aptitudinal, habitual and actual,* that is to say, by means of that ecstatic love which transforms the one who loves into that which he loves. The reason for this impossibility is that divine nature, due to its Simplicity and most perfect Oneness, cannot concur with another to constitute a third, nor can any other transform or convert itself into it.

The second point is this. The lover will join the beloved in two ways. One concerns existence. The existence of the loved one has to be presupposed if another is to join to it. Aristophanes, a philosopher referred to by Aristotle, said that those who love each other would wish that both could become one, were it not for the inconveniences that follow, i.e. the corruption of both, or of one of them. And so they opt for tangible union, that is to say, to converse, to live, to do things together and unite in other ways and as intimately as they can.[3]

But there is another type of union in regard to the affection of our soul that induces and formally causes love, which is its very cord and bond. This union proceeds from prior knowledge because desire moves to strive and aspire towards the known good. This can clearly be observed not only in concupiscent love, which is to love and covet that which we learn is favourable to our own being, but also in *amicitia*, or love of friendship, because if I am somebody's friend, I will want for him the good that I want for myself; I see him and know him as another I, and wish for him the good that I wish for myself, which is what the Philosopher meant when he said: *My friend is another I.*

Note the third point, that in conformity with the diverse modes in which God exists in his creatures, the affinity, love, and union that arises between him and them will also vary. And so that we may not stray from our purpose, we should note that God

---

[3] The author is referring to Aristophanes's discourse in Plato's *Symposium*, 189-93.

exists, or is in his creatures, in a *natural, aptitudinal, habitual,* and *actual* inexistence from which originate four different types of union between him and them, to wit, *natural, aptitudinal, habitual* and *actual* union.

God exists naturally in his creatures in natural inexistence, that is, in Essence, Presence, and Might, which can be translated into three types of causes: efficient, formal and final. The efficient cause is appropriate to Might, the formal to Presence, and the final to Essence. Nothing, no power in heaven or earth can prevail against the infinity of divine power. Nothing hides from the purity and clarity of divine presence. Nothing lasts outside the immensity of divine essence, for its virtue extends to all things, and all things are naked and evident to his eyes, and he is in all and all are preserved in his Being. And if it were deemed impossible for all things to be dependent upon God by any type of cause, one could say that by his immensity alone he would be in all, for no things can be outside God who penetrates all, nor, for the same reason, God without them.

The second union is *aptitudinal,* in accordance with the three natural faculties of the rational soul in unity of essence: memory, understanding and will, for it is in relation to them that the soul is a natural image of God. It is called *aptitudinal* because the soul, in its creation, is like a *tabula rasa* upon which no painting has yet been drawn, but is ready, nevertheless, to be perfected by intellectual, moral and gratuitous, and infused or acquired habits. Because it is by these habits that the mental and sensuous faculties of the soul are dressed, beautified and reformed to likeness with God. This refers to the three natural forces or faculties by means of which the soul is made capable of embracing God: knowing him by means of the intelligence, remembering him in the memory, and loving him with the will. They are called natural faculties because they cannot be erased from the soul so that their light, a light that even from devils cannot be extinguished, continues to illuminate and shine forth. As is the case with the sun which would not cease to be luminous and give light if it had nothing outside itself to communicate its light to. This is why man who, through original sin lost the rectitude with which God created him, preserved nevertheless the aptitude to recover it. He lost the habit not the appetite. Gratuitous is the likeness of the soul to God because by this means she is made a participant with him through being caught up into the divinity: as *pilgrim*, through the habits and efficacy of the theological virtues, and as *beholder*, by the three glorious graces.

The third type of union is called *habitual* and is of two ways: of pilgrims and of beholders. The former, the only one we shall consider here, evolves from gratuitous love which brings together the affection of the superior part of our soul with God, and is firmly rooted in grace, *gratum faciente*.[4] This union presupposes the three theological virtues, the gifts of the holy Spirit, the beatitudes and the other habits, especially those infused, of which this grace that makes us pleasing to God is their root, their form, and their end.

We call the fourth union *actual,* and it is also of two ways: according to the state of being in exile, or in the heavenly Fatherland. The first refers to the perpetual and experiential operation of the three theological virtues from the root of *gratum faciente*, one in essence and root, and enlivens the habits and theological virtues based on and moulded in it, for the soul has three faculties in imitation of the Most Holy Trinity which is one essence and three distinct Persons. This union is called *actual* because it results from the *habitual* and formal *gratum faciente*, which extends and is manifested in its operation. It is more perfect in this second effect, that is, as reflected in its operations, than in its first *formal* and *habitual* act, when it informed and beautified the rational soul with its presence. I am saying that grace brings out and manifests the effects of the theological virtues, not immediately, but through the will which is ruled and guided by it; and the rational, irascible (or passionate), and concupiscent faculties, through the theological habits and virtues – faith, hope, and charity – bring forth manifestations of that grace, the experiential and actual perceptions and tastes that, in its present condition, bring the soul to God. Faith leads the soul that believes and assents to that which absolute truth teaches. Hope

---

[4] This is to say, grace that makes us acceptable to God, in contrast with what we call *gratis data*, which does not presuppose justice in the soul and is solely a favour bestowed by God.

uplifts her to supreme majesty and divine abundance. Charity, in its kiss and embrace, locks her with the Supreme and inviolable goodness. It is because of this that charity, inasmuch as it is a theological virtue, signifies habit and causes *habitual* union, as that existing between God and recently-baptised children; but in *actual* union, a real sense and experience of God is required; it is this union that causes and pours forth the fervour of charity. And in this consideration, charity, inasmuch as it is a theological habit, is the same as gratuitous love, supernaturally infused in the soul by divine influence. From this *habitual* and *gratuitous* love, *actual* ecstatic and *fruitive* love is born and it is to be found in charity, a gift of the Holy Spirit. And this union is called *experiential* and *actual* because it consists in the experiential apprehension and taste of the most intimate tenderness, consolation, joy, and delectation, which erupts from the coming together and bonding of the soul to the supreme object of her love, which is God, through *actual* intense and fervent love, resulting in a perception of this delectable and delicious union; because delectation is the fusing of one affinity with its identified loved one.

The Chancellor of Paris[5], in the treatise written on the *Magnificent grace of experiential union with God,* says that it is a simple and actual perception and taste of God by means of his *gratum faciente.* And he says *perception* and not *knowledge* because the former is a general term that applies to each and all mental powers, to wit, the rational, the irascible, and the concupiscent, to the cognitive and affective faculties.

This experiential union is a pre-tasting or an anticipated taste of glory and, so to speak, its representative ambassador. And it is a token and pledge of eternal happiness, which commences here and perfects itself in the Homeland by consummate grace. Though it is one, it is afforded several names: sometimes it is called *transformation,* on other occasions *perfect prayer,* elsewhere *mystical theology,* elsewhere still *divine wisdom.* The reason for this variance is that for the contemplative soul all these things are one and the same for they all presuppose one another.

---

[5] Gerson.

To conclude and sum up all we have said about union so far – this union through which the undivided soul joins and fastens to God, when we consider the world in its totality, from without and from within, externally and internally – I would say that the world was created for union, that is, created so that all things may be consummated in one, for as Dionysius says, they all participate and partake of the one. And so he founded and constituted his *Mystical Theology* upon that union that is effected on the *mens*, or mind, understanding the mind here to be that superior part of the soul that contains the three eminent faculties: intellectual memory, intelligence and will.

From this we deduce that the most perfect state of being man can reach is union with God. With all the powers and faculties of the soul recollected and brought together in one, she is now one spirit with him, and in this way deified and sanctified, she feels, understands, and loves nothing outside of God; and only in God do all her affections and desires rest.

Since the image of God in the soul is present through these three faculties – memory, understanding and will – if these be not wholly stamped and impressed in God, this soul cannot be properly said to be deiform. God is the form to which she has to adapt, as wax adapts to the seal, the form and shape of which it acquires without one single flawed line.

Our soul, then, will be a perfect image of God when our intelligence, in proportion to its capacity, is perfectly illumined to understand God, who is Supreme Truth; when our will is perfectly disposed towards loving the Supreme Goodness; when our memory is thoroughly absorbed in contemplating, possessing and delighting in the Supreme Joy.

And since the perfect blessedness we hope for depends upon the perfect consecution of this, it follows that it is upon their perfect beginning and initiation that the perfection of pilgrims depends.

Great considerations are these, to be sure; they exceed our strength, industry and efforts; but they are not impossible when helped with grace and the favours of heaven, and when in humility we do the best we can on our part, clean of all sin and severed from all covetousness of eyes and flesh; free from arrogance, from which all evil in the world comes.

Chapter 11

On prayer: mediator between God and the soul.

Think of prayer as the "match-maker" between God and us. Just as a mismatched marriage, or an agreement between unequal partners, is difficult to arrange save for the good offices of a broker who can bring both parties together, in the same way, it is only through the intercession of prayer that union between God and us will ever take place. After renunciation and surrender of the self to the will of God, and rejection of all things temporal before him, prayer is a most virtuous exercise and one that should be continued throughout one's entire life.

But what is the best and most efficacious way to pray, you ask! Well, I'll tell you. Have you ever noticed a mother weaning her baby off her breast, gently pulling him away from her body, softly laying him by her side? Did you hear the cries? And those huge, beautiful tears, did you see them? The little rascal knows what he wants and will not give up until he is back where he wants to be: suckling at the warm and comforting breast. And isn't that just what we should be doing when we feel banished or distant from God? Pestering him continuously with our cries, bombarding him with our insistent pleas until we leave him no choice but to draw us up close to his divine bosom and hold us there, caressing us, feeding us with his love, soothing us with his forgiveness, a balm more precious than any alleviation the world will ever have to offer.

People who do not appreciate the worthiness of prayer and laugh at and scorn those who do pray and turn to God were viewed by Plato and his disciples as orphaned from mother and father. The most virtuous people of all the nations of the world have always been people respected for their insistence on prayer to the gods. This was the case of the Brahmin, among the Indians; the Magi, with the Persians; the Theologians with the Greeks; the Chaldeans, with the Assyrians. These were the people who would institute feasts to their gods and celebrate them with propitiation and prayer offerings. And should not a Catholic, who already knows the true God, and for whom the gates of heaven have been left ajar, should he not, I say, with much more reason, be continuously at prayer to His Majesty with a pure and humble heart?

Every time we ask God for what we are missing, we are sighing soft, sweet songs in his ear, says Proculus. And it is to these songs and divine motets that the spouse is sweetly cajoled by the Beloved: *Let thy voice sound in my ears: for thy voice is sweet and thy face comely.*[1]

The Hebrews understand this voice of the spouse, so dear to God, as the prayer of saints, a melody sweeter to him than all other music and harmony. The Chaldean paraphraser interprets the above passage in this way: *Pray that I may hear your voice, because your voice is sweet in prayer and in the tabernacle's home, and your beautiful countenance is in thy virtuous deeds.*

Psalm 49 can be understood in this way when God himself speaks of the sacrifice of prayer and praise: *Offer to God the sacrifice of praise: and pay thy vows to the Most High.*[2] A sacrifice of pure, clean and simple prayer is most pleasing to God. It is a sweet song of love that can be whispered anytime, anywhere.

God tells us, through St. Luke, that he wants this ardent and persevering prayer to be continuous:

And He spoke also a parable to them that we ought always to pray and not to faint, saying: There was a judge in a certain city, who feared not God, nor regarded man. And there was a certain widow in that city; and she came to him, saying: Avenge me of my adversary. And he would not, for a long time. But afterwards he said within himself: Although I fear not God, nor regard man, yet, because this widow is troublesome to me, I will avenge her, lest continually coming, she weary me.

And the Lord said: Hear what the unjust judge saith. And will not God revenge his elect who cry to Him day and night? And will He not have patience in their regard? I say to you that He will quickly revenge them. But yet, the Son of man, when he cometh, shall he find, think you, faith on earth?

And to some who trusted in themselves as just and despised others he spoke also this parable:

---

[1] *Sonet vox tua in auribus meis: vox enim tuam dulcis…* (Cant. 2:4).
[2] *Sacrificium laudis honorificavit me. Et immola Deo sacrificium laudis. Et redde Altissimo vota tua* (Psalm 49:14).

Two men went up into the temple to pray: the one a Pharisee and the other a Publican. The Pharisee, standing, prayed thus with himself: O God, I give thee thanks that I am not as the rest of men, extortioners, unjust, adulterers, as also is this Publican. I fast twice in a week; I give tithes of all that I possess. And the Publican, standing afar off, would not so much as lift up his eyes towards heaven; but struck his breast, saying: O God, be merciful to me a sinner. I say to you, this man went down into his house justified rather than the other; because everyone that exalteth himself shall be humbled; and he that humbleth himself shall be exalted. [3]

The prophet, also, says: *I will sing to the Lord as long as I live: I will sing praise to my God while I have my being. Let my speech be acceptable to Him: I will take delight in the Lord.* [4]

And Lactantius: *The highest means to honour God and the most propitious sacrifice is the praise that comes out of the mouth of the just directed to God which, in order to be accepted, has to be accompanied by great humility, awe, and devotion. And let no one think that prayer can only be done in church. But in one's own house, in one's own room.*[5]

As Christ himself said: *Intra in cubiculum tuum, et clauso ostio ora Patrem tuum.* [6]

The holy king, pursued by Saul like a wild beast through the forest, prayed as if he were in the temple: *O God, my God, to thee do I watch at break of day. For thee my soul has thirsted. For thee my flesh, O how many ways! In a desert land, and where there is no way and no water, as if in the sanctuary have I come before thee, to see thy power and thy glory.* [7]

Proculus singles out five factors for this sweet music to be perfectly well tuned and most melodious to God:

1) Recognition of the Divinity to whom we are praying (for there cannot be prayer otherwise). This is why, with the Oracles, it was mandatory to light and hold a candle before addressing the gods for guidance. A candle - light - representing *understanding* of

---

[3] Luke: 18:1-14.

[4] Psalm 103:33-34: *Psalm Deo meo quandiu fuero...*

[5] Lucius Coelius Lactantius (240-320 A.D.), *De divinis institutionibus adversus gentes*, Bk.6, chp.25: *Summus igitur colendi Dei ritus est, ex ore justi hominis ad Deum directa laudatio. Quae tamen ipsa, ut Deo sit accepta, et humilitate, et timore, et devotione maxima, opus est. Neque tantum in templo, sibi putet hoc esse faciendum aliquis, sed et domi, et in ipso cubili suo.*

[6] *Go into your private room and close the door, then pray to your Father,* Matt. 6:6.

[7] *In terra deserta et invia, et inaquosa, sicut in sancto apparavi tibi, ut viderem virtutem tuam, et gloriam tuam.* (Psalm 62:3-4; note: Vulgate says *sic* not *sicut*).

what was being asked as well as *acknowledgement* of the divinity of whom it was being asked. For us, it is not only that but what God wants us to do, for, as Philo the Jew confirms in his writings,[8] God commanded that fire be forever burning in the sacrificial altar, and it is in this context, he says, that chapter six of Leviticus has to be understood: *And the fire on the altar shall always burn, and the priest shall feed it, putting wood on it every day in the mornings: and laying on the holocaust, shall burn thereupon the fat of the peace-offering. This is the perpetual fire which shall never go out on the altar.* [9]

2) It is written: *For whosoever shall do the will of my Father that is in Heaven, he is my brother, and my sister and mother.*[10] And so Proculus gives *Sincerity, Purity and Fidelity*, as the second consideration for efficacy in prayer. What he means is that these are fundamental qualities that must be embedded in the soul so that, with pleasure, we may do what we understand to be the will of God, and in so doing, become brother, sister and mother, that is, kindred with God. So next to an understanding of what we are asking and awareness of he whom we are addressing, the most important thing in prayer is absolute sincerity, accompanied by the most faithful readiness to do and accept God's will. Essential qualities for the affinity and kinship that the soul, through prayer, is to covenant with God.

3) Once the superior part of our soul senses and touches him, and standing on nothing but the rock of *Humility*, we must acknowledge – confess – our unworthiness. This contact, this touch, it would seem to me, is what St. John was referring to in his first canonical epistle: *That which was from the beginning, which we have heard, which we have seen with our eyes, which we have looked upon and our hands have handled, of the word of life.*[11]

4) *Assiduity, Attachment, and Steadfastness* to the Supreme Good come next, of which the prophet so specifically speaks: *It is good for me to draw to God.* [12] And elsewhere in the Psalms, having spoken of this continuous prayer, he says: My *soul came close to you and your*

---

[8] *in lib. De victimis, vol. II. Pag. 194, and in lib. De victima afferentibus, pag. 200.*

[9] Lev. 6:12-13.

[10] Matt.12:50.

[11] I John 2.

[12] *But it is good for me to adhere to my God, to put my hope in the Lord God: that I may declare all thy praises in the gates of the daughters of Sion,* (Psalm 72:28).

right hand received it.[13] In one oracle it is written that when mortal man draws near to fire, he will have divine light, will be deified, and will remain deified. This attachment and application to divine fire is of utmost importance. It is through these means, more than any other, that God reveals himself to us allowing us to partake of his light and affection, mirroring him in our works.

5) We are almost there: union with God. But not quite yet. Union is not accomplished in prayer because prayer itself is not the target. The objective, our desired aim, is union with God. I say it does not take place in prayer because, in prayer, we are asking for what we do not have, and we can hardly be asking for what we do not have if we have already got it. Union takes place only in perfect contemplation, by means of which whatsoever is in our souls is placed in union with God, and we are then made whole, steadfast and one in him, no longer in ourselves but in God; and unflagging in this divine light, embraced and embellished like bottles in their racks we remain. As the woman St. John saw adorned and robed in the sun, of whom he speaks: *A woman clothed with the sun, and the moon under her feet, and on her head a crown of twelve stars.* [14]

In contemplation, says Richard of St. Victor, the soul is avidly witnessing the pageantry of divine wisdom and, in admiration and awe, she is made to take leave of herself.[15] Pageantry is what is staged and manifested during contemplation for the soul to witness, consider, and reflect upon. And the soul finds herself astonished, aghast, wonder-struck and, one might say, out of herself at such origination and magnificence.[16] It was upon this pageantry that the prophet had his eyes fixed when he urged us to glorify the Lord as much as we can, from the depth of our soul, from the bottom of our heart, with all our strength; we will never exalt him enough, for he exceeds all praise and can never be glorified enough by either one creature alone or all of us together. *Glorify the Lord as much as ever you can: for he will yet far exceed, as his magnificence is wonderful. Bless the Lord, exalt him as much as you can: for*

---

[13] *My soul hath stuck close to thee: thy right hand hath received me,* (Psalm 62:7).

[14] Apoc. 12:1

[15] *Speculum dicitur, quod spectandum oculis exibetur.*

[16] *Redeunt spectacula mane,* Virgil.

He is above all praise. When you exalt him put forth all your strength and be not weary: for you can never go far enough.[17] Do not tire, do not grow weary, my soul, of praising God. Take courage; keep striving for as long as you can, knowing that you will always fall short however much you praise him.[18] All this that you see in this world, and all that you have heard and read is very little, almost nothing, compared with what is secret and hidden in the private chambers of God, unfolding and revealing themselves during contemplation. Even the Blessed see and know little of it. Although they see God as He is, they cannot apprehend all that he is, for God is boundless, and the degree of their virtue, however great, is still finite. Prayer can arrive at the taste, the savour, the wonder of God, but only in contemplation can it actually be savoured and tasted. Prayer opens the door. Contemplation enters in, and sees things not licit for man to speak of. Nor could one do so, however willing. It is something not absorbed through the bodily senses and, consequently, these senses are not equipped to define it.

Of both aspects of prayer was Holy Job speaking when he urged us to appease and praise the Lord, for he will uncover his face and we will rejoice in him with great jubilation. *He shall pray to God, and he will be gracious to Him. And he shall see his face with joy: and He will render to man with justice.*[19]

The soul, uplifted in such glory to the mirror of divine brilliance, and marvelling at the felicitous sight of such bounty and satiety of Good – at which angels undeviatingly wonder – begins to feel an all-embracing fire-like warmth, the warmth of that Reverberating Light, which wounds and burns with its Rays. And the soul softens and melts in this heat, in this fire. And so melted and softened, she immerses herself in God himself who ignites and inflames her as metal in a foundry. And perfect union occurs.

And let the sages of the world issue me a reprimand now. I mean all those ever trying to measure God in yards and inches, trying to fit and encircle him in the realm of mathematical

---

[17] Sirach 43:32-34.
[18] *Multa abscondita sunt maiora his; pauca enim vidimus operum eius.*
[19] Job 33.26.

theorems, pigeon-holing him who has no boundaries and is free of all laws. The very first thing I said at the beginning of this study was that these words were not written for them. They are of the opinion that, since there is no proportionality between finite and infinite, that union cannot take place. They will also dispute this point from the argument of the Simplicity of God, saying that, since he is Most Simple, as he is, he cannot, by necessity, partake of any mixture. But I hope they will grant me that the sun, one and simple, shedding its light in all places and parts of the globe, remains one. And though it heats and illuminates everything and everywhere, still, it admits of no mixture, nor is it touched by the impurity of the things it touches, nor is it contaminated by them. And is not this One and Most Simple God above the oneness and simplicity of the sun? Can he not, he who creates, impregnates and permeates all and everything, will them to revert back and fuse in him? Plato said that this was, precisely, the life of gods and men divine who, circumvently, come round to God, and nourished on his delicacies and transformed in him, repose. Why should we marvel or be surprised at hearing that God brings a soul into union with him and transforms her in himself! Even ordinary fire does that. When fire burns a tree, fire does not become the tree. Nor could it be said that fire is less pure, or its essence now mixed, because the tree is joined to it. The tree partook of the fire, and was converted and transformed in it, but the essence and purity of fire itself remains. Why would our impurity stick to that infinite fire (of which Deuteronomy says it "consumes" and "scorches"), when it converts souls in itself? Nor is quantitative proportionality required in this First Cause, free, and exempt of all predicates, on which First Cause they inevitably depend for their operation. For this primary and supreme cause, although infinite and complete, enfolds and imparts itself to each and every thing, however small, even though the disparity be so great and the magnitude of difference so vast. The laws of proportionality in causes is valid for those of finite and limited qualities, but not for God, most excellent agent, who exceeds and surpasses all natural faculties, and at whose blinking of an eye, all things obey and all creatures make ready – those that are not, in order to be; and those that are, to act so as to return to him. And this is so especially of man, with his built-in capacity for the divine, born to be united with God through the means of love. Love, by which the lover steals into the beloved and two are made into one. Love of which it is written: *God is love and he who loves is in God and God in him.*[20]

Chapter 12

Of the reciprocal union that exists with God through the

Most Sacred Sacrament of the Altar

Christ clearly showed his intention to give himself to us transubstantiated, when he said through St. John:

I am the bread of life. Your fathers did eat manna in the desert; and are dead. This is the bread that cometh down from heaven; that if any man eat of it, he may not die. I am the living bread, which came down from heaven. If any man eat of this bread, he shall live forever: and the bread that I will give is my flesh, for the life of the world. The Jews therefore strove among themselves, saying: How can this man give us his flesh to eat? Then Jesus said to them: Amen, Amen, I say unto you; except you eat the flesh of the Son of Man and drink his blood, you shall have not life in you. He that eateth my flesh and drinketh my blood hath everlasting life; and I will raise him up in the last day. For my flesh is meat indeed; and my blood is drink indeed. He that eateth my flesh and drinketh my blood abideth in me; and I in him. As the living Father hath sent me and I live by the Father; so he that eateth me, the same also shall live by me. This is bread that come down from heaven. Not as your fathers did eat manna and are dead. He that eateth this bread shall live forever. These things he said, teaching in the synagogue, in the Capharnaum.[1]

He said that by eating his flesh and drinking his blood we were one with him, as the head and other parts of the body are one body and one spirit, and partake of one and the same life. What kind of union is this that is effected by eating this flesh and drinking this blood? I shall try to elucidate this with some care and deliberation so that its significance may more easily be discerned.

The words of Christ are these: *He that eateth my flesh and drinketh my blood abideth in me and I in him.*

A spiritual metaphor, some say, a figure of speech on love, he uses them frequently. Well, we shall see.

---

[1] John 6:51-60.

We saw in the last chapter that St. John, in his first Epistle, says that *God is love and he who loves is in God and God in him.* [2] Let us talk about love a little.

Love makes the lover forget himself. He lives, not in him, but in the beloved. We can see this everyday watching those passionately in love, what they do, how they act, the thousand and one silly nothings they will say to each other, and so on. When our love is true, we live in the other and for the other, not in ourselves or for ourselves. I am referring here to mundane love, but this applies to love divine as well. Spiritual love causes in those who love God and with love receive him in Communion, a holy inebriation by which they take leave of themselves and forget everything that is not of God. The favoured disciple was referring to this communion when he said he was left asleep and as in ecstasy, having Christ's bosom as his pillow.[3] It is a bold, perhaps perplexing thing for me to say, I know, that when we receive Holy Communion properly, we take leave of ourselves. But I consider this to be most true. Just as the humble serf will take leave of his lodgings upon the king setting foot in them so, when we receiving Communion worthily, we *come out of ourselves* as God enters in. Now, what do I mean, exactly, *coming out of oneself, taking leave of oneself?* I mean surrender, I mean renunciation and self-denial, I mean extricating self-love from our hearts so that only God may live and reign there. I mean saying "no" to our egotistical "yes", and "yes" to our bull-headed "no". I mean shedding one's old life and receiving the new. I mean ridding our soul of all sin because, for as long as it is there, neither are we in God nor God in us. *If we were in God*, St. John says, *we would not sin.*[4]

St. Augustine asked[5] why God gave his flesh and blood to us specifically under the species of bread and wine. Why not under the form of a chicken or a partridge, or anything else? And he answers himself saying that, as bread is made into one substance from many grains of wheat, and many clusters of grapes are

---

[2] I John 4::16.

[3] *Now there was leaning on Jesus' bosom one of his disciples, whom Jesus loved* (John 13:23).

[4] *Whosoever is born of God committeth no sin, for his seed abideth in him. And he cannot sin, because he is born of God* (I John 3:9).

[5] Reference not found. It does not look like St. Augustine [Ed.].

pressed to become one wine, in like manner, Christ and those who eat him are made one through love. Signifying, he explains, the union between God and the soul that receives him transubstantiated, and the union that is to exist among the faithful who worthily receive him. God took our flesh because of the depth of love he felt for us, and so that we may truly love him, he gives us his in return. He wanted this reciprocity of love so that we could all, in truth, say: *This now is bone of my bones and flesh of my flesh.*[6] St. Augustine called this food and drink a sacrament of mercy, a sign of unity, the ligature and bond of love. My own opinion is that these words of Christ indicate, above all, union; a union so close, that Christ likens it with that existing between the Father and him. *As my Father who lives, sent me, and I have life through him, so he who would eat me will have life through me.*

Again, what kind of union is this?

Modern heretics err when they say the Sacrament represents a spiritual union of wills brought about by charity. They do not accept that it is the Flesh of Christ that is being eaten, nor His Blood that is being drunk. A representation, a union in spirit, they say, not a real, an actual, one. We, Catholics, judge this on a much higher plane, for we firmly profess that in the Sacrament of the Altar and the consecrated Host we receive Christ in reality and actuality, and since we verily and truly eat him we are, in reality and actuality, joined to him. This union comes about, not by spiritual congeniality, but in reality and in fact, physically, by means of the flesh.

We believe that, by means of this divine sustenance, the soul, being spirit, is nourished through her own natural faculties with grace and virtue; that she is renewed and regaled with joy, maintained with peace, strengthened in faith, confirmed in hope; that she becomes more fervent in love, more predisposed to do good. But those things that are of the flesh are also affected. For when we receive Holy Communion worthily, we participate, as much as our own capacity will allows us, in the condition and quality of the Body of Christ: chastity, purity, a refreshing temperance, an invigorating tranquillity, a detachment from the

---

[6] Gen. 3:23.

world that secludes us from the ardent passions of living by the senses.

This Divine Food is more than a spiritual metaphor. We are dealing here with the Flesh and Blood of Christ in real presence and real existence and, it is precisely through Communion that we are made one with him and partake of his qualities and virtues, as members of a body to its head, as branches to the vine.

So, in order to rouse Catholic believers to reverence of this most royal fare, and so that their faith be strengthened, their conviction deepened, and their desire to receive him worthily and continuously may grow, I thought it appropriate to cite some examples here of what some saints have written about this matter; those especially who, with particular devotion and fervour, wrote about this truth which all the faithful know and cherish: that in the consecrated Host we are truly receiving the Body of Christ.

Saint Hilary, in the dispute against the Arians[7] concludes with the assertion the Catholic Church professes: that the natural union between Christ and those who worthily receive him transubstantiated is the same union existing between the Father and the Son. He says Christ wanted this type of union to take place because, praying to the Father just before his death, he said to Him: *Father, I will that I and mine be one thing, as I am with you.* Now, the Father and the Son are not one in the other because they love each other, or because their wills are one. The Father and the Son are one in the other because they are of one essence. The words of Christ are:

That they all may be one, as thou, Father, in me, and I in thee; that they also may be one in us; that the world may believe that Thou hast sent me. And the glory which Thou hast given me, I have given to them; that they may be one, as we also are one, I in them, and Thou in me; that they may be perfect in unity.[8]

The Father lives in the Son, and the Son lives in the Father, and they are both one Being, and there is but One living in them.

Undeniably a union of wills takes place, impregnated in our hearts by the Holy Spirit. But Christ is referring here to much

---

[7] St. Hilary of Poitiers, *Contra Arianos*, Book I.
[8] John 17:21-23.

more than a meeting of wills. He is talking about a unity of Being, of body and soul, so that all of us, each according to his capacity and individual condition, may be one with him. And because it is one and the same spirit, one and the same nourishment, one and the same food we all partake of, all of us are made one spirit and one divine body. A body and a spirit that joins most closely with his, and that in so doing conforms, in this capacity and no other, to the one that is substantive of that divine body and spirit. This is the greatest union that could ever be made or imagined for beings so far removed from him.

St. Hilary continues: What I ask of those who correlate Father and Son solely in terms of the will, is whether, in the same way, Christ is in us only because of his will and ours coming together. If the Word really and truly became flesh, which they are willing to accept, and we are truly receiving the Word incarnate in this divine meal, how can it be thought, or imagined, that it does not hold good in us, he that by being born man, joined indistinguishably to himself the nature of our flesh, and that this flesh and ours are brought back together in the sacrament, to communicate to us eternal life? We are one because we are in Christ and Christ is in the Father. And whosoever denies that Christ is not in the Father, by necessity has to admit first that he is not in Christ, nor Christ in him, because the Father in Christ and Christ in us are all in union. And if truly Christ took of our flesh, and truly that man who was born of the Virgin Mary was the Christ, and we, under the mystery of the Sacrament truly eat of the flesh of his body, truly, then, we are one with him, because, again, the Father is in Christ and Christ in us. How, then, can anyone dare affirm that this is, merely, a union of wills, a unity in spirit only, and not a real one? The purpose of the Sacrament is to join, not to agree.

But please note, Catholic reader, that you will fall short of apprehending these truths if you simply examine them through the eyes of the flesh, as do those so domiciled in the world. Let us mindfully read what is written, and let us comprehend what we read. Let us hear the words of the Lord: *He who eats of my flesh and drinks of my blood is in me and I in him.*

And so that no one would doubt that the union we are talking about here is more than a spiritual metaphor, let us deliberate as to what Christ himself might have meant when he spoke these words to his disciples: *I will not leave you orphans; I will come to you, yet a little while, and the world seeth me no more. But you see me; because I live and you shall live. In that day you shall know that I am in the Father; and you in me, and I in you.*[9] The only way you can dare untie this tight knot between Christ and us is if you are willing to deny the unity between the Father and the Son.

But this is a complex issue and one can legitimately have questions. How can it be that only by our touching the flesh of Christ, and Christ ours, can such an intimate union come to pass so that one could say, with certainty, that Christ and us are one same body? The answer is, leaving aside many subtleties of thought, that Christ's flesh and our flesh are not one merely because they touch or, as Theodoret says, kiss, in the sacrament. Not even the saints assert that union results from contact alone. If this were the case, those who receive Communion unworthily would also be one in him. It is, rather, because, when receiving his flesh worthily, by means of the grace bestowed on us when his body touches ours, our body comes to resemble his a little more closely, by affinity being called one.

When our body strips itself of its own qualities and clothes itself with the qualities of the body of Christ, we become, unequivocally, one with Christ. Just as red-hot charcoal is called fire, not because it is itself fire, or has the essence of fire, but because it resembles it in all its properties and characteristics, in its ardency, combustion, colour, effect and consequence, why should not it be said that our flesh is in Christ when so adapted and conditioned to his? Doesn't the Apostle say that *he who is joined to the Lord is one Spirit?*[10] What does it mean for man to join to God but to receive his grace, a celestial manna that when poured on the soul conditions and perfects it in Christ? If St. Paul calls our spirit and that of God one spirit, then, by affinity, resemblance, and

---

[9] John 14:18-20.
[10] *Know you not that your bodies* are *the members of Christ?...but he who is joined to the Lord is one spirit?* I Cor.6:15-17.

condition of our body to his, why cannot it be said that his and our body are one as well?

Let us add to this notion of affinity another not less important reason: the virtue of the flesh of Christ. If our hands can retain the fragrance of the amber scent-box we carried leaving a trace that can still be perceived long after we laid it aside, the flesh of Christ, more virtuous and efficacious than any amber, being joined to our body, having boosted our soul with grace, will it not transmit its virtue and fragrance to ours? Does any body joined to another body fail to communicate itself? The fresh air refreshes us, heat warms us, do they not? I am not saying that it is a law of nature that the amber must leave its fragrance in my hands, that a mild breeze must cool me. I am saying simply that they do. In the same way, I am not saying that, by necessity, Christ's body will communicate its condition to ours when union occurs, for then, both the worthy and the unworthy would be communicants in such a union, which is not the case, for we know that, if we receive Communion when unclean, what we in fact receive is not grace but judgement and condemnation. But what I am saying is not an irrational assumption.

Let us add to all said above another more congruent reason. If the whispering of the serpent confounded our souls, and the eating of the forbidden food tainted our bodies, who can doubt that this benevolent food, so ordained to counteract the malignant other, will deliver not only justice to the soul but also sanctity and purity to the flesh, and to this extent, how can the divine mediation of the Sacrament be overestimated? Can we now see how much a clean soul that with purity, reverence and devotion receives Communion, has to gain?

Tertullian declared this truth in a few simple words.[11] Those who share one soul, he said, meaning those who are, together, one body and one will, can never doubt partaking and sharing of what they have with the other. It is plain that if I am willing to give you my heart, I am not going to fear sharing my property, or anything else that is mine, with you. Marriage is an example of this: a mutual giving, between husband and wife, of each other's bodies

---

[11] Tertul. Apolog. c.39.

and all other goods, so that they partake of them with no variance, there no longer being a "yours" and "mine" but an indivisible "ours". So it is in the Sacrament. When Christ gives himself to us, there is nothing hidden or stacked away under the floorboards, for a rainy day. He gives himself completely. We saw this taking place in the early Church, when each day the faithful would receive Communion, their wills being one and their properties held in common. *And the multitude of believers had but one heart and one soul. Neither did anyone say that naught of the things which he possessed was his own; but all things were common unto them.*[12]

St. Paul called the consecrated bread that we eat, the participation in the Body of Christ, and the chalice that we drink the communication of his Blood, and to one and the other, the partaking of his magnanimity and honour. *The chalice of benediction which we bless, is it not the communion of the blood of Christ? And the bread which we break, is it not the partaking of the body of the Lord? For we, being many, are one bread, one body; all that partake of one bread.*[13]

St. John Damascene[14] says that if, through fire, those things that touch gold become golden, and of such a beautiful colour that, rough and coarse metal though they were, they now seem to have drunk of the essence of gold, how much more united and deified could faithful Catholics become if only they were to receive the Most Sacred Body of Jesus, our Redeemer, properly! If only, in such way nourished, we could disrobe ourselves of the world and clothe ourselves with golden garments of love?

The Catholic Church is called the Body of Christ in Scripture, and the reason for this is that, by her feeding on Him she converts back to Him becoming His Body, and each of the faithful, in consequence, a member of that Body. The transubstantiated Christ brings the Church to Himself, and by its virtue, makes it one Spirit and one Body with Him – as yeast, stealing the dough to itself, giving it meaning, bringing it life. Maturing it.

---

[12] Acts 4:32.
[13] I Cor. 10:16-17
[14] St. John Damascene, *Expositio*, IV, 16.

Chapter 13

On the relationship that exists between God and the soul
that receives him transubstantiated.

Medical doctors say that the physical sustenance of the body is dependent, primarily, upon nourishment from food being absorbed, assimilated, and distributed throughout. I thought it appropriate to use this analogy of the body and of food as a means of explaining the wondrous relationship that exists between God and those who, worthily, receive his divine nourishment in Holy Communion.

It is worth noting that doctors view food, or rather, estimate its nourishing potential in three different stages: Non-nutrient, quasi-nutrient, and nutrient. Food in its non-nutrient stage is said to be food that has not yet been eaten: a piece of bread, for example. Quasi-nutrient is food that has been eaten, masticated, and swallowed. But it is only when food has been digested, distributed through arteries and veins and absorbed by all body parts, that food can now be said to have nutritious value. Only then can it nourish and be of sustenance to the body, each part converting its equivalent into its own. The lungs, nimble and light, attracting the choleric and irascible elements; hard bones, the earthly and melancholy; nerves, cartilage, bowels and joints, the phlegmatic and apathetic; and the heart, most noble lodge and chamber of life, the purest and most virginal blood. We understand, then, that for food to sustain and nourish, it has to be assimilated first by each part of the body that is in need of its sustenance.

Likewise, for the Sacrament to nourish and for the conversion that God intends to take place in Holy Communion to take place, there must be a correspondence between him and us; and because such conversion is not of Christ in us but of us in Christ, we have to assimilate ourselves to him inasmuch as our own individual capacity will allow so that, as the ingested food and recipient body evolve and become one, so, with Christ in us and we in Christ, one love and one spirit will emerge.

Consider the means with which nature has provided us to absorb and dispose of our food: how the body refines, filters and purifies it to become an integral part of our bodies, a process, in itself, worthy of admiration. We have teeth to break and divide it, molars to crumble it, warmth in the stomach to dissolve and separate the gross from the fine, mesenteric veins to suck the useful and ignore the rest, filters that seep and purify, dense and narrow pores that receive this filtered refuse; and, finally, a *sponginess* common to all body parts, that enables them to absorb its nourishment.

We shall need to go through more twists and turns than these do to become worthy of God's nourishment in Communion! We shall first have to be crushed and broken with abnegation and contrition, emaciated with penance and consumed with the fire of love and devotion in order to be commensurate with Christ who, crushed, emaciated and broken with the immensity of his love for us, offered himself to the Father on a Cross. Or, to say the same thing differently, when I celebrate Mass and you receive Communion properly, in order for us to benefit from the Sacrament, it is essential that we reconcile ourselves to Christ and adapt ourselves to his image once again, for it is an illusion that the arrogant could blend easily with the humble, the carnal with the chaste, the haughty with the meek, the cruel with the gentle lamb, unless it be a monster you want as a result. Considerable mastication and rumination will have to take place beforehand, a rigorous examination of conscience, and an arduous groundbreaking preparation; all of it enveloped in the warmth of devotion, for us to be worthy of receiving him. And nothing less will do. For we are readying ourselves for union with God himself and to be converted, spiritually and bodily, into him.

Let us hear how the learned and holy Cajetan uses this analogy of body and food to explain the words of Christ, *He who eats of my flesh and drinks of my blood abideth in me and I in him:* This divine food will be of no benefit, nor will union take place if we do not remain in Christ and Christ in us once the Sacrament has been received. According to doctors, says Cajetan, there are two essential prerequisites for food to get to the nourishing stage. First, it must repose in the stomach for a length of time: having eaten a nutritious meal will be of little value if the food is not retained in the stomach to allow digestion to take place; indeed, non-retention might well be a sign of intestinal damage. Secondly, it is important that we are mindful of what we are doing when we eat, concentrating on just this one activity; for example, taking our time masticating, I mean, enjoying our meal. If not, all we'll get is indigestion and constipation, to which studious professors will testify.

What Cajetan means is this. For the Flesh and Blood of Christ, our soul's true food and true drink, to be of benefit when received in Communion, it is essential that we hold him, retain him, keep him within. If we immediately return to our old sins and vices, what we are simply doing is throwing up God. I am saying here that those who, having just received Communion, blatantly and shamelessly go back to their old ways as if nothing had happened, are emptying themselves of Christ, they are ejecting him with such force and violence that, yes, one could almost say they are vomiting him. It is such a violent act of aggression of the soul against God that they could not torture him more cruelly were he able to feel it.

Let me make this clearer with an example. When I eat something, a partridge, say, it goes first from my mouth to my stomach, then to my kidneys from where, once digested, there arises a type of *sap*. From there it gets distributed to my veins and finally, through them, to all the parts of my body. Now, the nourishment that goes to the eyes, for example, will not stay in the eyes as nourishment to the eyes, separate and independent from them but will become, instead, an inseparable part of the eyes themselves. The part that goes to the tongue, will become part of the tongue, the part that goes to the heart, part of the heart, what goes to the hands, part of the hands, and so on. Now, I ask you. If someone were to extricate this partridge from me with an iron hook, this partridge that has already become an integral part of the body itself, what degree of pain, do you think, would I have to sustain and endure for that part that is already eye to leave the eye? The part that is already tongue to leave the tongue? The part that is already heart to leave the heart? The part that is already hands to leave the hands? Is this even imaginable?

My brothers and sisters in the Catholic Faith, please listen to what I am saying here. When we receive Christ in Communion, Christ does not convert himself into us. We are too small. He is too big. It is us who convert into him and, as in the analogy of food, become part of his eyes, part of his hands, part of his heart. Do you see? Part of him! When you receive the Sacrament worthily you are embodied and converted in the Body of Christ himself.

Now, then. Think of mortal sin as an iron claw from hell. If you then go on to sin, this hook will rip you apart from his Body in the way I have just described, with great injury, pain, and suffering to the Lord. It is an abominable offence, a horrifying insult to God. In my opinion, it might well be what the Apostle had in mind when he wrote to the Corinthians:

Know you not that your bodies are the members of Christ? Shall I then take the members of Christ and make them the members of a harlot? God forbid! [1]

God forbid, indeed, that what was and is eye of God, hand of God, foot of God, heart of God, we would go on to profane and turn into eye of the Devil, hand of Satan, heart of Judas, foot of Lucifer. If you want Communion to be of benefit, first make sure you are clean and worthy to receive Christ. Then hold him when you receive him, hold him there, hold him tight, don't just throw him out, embrace him with the warmth of living faith and perfect charity. Don't let go, keep holding him close to you by believing, loving, and acting in a way that his loving wish for us may come to pass: to join us to him and make us one with him, letting us share in the treasure of his divine Flesh and his divine Spirit.

St. Cyprian[2] maintained that Christ, at the end of his life, gave us his Flesh so that our own could be renewed and restored. We were made of corruptible flesh and blood, and it would not have been possible, given the frail nature of our body and soul, for us to be renewed and restored back into his image, immersed, as we were, in our old and haggard affliction. He gave us himself as Life to remedy our terminal disease.

---

[1] I Cor. 6:15.

[2] St. Cyprian, *In Serm. Coenae.*

These are the words of St. Cyprian whose teaching is clear. The reform of our being, of our body, would not have taken place save for the Flesh of Christ and ours being joined. This physical coupling between Christ and us was essential so that the impure nature of our bodies could be reformed. Is it not the case, he asks, that a poultice is applied to the wound in order to help it heal? In the same way, Christ fastened himself to our body to bring it back to health, to restore its innocence of old, and what is more, to restore it to immortality so that our body and soul may be free from perpetual corruptibility.

St. Cyril says[3] that in no other way could this corruptible nature of our body have been saved unto incorruptibility and eternal life, but by this body of natural life joining us to itself. Do you not believe my words? he asks. If you do not, then believe Jesus, whose words are these: *In truth, in truth, I tell you, that if you do not eat of the flesh of the Son of Man, and do not drink of his blood, you will not have life in you.*[4]

Don't you realise, my dear Catholics, that more than union of wills, much more than symbolic acts and spiritual metaphors would have been needed to restore us to health? It is only because Christ gave us his Flesh as food that we have a chance to enjoy eternal life.

And, in another passage, St. Cyril says: *we do not deny that a supernatural union exists between Christ and us brought about by righteousness, faith and sincere charity; but we do manfully and in the strongest possible terms affirm, that that is not the only benefit the Sacrament confers to us. To believe and say otherwise is to see things differently from Holy Scripture, and to stray dangerously from the truth.* And, again, elsewhere, he give us the following example as illustration: *as water, whose nature is cold, forgets its natural coldness when heat is applied to it and comes out of itself boiling, in like manner, since our bodies are mortal by nature, it is by participating in that Life that sequesters us from our natural weakness, that we come to live again. In other words, the soul is not the only one to gain by this virtue communicated to us by the Holy Spirit. This coarse and ephemeral body of ours gains, too, in accordance with its own faculties.*

---

[3] St. Cyril of Alexandria, *In Io.*, c.13.
[4] John 6:53.

Since the Flesh of our Saviour is flesh that vivifies by the nature of the Word to whom it is united - Life itself - it is by this virtue of being united with him who is Life that, when we eat him, Life is given back to us. When Christ raised the dead and healed the sick, he did not just use words and issue commands, as he could have done. Often he would touch, he would apply his body, too, and his flesh would join in, showing us that his body had the same life-giving virtue. These are the words of St. Cyril.

We can add something else. Christ aimed in all his deeds to reveal and communicate his love for us, to unite us to him. The more pure and excellent love is the closer the union becomes. We know that Christ joins us spiritually in many ways, endowing us with grace, invigorating and enlivening our soul, drawing her to his image. But we are made of flesh, too, are we not? Loving us as he does, would he shy off from physical proximity, he who took our flesh? There is no shortage of those who would place fault with the former and doubt with the latter. Let us answer them with the words St. Paul used to remind the Romans that, just as we had all died in Adam, we all rise in Jesus Christ.

Wherefore as by one man sin entered into this world, and by sin, death; so death passed upon all men, in whom all have sinned...Therefore, as the offence of one, unto all meant condemnation; so also the justice of one, unto all men the justification of life...For if by one man's offence death reigned through one, much more they who receive abundance of grace and of the gift and of justice shall reign in life through one, Jesus Christ.[5]

By Adam we inherited injury and harm to both body and spirit. There was spiritual temptation in the breathing of the serpent, but there was also consumption of forbidden earthly food. Life is the opposite of death, medicine remedies injury, and disease; so Christ with his most excellent love grants us wholesomeness and well being, remedying both: the soul with his Spirit, the body with his Flesh. The venomous apple, making its way to the stomach, so distempered our bodies that one thousand and one diseases revealed themselves as a result. His sacred body, duly joined to ours by grace, counteracts this malady with freshness, vigour, and youthfulness. The forbidden fruit intoxicated and poisoned our bodies and death came as a result. This sacred Flesh, inundating

[5] Rom. 5:12-19.

us with his grace, immerses our bodies in his, cleaning, purifying them, giving them life, raising them. *We are one body in Christ,* says St. Paul writing to the Corinthians, *because all of us participate of one bread and drink of one chalice,* meaning, of the Flesh and of the Blood of Christ.[6]

It is our duty, says St. John Chrysostom,[7] *to speak of the wonder of this mystery, the reason why it was granted, its worth and its significance. We are one body: members of his. And, because the union that Christ intends us to have with him is not only spiritual but also tangible and real, he gives us his Body as food, so that we may be transformed in him, each one according to his individual capacity and condition. He was made man. Not content with declaring his love, he wanted to convey and fulfil it by means of his Body as well. And now he continues to do so by coming to us and embodying us to him, so that we may all be one. And in this way, in order to regale us with his love and better show us that union is what he desires, he allows himself not only to be seen by those who cherish him, but also to be touched and eaten, for his flesh to be ingested in ours. As if he had said: I wished and tried to be your brother, and with this aim I dressed myself as man in your flesh and blood: that by which I became your kin, I am now giving to you.* These are the words of St. John Chrysostom.

The Ancient Fathers made use of the marriage between Christ and his Church to describe this union between Christ and ourselves. The Apostle Paul celebrates this marriage by analogising it with matrimony, when he writes to the Ephesians:

The husband is the head of the wife, as Christ is the head of the Church and he is the saviour of her body. Therefore, as the Church is subject to Christ, so also let the wives be to their husbands in all things. Husbands, love your wives, as Christ also loved the Church and delivered himself up for it. That he may sanctify it by the laver of the water of the word of life, that he might present it to himself, a glorious church, not having spot or wrinkle or any such thing, but that it should be holy and without blemish. So also ought men to love their wives, as their own bodies. He that loveth his wife loveth himself. For no man ever hated his own flesh, but nourisheth and cherisheth

---

[6] Cf. I Cor. 10:14-17.

[7] Chrysostom, *Homilies on St. John,* 4.

it, as also Christ doth the Church; because we are members of his body, of his own flesh and of his bones [8]

These words are quoted from the words in Genesis of Adam to his wife: *This is bone of my bones and flesh of my flesh.*[9] She will be called vigorous and robust for she was taken and formed from the male:

For this cause shall a man leave his father and mother; and shall cleave to his wife, and they shall be two in one flesh. This is a great sacrament; but I speak of Christ and of the Church.[10]

This inference does not depend on the formation of Eve out of the rib of Adam, which Christ never mentions, but of Adam and Eve joining together and becoming one flesh.   As in matrimonial union, where two that were separate are no longer two but one, so by our eating the Body of Christ we are made one with him and joined with him.

In summary: this is the great Sacrament the Apostle himself lauds and extols and one which imparts benefits more excellent than the marital union to which he was likening it can ever provide: for the bond between the participants is closer, the purity, greater.   In the marriage between Christ and his Church, souls are deified and bodies sanctified.   In a physical union bodies cannot escape vitiation and decay; in divine union, the joy and exaltation is of such calibre and magnitude that it floods and inundates body and soul; it is so noble and majestic that it is glory itself; it is so pure that pain neither precedes nor follows it, nor is it ever in its midst.   In physical union the richest wine is always watered, the delight only too brief. From afar its gold may shine more brightly, but it is, and remains, a lower carat, poorer quality gold.

Let us confess with the Apostle that what Christ has, he has given to us, and is ours for the taking; that Christ is in God and we are in Christ.

As for me now, I have nothing left worth saying. Because, when I meditate on this glorious mystery (and I do often) after a

---

[8] Eph. 5:23-30.
[9] Gen. 2:23.
[10] Eph. 5:32.

while words escape me, my heart overflows, and I confess I can think of nothing to say but cry out with St. Augustine: O Sacrament of mercy! O sign of unity! O bond of charity! All ye who desire life and joy everlasting, come, draw near! And believe.

Addendum to this chapter

Some reflections and personal sentiments of a priest about the Most Sacred Sacrament of the Altar.

The Sacrament of the Altar is God's own and unique way of communicating his infinite love for us. This becomes very clear to me when I meditate on this august mystery of the Mass. Through this Sacrament God is giving us his holy Body and precious Blood, and this he does each time we ask for it.

Are we fully aware of the extent of love involved in this act? Here we have God himself eager, ready, almost pleading with us to become intimate with him, and all we have to do is to want him. Patient, hopeful love, this, forever waiting. I reflect on this often and I confess that every time I do I am left trembling.

I don't know whether other priests would put it in these terms, but I have become convinced – and more so with each day that passes – that when I celebrate Mass and offer the Sacrament to the Eternal Father, the joy, the delight, the glory with which he receives his beloved Son is so immense that nothing compares with the worth and merit of the sacrifice I am offering.

Our actions, however worthy and noble, are still actions of human creatures. And even all the glory and praise that angels and saints perpetually offer the Creator in the blessed Homeland are little, I would say nothing, compared to the sacrifice a humble priest is able to offer the Lord. For here, in the Mass, through the unworthy, God is being offered to God. God is offering himself for us. And so what I am saying is that the praise, the honour, the delight, the glory that is being offered in the Mass is not just a little praise and a little honour, here and there, but infinite praise, infinite honour, infinite delight and infinite glory: beyond any praise and glory that we, or even angels and saints could offer him, for what we are offering is God himself, eternal goodness, eternal righteousness, eternal justice and eternal truth.

And the question of whether the priest is in grace or not in grace is of no relevance here. Because the magnitude - the worth and merit of the offering - does not consist on who is doing the offering, but on the offering itself, on the fact that what is being offered to the Father and the Holy Trinity is still the glorious Person of Jesus Christ, as the Council of Trent firmly declared in Section XXII, chapter II. And because it is his most beloved Son that is being offered, God will never refuse this sacrifice. The priest, though unworthy, when celebrating Mass is the minister of God and of his Church. Who he is, as an individual, is of no consequence when considering the efficacy and merit of the sacrifice (*ex opere operato*). The offering is still the offering of Christ, and by offering his most beloved Son, in whom he is infinitely pleased, as he himself said through St. Matthew, eternal glory, honour and delight is given to the Eternal Father.

And lo, the heavens were opened to him, and he saw the spirit of God descending as a dove and coming upon him. And, behold, a voice from heaven, saying: This is my beloved Son, in whom I am well pleased.[11]

I was reflecting and mulling over these thoughts, on how God continuously bestows grace and great gifts upon us, and about all the reasons why we should always, untiringly, love, honour and praise him, when I felt something like an inner voice telling me most clearly, I sensed, that, if this was what I most desired, I would find no better way than to receive the sacred Sacrament, and having done so, to keep him tightly within me, to make him mine, and then to release him and give him back to the Eternal Father with my praise and my prayer.

And this is what I always do now. When I receive communion, I don't just swallow the sacred Host right away. I hold God. I hold him tight inside of me. I hold him for as long as I can, the longer the better, until the Host dissolves itself naturally by means of my body's warmth. And all this time, I am with God and God is with me, and we are both together and I offer God to God with my prayer and with the most intimate and

---

[11] Matt. 3:15-17.

loving sentiments of my heart and of my will, and with all the humility and the reverence of which I am capable, for what I am doing is offering to God his most beloved Son.

And if I want to give the glorious Queen of Angels as much praise, glory and honour as she deserves, I do that too. With fervour, humility and reverence I put her Son back in her most pure arms, and this is an offering that she receives with great delight, for it is her Son that is being offered. And we can all do this. We can do this every day. And the same offering can be made to the saints for their honour and glory and that of God himself.

But mind, reader, that you do not misunderstand what I am saying here. Christ, our Lord, cannot be offered to anyone but God. Not even to the Virgin or any or all the saints. Nor can the Mass be offered to anyone but God. Only to God can God be offered. What I am simply suggesting is that you can offer him to the Father through the honour and memory of the saints, or of the Virgin, so that they, cleaner and purer than we are, can themselves present the sacrifice to God on our behalf, for God is pleased with them.

And it is so clear to me, that all priests and all Catholics should give glory, honour, praise and delight to God and to our sovereign Lady, the Empress of Heaven, and to all the saints of the Heavenly Jerusalem through the Most Sacred Sacrament of the Altar, that all I want to say loud and clear now to those who can hear me and receive this news is to try to give all of your love to God and strive as much as you possibly can to be always ready and in grace so that not one day passes that a priest does not celebrate Mass or a layman receive Communion – always preceded, of course, by the counsel and approbation of your religious confessor and spiritual father.

It seems to me that the loving and paternal heart of God is always more eager to bestow gifts on us than we are to receive them. Let it hearten us to know that this most rich sacrifice we are offering with our prayers will always be answered. As the spouse says, his hands are generous and filled with hyacinths. We are offering the Father such a highly esteemed gift that we will receive the favours we hope to receive if our soul is adorned with virtue and esteemed beautiful in his divine eyes. And even more so, it would seem to me, if we do it through the Virgin or the saints, asking them to take the offering to the Father, pleading with them to act as our intermediaries and intercede to God for us, for God is pleased with them and will not refuse them favours.

It is our choice, isn't it?, to accept or to ignore God's sacrifice. To accept the gifts he has chosen to give us so that we may prepare for life everlasting, or to pay no heed and throw it all away. Think about it this way. Imagine you had a lawsuit filed against you claiming your property, your honour, even your life. What would you do? Would you prepare to defend yourself or would you simply ignore it? And if you were so careless, negligent and outright lazy that you didn't even bother turning up in court and the judgement went against you, who would you blame?

My dear Catholics everywhere: know that what had been promised you has been faithfully made ready and delivered to your doorstep. If you are so negligent, careless and lazy that you fail to procure for yourselves these vast spiritual riches, and if you do not, with due readiness, come and frequent these divine mysteries, you will justly suffer poverty and dishonour and will die forever in misery and need. Let the soul ask God, ask whatever she desires because, by these means, the prayer will always be heard. It may be answered then, or later, when he knows the time is right, *adiutor in opportunitatibus*. But the prayer will always be heard!

Chapter 14

On the ultimate triumph of love:

the transformation or death of the soul

After union comes transformation which, when rightly considered, will be seen to take place at a stage of higher union. Union here (speaking in spiritual terms) is a coming together of two in one will and in one love. Transformation, however, means a modification of one thing into another and this with enhancement and benefit. St. John promises this in the name of Christ when he says *he gave them power to be made sons of God,*[1] a power not given to all, but to those only who are no longer of flesh, or blood, or human will, for they are now of spirit, distilled, parched, squeezed of all sogginess, as the strings of a psaltery which, unless well dried, cannot produce flawless harmony and pure music. The Hebrews called this transformation "dying in a kiss". It is the one the spouse yearns for at the beginning of the *Songs,* the one the prophet spoke of as *precious death in the eyes of the Lord.*[2]

Happy indeed, many times felicitous the soul when God, wholly by means of a kiss, brings her to him, and she is transformed and deified, and in this kiss she dies, and in dying to all that is not of God she lives, exclusively in him. This death, the saints say, takes place when the soul gently coasts and steals away into the arms of her Beloved and there, well anchored now, moors, her eyes away from the world, all things spiritual now. When speaking of this death St. Bernard cried: O glorious death that takes not but enhances life![3]

Why fear lust when sensual life is not felt! Can one sin when the inclination to sin has been transcended? Truly, such beautiful death has to be an angelically pure death; a death caused by pure love and nothing else, love as powerful, more powerful, than

---

[1] *He came unto his own, and his own received him not, But as many as received him, he gave them power to be made the sons of God, to them that believe in his name. Who are born, not of blood, nor of the will of the flesh, nor of the will of man, but of God,* (John 1:10-13).

[2] *Precious in the sight of the Lord is the death of his saints,* (Psalm. 115:15).

[3] *Commentary on Cant.*

death itself. And the more she burns in love of her Beloved, the more she dies to the world.

Just as physical death separates the body from the soul, so divine love separates the soul from the vanities of the world and some times, a few only, from the body itself, as Gerson said. When speaking about this subject he would sometimes tell the story of a simple, devout woman who, after hearing a sermon during the feast of Pentecost on the transformation of the soul into God, started sighing, weeping softly, her sobs becoming ever more uncontrollable. Reproached and even struck by some of those present because of the disturbance she was causing with her cries, tense and intensifyingly taut in spirit, she expired right there in church, her veins broken, a martyr of love; like fermenting wine that bursts out of the vessels that contain it, being unable to constrain its fullness and abundance for want of adequate vents. Fortunate and blessed she was, being able to say with the spouse not only *I wane in love* or *I am wounded in charity* but *I languish, I am dying in love.*

Truly admirable, that a man can reach a state of contemplation such that he can be transported to heights where the body dies to the soul, and before the soul abandons it, the body neither feels, understands, sees nor hears, nor does it seem to be alive.

In order to comprehend better what I am discussing here, the difference between transfiguration, transubstantiation and transformation should be noted. Transfiguration is a transposition of one thing into another thing, the original corporeal substance and form remaining, as Christ was seen transfigured in Mount Tabor. Transubstantiation is a conversion of one substance into another, the same accidents remaining, as is the case with the Sacrament of the Altar. But transformation is when our soul, by virtue of ecstatic love, moves into God whilst retaining its own being new attributes ensuing, not material, not imagined, but sanctifying, the divine brilliance gleaming upon her. This transformation, as St. Bonaventure remarked, takes place when the lover is acting, not after his own way, but according to the form, that is, the will of the Beloved and partaking of his qualities because our soul, the substantial element of man, operates in a two-fold manner. The first is to animate and vivify the body, and this it does as one more life-giving force, in conformity with all the others. But the soul operates at another level, too, as spirit, and as such through the most eminent qualities, to wit: memory, intellect and will, by means of which she remembers, understands and loves. It was in regard to this quality of the soul as spirit that St. Bernard and St. Augustine coined the celebrated phrase: *she is not where she lives but where she loves.*

Let us put this concisely. When the soul converts herself into her beloved she appropriates his form and his mind. In other words, she thinks, understands and loves, not as herself but through the beloved. She is now operating within the primary level of his essential being, as a life-giving force, not in the secondary level of herself or any other creature.

The Apostle did not forget this wondrous effect of love. When writing to the Corinthians he said: we are transformed from light to light,[4] meaning from elucidation to elucidation, from the clarity of common knowledge, rational and acquired, to the clarity of faith, knowledge divine and infused; from the clarity of faith to the clarity of discernment and from this, ultimately, into the clarity of wise and delectable experience. Blessed is the soul who knows of this transformation. More blessed still she who can enjoy and experience it.

But let us hear what the great contemplative Gerson had to say about this. As has been previously noted, he takes iron and charcoal as examples of things incorporating the properties of others into themselves, in their case, incorporating fire and heat. Iron, he says, can clothe itself in the qualities of fire or heat, losing in the process some of its own, to wit, coldness, hardness or blackness, and this it can do to the point where iron might seem to be what it is not rather than what it is; however, iron is still iron, it retains its own substance. Likewise does the soul retain her own being whilst, by similitude only, she is said to be transformed. And this is why we can say that in loving, the soul and heart of the one who loves takes on some of the qualities of the beloved.

---

[4] Cf. II Cor. 4:6.

Now, it can be seen how man may, by assimilation, transform himself into God, if we consider the end for which he was created, which was none other than to unite in friendship and love with his Creator; by means of meditation and contemplation in this present life, and in perpetual fruition, consummate and pure delectation in the one to come. Others explain this transformation by the correspondence between air and light, air incorporating to itself the light of the sun to the extent that both appear to be one and the same thing. Still others say that it is similar to the union of matter and form, for before receiving form matter is imperfect, undefined, without beauty, purpose, or movement. Likewise the soul, before joining God through life-giving love, exists as if in a spiritual death, without beauty, without any aspiration towards eternal life. But by uniting to God, the primordial spring of all life, in some way it partakes of life divine, not because God factually combines with the soul, for that would contravene divine perfection, but by an intimate spiritual penetration, all imperfection deserted. And this solely by love as its qualitative and compatible condition, commensurately, like the arrangement of matter ready for the receiving of form.

Man having been created, then, in the image and likeness of God and disposed of his three supreme powers: rational, passionate and concupiscent, journeys and transforms himself in God so that he can be a participant in the likeness of God. And by transformation here we mean a participation in the power, wisdom, and goodness of God, which are the main attributes of the three divine Persons.

We could expound at length here about the many who were raptured to the sweetness of the kiss of God, and by this were divinized and transformed in God, but I will only mention here that admirable transformation, that perpetual, divine, precious death of St. Paul's who, existing in mortal flesh, did not live in himself but in God, as he confessed to the Galatians *And I live, now not I, but Christ liveth in me.*[5]

---

[5] *For I, through the law, am dead to the law, that I may live to God. With Christ I am crucified to the Cross And I live, now not I; but Christ liveth in me. And the life that I live now in the flesh, I live in the faith of the Son of God, who loved me and delivered himself for*

Let us pause here and philosophise a little.   Let us turn our attention to the best though most arduous and difficult part of this passage, availing ourselves of what sages, though pagan, had to say in this instance. One of them tells of a lover whose soul was dead in him but alive in another's. That this is true, that he who truly loves dies, is sufficiently clear because the lover forgets himself and his thoughts and occupations and finds himself in the beloved. He neither thinks in himself nor of himself, and if he does not think in himself he cannot act for himself either, for thought is the principal act of the soul. If he does not act of himself, it follows that he is not in himself because these two things, to be and to act, are commensurate with each other, for there is no being without action nor action outside being. As the Philosopher says, all entity acts in equivalence to its being, and so it is that no one can operate where he is not, for all actions are where the agent is. Consequently, if the spirit of the lover does not act where the lover is and is not to be found in him, then we will have to consider it to be dead in him. But if, in loving, his love is reciprocated, although dead in himself, he lives in the beloved, which is what our father St. Paul is saying: *I live and I live not. Not I in myself but in Christ, because Christ lives in me.*

Love is of two types: singular and reciprocal, and this we need to remember in order to understand this holy philosophy better. We say "singular love" when I love but I am not loved in return. Reciprocal love, on the other hand, is when I love and I *am* loved back in return. In singular love, the lover dies in any case because the lover neither lives in himself nor in the beloved, for he is not loved. But when the beloved responds to the lover with love, the beloved, at least, lives in him. Amazing and ingenious is this give-and-take of love, that I by loving you, and you by loving me, you live in me and I live in you. We exchange lives and give ourselves one to the other. I do not have myself, and you do not have yourself, but you have me and, therefore, yourself within me; and I have you and, therefore, myself within you. So my beloved is more myself, is closer to me than I am to myself, because, in

---

me. I cast not away the grace of God. For if justice be by the law, then Christ died in vain (Gal. 2:19-21).

loving, I die, and if I live it is because my beloved requites my love and in so doing, gives me life; and I benefit and gain from it, and this life is more important to me than myself.

Great is the virtue and efficacy of reciprocal love because it brings the lover closer to the beloved than to himself, and because – although dead in himself – he is reborn in the beloved. And it is worth noting that, although only one death occurs in reciprocal love, the renascence or rebirth is nevertheless two-fold. In this way – since in my loving you, you possess me, and in your loving me, I possess you – by loving and possessing each other I give you life and at the same time regain mine in you. O blissful death from which two lives are born! Oh how blissful this intercourse by which I give myself to someone and in return I gain, not only myself, but that someone as well; and having had but one life to begin with, through death, simply by loving, I now have two.

So now, if we extrapolate this consideration to love divine, and to the reciprocity that indeed exists between God and the soul, can one possibly begin to explain with mere words, can any amount of elucidation help us conceive what man will gain by loving God – in whom he lives, not just his own life, but the life of God (as St. Paul relates)? Whether we love God or we do not love God, to say that he himself does not loves us is a defamation we raise against him, and if that is what you think, reader, if you think that God doesn't love you, go back to the beginning of this book and start reading it again.

Oh, how many deaths God dies for loving those who do not care to love him! I can accuse myself of being the cause of many of your deaths, my loving God, for knowing that you loved me infinitely with your infinite love,[6] I did not return your love, my dear Lord, I did not even remember you, and in this I committed a *crimen laesae maiestatis*, my God and Lord, because by loving myself and wanting to have life in myself, for my part I gave you death as many times as you wanted to give me life.

Plato said that if you do not repay the debt of love, you deserve to be killed three times on account of the three crimes you have committed by not reciprocating that love: homicide,

---

[6] Cf. I. John 4:10.

theft and sacrilege. In other words, you destroyed your lover's body, stole his property, and killed his soul. Money and property are possessions of the body, but the body belongs to the soul, and if you steal the soul, you steal everything, body and property included.

But homicide would be an impossible charge against that soul who, knowing the love the heavenly Spouse had for her – such tender and bounteous love – gave herself freely to him and said: *I am for my Beloved and my Beloved will be in me*.[7] I don't know whether more beautiful words could be found in the world to express this most tender love that God has for the soul than these words voiced by the spouse. She does not say that she is for God and God is for her, she says *she is for God and so God is in her*. And to understand this, we need to remember that when our first parents sinned, God said to Eve (the first married woman, by the way): *you will be subject to your husband*.[8] The Seventy paraphrased this sentence as *Ad virum tuum conversio tua: you will be subject and converted to your husband*. From this and other passages one could infer that to be converted in another is a phrase that means to be subject and subjected to him. We have no problem understanding this metaphor when it refers to herbs and plants, especially the one called "the sunflower", which always turns towards the sun; and in the mornings, before he rises, she is already in wait, facing east. The flower is subject to the sun, as one who knows that it is from him that she derives life and growth. In the same way the wife is subject to her husband, gazing at his face, rejoicing in his presence and happiness. This is the condition of married women, queens though they may be. But the soul, the spouse of Christ, takes leave of this common law, and this curse has turned into a copious blessing such that she is able to utter those words with utmost confidence, "I am for him and he is bound to me. I am joyful, I am so blessed! All other wives in the world are subject to their husband; they are servants of their husband, but I am mistress of mine. He loves me, he desires me, he adores me, he

---

[7] *I to my beloved and his turning is to me*, (Cant. 7:10).
[8] *To the woman also he said: I will multiply thy sorrows, and thy conceptions. In sorrow shall thou bring forth children, and thou shalt be under thy husband's power, and he shall have dominion over thee*, (Gen. 3:16).

so has me in his regard he makes me his equal, nay, he wishes to subject himself to me. He seeks me, he conforms himself to my will."

And tell us, most happy spouse, do you not requite this rare love to your spouse? What do you give him in return for that amorous dependence?

Ego dilecto meo. I am wholly for my beloved. All that I am, all that I have, all that is mine is his: my property, my thoughts, my hopes, my soul, my life, all his. I want nothing of mine, I want nothing else within me. I want only him.[9]

A story is told of a certain illustrious lady in Persia. She was invited along with her husband to the dining table of the great king Cyrus who came to the feast richly dressed and arrayed, his natural gentility as well as his adornments being the cause of much admiration. When the feast was over and upon returning home, the husband asked his wife what she thought of the king, and she replied genuinely: "My dear friend, how could my eyes, which are for you only, remember what king Cyrus looks like? Where you are, my lord, there is no prince or monarch worthy of being seen." A response from a virtuous, prudent and happily married woman, for a married woman should not have anyone but her husband in her regard. Whatever he is not, she is to consider as adverse, disagreeable, and unfavourable. This lady could have very well said the words of the spouse: *I am for my beloved.*

Blessed is the soul that has reached this point of perfect love where all of herself is for God only, where nothing else will satisfy or delight her; she will have eyes for no one but her Spouse, God, in whose sight and in whose company she reposes, serene and at peace with herself. As another Mary at the feet of Christ who, reprimanded by Martha, neither excuses nor troubles herself, absorbed as she is in the word of God, hanging on his every word, melting as she hears him speak, having left the administration and management of the house to her sister. *Now it came to pass, as they went, that he entered into a certain town; and a certain woman named Martha received him into her house. And she had a sister called Mary, who, sitting also at the Lord's feet, heard his word. But Martha was busy about*

---

[9] The author refers here to "Francis Senense". This writer has not been identified [Ed.].

much serving, who stood and said: Lord, hast thou no care that my sister hath left me alone to serve? Speak to her, therefore, that she help me. And the Lord answering, said to her: Martha, Martha, thou art careful and art troubled about many things: but one thing is necessary. Mary hath chosen the best part which shall not be taken away from her. [10]

The life of holy, deified men or of gods by grace and transforming love, said Plotinus, is to disdain and ignore all delights of the earth, which consist of many of the things that unsettle and preoccupy Martha – a worried and perturbed world – and to escape to the world of Mary – the essential world.

"Little man", says St. Augustine, "what are all those flights of fancy and all those rationalisations in which you so occupy and distract yourself? Seek the one in which everything is found and be off!" Oh, if only we could arrive at that one supreme and infinite good that we might stop searching, and then rest, at one with him. Of which blessed estate Jeremiah said: *Sedebit solitarius, et tacebit, et levavit supra se.*[11]

Four very important matters are raised in this short sentence. *Settle down,* viz. the quietness and stillness to be found in God. *He will be alone,* the nakedness and isolation from the multitude. *He will keep his peace,* meaning the strict silence to be had in that place. *He will lift himself above himself,* giving to understand this transformation in God. Because the only thing above man is God himself, and man will arise above himself and terminate in Him. In agreement with this the prophet David says in one psalm: *In peace in the selfsame I will sleep and I will rest.* [12]

And let these be the last words uttered for there is nothing else to be said. Hush, now. Silence. We have finally arrived where he is in us, where we keep him, where we become most intimate with the Most High. Forget all and part with all. No need of words to him who knows, and hears, and sees all. No words because what we are now seeing and contemplating could not be retold, even if we tried.

Et tacebit, quia levavit supra se. Quia onus supra se. She will grow quiet because it is all too much, because the load exceeds her

---

[10] Luke 10:38-42.
[11] Lam. 3:28.
[12] Psalm 4:9.

strength. She will grow quiet because she feels she has been given more than she deserves. Yea, those who enter into the secrets of God bear a great weight, and his Majesty demands it as a duty not to disclose the secrets he communicates to them intimately without his consent. It is for a soul without religion to disclose these divine secrets to the crowds, because feeble souls, immature souls, will only vulgarize and debase them.

Chapter 15

On the inebriation of love

Oh, come to the wine cellar! Let us see if we can taste what the spouse tasted, as she came out of that glorious place saying: *I have eaten the honeycomb with the honey. I have drunk my wine with my milk* [1]

And because the wine is rich, and because she is generous, she invites some of her best friends, not all, to taste the wine. To drink until drunk with wine. *Drink and be inebriated, my beloved,* she says.

Isaiah the prophet had invited all to drink of the water, and then to drink of the milk and the wine. To eat well, with no need of money. To eat food that gratifies the soul with its fatness.[2]

It is the mystery, it is the secret of this passage, as indeed of the whole of the Song of Songs, that the love of God to which we are all invited because of what it is and what it does for us all, is sometimes called wine, sometimes milk; at others honey – honey in its honeycomb – at others water, and at still others "that which is good".

Rabanus explained it most elegantly in one of his sermons. He said:

In meditation, divine love is fire. Fire that purifies the soul of the filth of vices.

In prayer, it is light. Light that enlightens the soul and bathes her in the radiance and lucidness of virtue.

In grace, it is honey. Honey that sugars and sweetens the soul in the delectability of divine gifts.

In contemplation, it is free wine. Wine that inebriates the soul in jovial and merry delight.

In eternal blissfulness, it is a luminous sun that with its most serene light, cheers her ineffably and fills her with jubilation.

---

[1] *Let my beloved come into his garden, and eat the fruit of his apple trees. I am come into my garden, O my sister, my spouse. I have gathered my myrrh with my aromatical spices. I have eaten the honeycomb with my honey. I have drunk my wine with my milk. Eat, O friends, and drink, and be inebriated, my dear beloved,* (Cant. 5:1).

[2] *All you that thirst come to the waters; and you that have no money, make haste, buy and eat. Come ye. Buy wine and milk without money and without any price. Why do you spend money for that which is not bread and your labour for that which doth not satisfy you? Hearken diligently to me and eat that which is good; and your soul shalt be delighted in fatness,* (Isaiah 55: 1-2).

From these and the words of the spouse we can surmise that love induces *drunkenness*, or to speak more precisely, a laxing of the senses. And if one betaken with wine forgets himself and all about him, he who drinks of this divine wine so turns his love towards him that remembers nothing else.

Of this drunkenness spoke the prophet: *They shall be inebriated with the plenty of that house: and thou shalt make them drink of the torrent of thy pleasure.*"[3]

St. Bonaventure says that the delight of God is Christ; because those chosen are solaced, outwardly, by the sight of his flesh, and inwardly by the contemplation of his divinity.

Origen, commenting on the words of the spouse *I ate my honeycomb with my honey* affirms that honeycomb is the humanity of Christ, and honey is the most gentle divinity hidden in the virginal wax.

It is of this secret, this mysterious hiding place that St. Augustine is speaking: *O penetrable grace and sweet secret! O secret without tedium, mystery with no baneful thoughts, free from temptations and suffering!*

This is the joy into which the faithful servant is commanded to enter,[4] and of which St. Isidore said: *My heart is filled, my mouth is filled, my whole self is filled, and there is still joy left a-plenty.*

And the servant is invited to go in because the pleasures of the world can enter but do not fill; but the plenitude of this joy fills and there is much over.

The soul is commanded to go in: there are no sorrows in the taste of divinity. And she is bathed in joy and drenched in joy.

Happy is this opulent house where drink is ever abundant, this overflowing river from which everyone drinks and it never runs dry. From this copious river a few water drops will moisten the dry throats of the chosen, here in exile, and with delicacy invigorate them, and they will come out of themselves.

Said Richard of a man drunk of this wine: *He hears, and forgets the world.*

And St. Paul: *I did not know if I was in my body or out of it.* [5]

---

[3] Psalm 35:9.

[4] *And his lord said to him: Well done, good and faithful servant, because thou hast been faithful on a few things, I will place thee over many things. Enter thou into the joy of thy Lord* (Matt. 25-21).

Drunkenness causing forgetfulness of the world and of the self. But this glorious state of inebriation, says the same Doctor, means more than the estrangement of the bodily senses; it is an infusion of grace anew, and a wonderful manifestation of celestial secrets.

The wine is well chosen in the House of God. A wine, the prophet said, from which the dwellers of the House drink and of which they are drunk. And Richard urges: *Whosoever wishes for this inebriation, and to frequent its excesses and mysteries, love!* Love intimately, love supremely the Redeemer of man, love him with utmost desire, yearn all hours and all minutes for the joy of divine contemplation, and your soul regaled, intoxicated, with this plenitude of such inner delicacy, will forget what she is, and what she has been, she will forget herself. With exceeding joy she will be taken to the excesses of love and ecstasy, and for a brief moment be transformed above its humanity in a state of glorious felicity.

Do not be surprised at these words, said Vercelense,[6] *such is the efficacy of love, and goodness, and beauty, that not only make men and angels leave their natures, but in some way make God, with no necessity, almost come out of himself and lower himself to his creatures, and acquiesce and serve to them, and provide them with all.*

Brother David,[7] a high and most admirable contemplative, says that *inebriation of the spirit can be called any devotion of supreme love and supreme joy: that, like fermenting wine, the fervour of the spirit grows to the point where it can no longer be suppressed, or contained.* That was what was believed of the Apostles who, filled with the Spirit of God, were believed to be filled with wine.[8]

And a friend of holy Job confesses that he had the fermenting must of wine inside his heart, trying to break open. *For I am full of matter to speak of, and the spirit of my bowels straineth me. Behold, my belly is as new wine which wanteth vent, which bursteth the new vessels.* [9] My

---

[5] *I know a man in Christ; above fourteen years ago (whether in the body, or out of the body I know not; God knoweth) that he was so caught up into paradise and heard secret words which it is not granted to man to utter* (II Cor. 12:2).

[6] Unknown author, possibly John of Vercelli, *Intro. super Cant.* [Honeycomb].

[7] David of Augusta, d. 1272, *De exterioris et interioris hominis compositione*, P.III, c. LXIV.

[8]. Acts 2:7-13.

[9] Job 32:18-19.

belly, that is, my entrails, my heart, he says, was as wine fermenting without vents that bursts out of new vessels. New, he says, not old. Because in old hearts haggard with sins, devotion such as this is not infused. Or because the new are not readied to hold his devotion of the soul and break out in voices and gestures, weeping and joyous. As new wine bubbles in the glass, as when old it will be in quiet and repose.

We have a good example of this in the *Libro de Conformidades* of our Order. There, it is written of our Father, St. Francis, that, whilst at prayer, begging God for poverty, that richest of treasures, he was visited spiritually and in such a manner inflamed for love and covetousness of Blessed Lady Poverty, that it seemed his face was about to burst open and burning flames of fire were coming out of his mouth. And he went, as intoxicated, to his companion Brother Masseo and said: "Oh, Oh, Oh, Brother Masseo, give me of yourself". He said this three times. And Brother Masseo, bewildered and terrified at this intensity and fervour of spirit, having heard the request three times, threw himself into his arms and embraced him. And our glorious Father, inhaling deeply and with a loud outcry, his spirit overflowing and still saying "Oh, Oh, Oh", picked him up in the air and thrust him as far as he could, as he would a spear. Poor old Brother Masseo landed on the floor not knowing what to make of it all, but he later told the Brothers that he received more consolation and joy in being launched like a missile by our blessed Father than at any other time in his life.

Remember, too, that the body partakes of this superabundance of spiritual inebriation and our limbs may appear incompetent and unable to move. The reason for this may well be that, owing to the intense affection of the heart, the spirit overflows over the whole body and the limbs, in turn, lose their capacity to act owing to the over-extension of the nerves, the obstruction and blocking of the vents, or channels, of the physical, animal life-force. And to such a degree that the mouth can't talk, hands and feet move with no rhyme or reason, and this goes on until fervour subsides, and the channels necessary for the sensorial humours to operate are open again.

Do not be so surprised that divine affection can have this effect! Many human passions can do this sometimes – I am thinking of a sudden, unexpected fright, or excessive rage, happiness, hate, or carnal love. Ammon, son of David, took ill for love of Thamar, most beautiful sister of Absalom.[10] And we know of many other who suffered ecstasies, spasms, and other frenzies brought about by love, and their bodies were left shaking and their limbs with no movement, as dead. And if this is so, is it any wonder that in a state of overmuch joy, infused in the human heart by the Holy Spirit, there will be some that, unable to restrain this inner joy, will manifest externally what they feel? Sometimes we see them laughing, as if mad, with little reason, with no means to stop it. But who will have the means for this frail human body not to be affected by such overwhelming joy? It is not possible to keep fire in a bottle, especially in a bottle with its stopper on, without it breaking forth and into fragments. It is possible for the Spirit of God, which is fire, to enter inside the human heart, and this, enlarged and dilated, explode and reveal by external means that which burns inside. We read this of several saints who fell on the ground, their strength impaired, when visited by God, as Scripture says of Daniel.[11]

St. Bonaventure says that before our soul is come to that dream and rapture to which very few arrive, she will experience two kinds of inebriation. One is an overflowing of joy in the heart and a vehement jubilation in the soul, either because of intense desire for eternal life and a deeply-felt and thoughtful reflection on the Passion of Christ, or because of great ardour of one's love for God, as it comes to our mind: new, certain, infused light. And this joy so abounds in the heart that, as has been said, it spills over into the rest of the body as well, making it jump for joy. And this soul, overjoyous and as under the influence of wine, wanders about hastily, with no repose, embracing all she finds in her way, unconcerned with the temporal, because she sees its banality.

---

[10] II Kings 13:1-2.
[11] Dan. 8:16-19.

The second kind of inebriation happens when the heart is filled to the brim with ease and sweetness, resulting from its familiarity with God. This mellowness comes via the quiet of contemplation and spreads – as does the former – to the externals in such a manner that the inner and outer seem to be distilling and overflowing honey and sweet delight.

The first inebriation cannot suffer quietness because of the surfeit of joy, and if it is not so intense as to cause drowsiness, it does not completely take away consciousness, or prevent activity; although the inebriated soul – as one under the influence of wine – is not left altogether free either.

Both kinds of inebriation are advantageous and pleasing. But the second, caused by oversweetness, is a little suspect. One should be prudent and cautious because, as the Apostle says, Satan likes to transfigure himself in angel of light, and procures sweetness to contemplatives, not in order to regale them, but to gain them for himself, making them believe they are special so that, touched by conceit, they may be miserably cast aside by God.[12] He will let false lovers with their false sweetness start thinking highly of themselves, making slight of others, thinking they are close to God when they are in fact far away.

Oh with what diligence one must be on the lookout! Whenever we sense being close to God let us not take our heart away from him: let us allow delight to come only from him. And with our heart firmly in him only, should the delight grow and spread, then we will know it is from God, and should it shrink and come to naught, we can be sure it is from the devil. And so that we may do away once and for all with all his traps and loops, we must always judge ourselves unworthy of all divine visitation, and if we are indeed visited, let us persevere and grow in humility and thanks-giving.

There is one difficulty remaining in this chapter, not less important that what we have been saying so far.

When we consult the Latin language we see that inebriation means something excessive, without measure. And it does not seem right to say that while here, in exile, a soul can have an

---

12 II Cor. 11:14.

excess of love for God. Scripture tells us that this corruptible body, decaying, little by little crumbling, keeps the soul down and does not let her empty herself in God completely.

To answer this difficulty, let us consider love in three ways: first, in itself, so we say it is finite, something that can be measured as any other finite thing can be measured; secondly, according to the lover's circumstances - so it must be treated as any other virtue: to be exercised how, when and where it should be exercised because, owing to the tie it has with the body, and with contemplation leading to excess, it would endanger itself or receive notable damage. Thirdly, it has to be considered in relation to the object of love, that is, in that it is directed towards God who is infinitely worthy of our love. It is in this aspect that there cannot be excess, nor should it be restricted, as there cannot be excess in praising him, because he exceeds all praise, as Ecclesiastes says.

St. Bonaventure in his *Soliloquy* says that previous disposition to obtain that sweetest and temperate inebriation of the spirit is the uplifting of the mind by means of which the soul is separated from earthly considerations and raise above herself and above all creatures, in a way that she can say with the spouse: *the king entered in my cellar and gave me rich wine from which friends drink, and the closest friends become drunk.* O blessed drunkenness that causes such temperance of body and soul!

St. Bonaventure warns in the above-cited passage that the motive for loving God is God himself, with no number or measure, or prescribed formulae. In Deuteronomy, however, God specified in the law the way in which he wanted to be loved by us, saying *you shall love God with all your heart, with all your soul, and with all your strength.* But this is not to prescribe one way of loving God, but rather a guidance for how the faculties of the soul should love.

But what I ask of you now, my soul, is that you love God with singular love for the Father, who created you from nothing with such dignity. And love God the Son, who so ineffably reformed you by means of his death. And love the Holy Spirit who, consoling with his mercy, many a time took you away from sin and confirmed you in goodness. *Love your God gently,* says St.

Bernard, *until any other love you love becomes a wicked love in your eyes, and only this love may be honey in your lips, sweet music in your ears, jubilation in your heart. Love him prudently, so that this one and no other may burn continually. Love him mightily, so that your fragility will suffer all harshness with joy for Christ, and so that you can say: this suffering is transient, and should it last, I shall not know it: so great is my love.*

Chapter 16

On Rapture — different names in Scripture.

The greatest and principal property of love is rapture.

Rapture has been defined by saints as the uplifting of the soul's superior faculties over her inferior ones. The force and intensity of the superior faculties cause the lower faculties to be left behind, detached and separated from the soul and weakened in such a manner that they remain unequipped to stop or hinder the superior faculty in this operation.

In order to understand this definition, we should first consider that rapture, by its very name, implies a violent act against the natural propensity of things, as when a stone is thrown up into mid-air, or an iron is pulled away from its magnet. The same can be said of the soul that has been rapt and uplifted above all things from the external and sensuous to the inner and most high. It, too, undergoes violence of a kind, because this uplifting is not co-natural with the order of present life as we know it. What is natural is to climb from the visible to the invisible, and when this process is not being followed because the lower faculties have ceased to operate, the soul is said to have been enraptured. This is the first consideration.

The second is that, although our soul is un-compounded and simple in its substance, its quantities of operation are manifold and indivisibly bound, and for that reason when the soul diverts itself towards any one thing, it diverts itself in its totality. From which it follows that, when it applies itself intensely in the operation of one faculty, it will subside and slacken in the operation of another, whichever that other faculty may be. And so it is that when it is powerfully actuated during rapture in the exercise of the superior faculty, it is weakened, or ceases, in the exercise of the inferior ones. In Scripture, this weakening – or cessation – of the inferior faculties of the soul is called *fainting*. Thus, in contemplation, the higher the soul is uplifted, the greater its withdrawal from the senses becomes, and when contemplation is at its most intense, the senses cease to operate, and the soul is seen to disappear, as happens during rapture.

The third consideration is this. Since rapture occurs with the cessation and suspension of the operative powers of the lower faculties, he is said to be in ecstasy and *out of himself* who – with regard to the cognitive powers – will surpass self-awareness and the proportionate knowledge of the self in relation to others; and – with regard to the affective powers – by the attraction and pull the other exercises over him, leaves himself behind.

The former – the cognitive – is effected by disposition or inclination, wherein love is engaged upon reflecting on the thing loved, because intense meditation upon one thing takes us and abstracts us from all else.

The latter – the affective – takes place directly: in *amiticia*, or love of friendship, simply and absolutely; in concupiscent love only partly and *secundum quid*. I say partly because in concupiscent love, although the lover, in some way, *goes out of himself*, this is only because, not content with rejoicing in what he himself has, he seeks delectation outside of himself by means of the other. And since this good that he is procuring for himself is a good external to himself, it cannot properly be called *coming out of himself*, in the sense of going beyond, or above, himself, but rather, affection is placed lower to himself, in its aim. In love of friendship, however, one can truly speak of affection making the lover *go beyond himself* because the lover wants the good outside himself, not for himself, but for the other; he acts for the other as if the other was himself, and the only motive and reason and aim is the other, not himself, which is what the divine Dionysius had in mind when he said: *love does not allow lovers to belong to themselves, but only to the object of their love.*

We are now to consider the fourth point and it is this. Rapture can occur in three ways, to wit, by means of the imagination, reason, and *mens*, or mind. I shall concentrate exclusively on the latter for such is, after all, the subject of our inquiry (the first two being of a much lower carat gold in comparison).

Let me first say that by mind here I mean the whole image of God in man in whose image and likeness he was made, that is to say, in the word mind I include intellectual memory, intelligence, and natural will, which dispose man towards God, to the divine in man, to things higher than himself, not just to any piece of meat that is placed before his nose. And man is quite capable of doing this.

Rapture of the mind over the lower faculties occurs by means of ecstatic love whereby our mind, recollected and focused in all its intensity and might, is moved to action, perfected, and uplifted to God, and she becomes one spirit with him. And she will see and know of nothing else. And through ecstatic love and by force of the natural will, or spark, which is the same thing, she now tastes the delectability of God.

In order that I might conclude on this subject of rapture, understood by so few and experienced by fewer still, I will say only that rapture is brought about in two ways: by the soul's cognitive and by its affective faculties. Through the former, one enquires into the nature of God, his essence and his works based on considerations founded on the Catholic and True Faith. And this contemplation is profitable for finding new truths within this Truth, or to confirm and inform those we already possess or have learnt by the Gospel's teaching. Through the affective faculties there is little in the way of inquisition and much in another kind of knowledge, a clearer knowledge – one that can be had by all, the clever, the unlearned and yes, even simpletons – for all that is required is to banish all cares of the world and keep a clean heart.

I'll tell you another true story. This one is about Brother Giles who was a faithful companion to our glorious Father, St. Francis. Now Brother Giles was not what you might call a scholar – dull-witted would perhaps be more accurate. But Brother Giles would experience ecstasies continuously, and to the extent of seeing the Divine Essence, as some say; and this he himself confirmed on his death bed. Now, St. Antoninus of Florence tells us that Brother Giles was so famous for his raptures that the shepherds and young lads of the village would tease him and laugh at him and the moment they saw him coming would call out: "Hey, hey, Brother Giles! Heaven! Paradise!" And off Brother Giles would go into one of his raptures.

The Pope himself invited him to dinner once – Pope Gregory IX – just to see if all this was on the level, and Brother Giles went into rapture three times, right there in front of him, and the

Pontiff saw for himself that he was left unconscious and even that no pulse could be discerned.

When the seraphic St. Bonaventure was our General, Brother Giles approached him one day with these words: "Father Bonaventure, clever people have really received a great gift from God, haven't they, but what can we do, we stupid, who know nothing?"

And St. Bonaventure replied: "The greatest gift God has granted to each and every one of us is our capacity to love him, and this gift would in itself be sufficient even if all others were lacking."

"Can an idiot like me love as much as a learned man?" asked Brother Giles.

"Brother Giles, can a little old grandmother love as much as a Doctor of Theology?" St. Bonaventure answered.

At these words Brother Giles in a heat sprang up from his chair, opened the door, ran into the garden and facing the city, at the top of his lungs proclaimed: "Hear me, all you idiotic little old grandmothers everywhere! Love God and you will be holier than Father Bonaventure!"

And off into rapture he went again. Three hours this time.

Good Brother Giles used to say he had been born four times: from his mother, in Baptism, in his Profession as a Religious, and the fourth time during a rapture he had had at Cetona, after which birth he said he no longer needed faith for he had now seen what faith teaches us. And questioned by his companion, Brother Andrew of Burgundy how, if he no longer had faith, he could go on and say *Credo in unum Deum* during Mass, simple Brother Giles could reply with these words: *I don't believe, I know, there's a God Almighty.*

So, to recapitulate: rapture brought about by means of the affective faculties is the most excellent of all, for the others can be brought about by the superior faculty in relation to the inferior ones, but ecstasy is effected by the whole of the mind in its totality, not only by a weakening of the lower faculties but also, because of its duration, by actually suspending them all.

These affective raptures are given difference names by saints and in Scripture. Sometimes they are called a *Division between Soul and Spirit*, sometimes *Entrance into Divine Darkness*, other times *Ecstasy*, still others *Rapture, Silence, Being in Spirit, Being out of Spirit*. For each one mentioned – and still others – the Doctors of the Church have had many and very important things to say but since, with God's blessing, I intend to treat of this elsewhere, I thought it prudent to end here, begging God our Lord to enrapture us and take us to him, that we may rejoice in his Light, by grace in this life, by glory in the next. Amen.

LAUS DEO

Subscribers to the Honeycomb series

The Saint Austin Press gratefully acknowledges the support of the following individuals who have made possible the publication of this edition by their subscription.

Rev. R.W. Hugh Allen, Coity, Bridgend.

Rev. C.W. Baker, Chatham, Kent.

Dr. G.J. Berry, Woodhall Spa, Lincolnshire.

Mr. Robert Binyon, London.

Rev. S.D. Brown, Leeds.

Rev. Christopher Connor, Edgware, Middlesex.

Mrs. J. Curtin, Helston, Cornwall.

Mr. Michael J. Doolan, Tremorfa, Cardiff.

Mr. Ray Duffy, Meols Wirrall, Merseyside.

Dr. M.D.E. Evans, Burghclere, nr. Newbury, Berkshire.

Mr. Lionel Gracey, Sunningdale, Berkshire.

Mr. George Grynowski, Raimals, Wellingborough, Northamptonshire.

Rev. Michael W. Hawkins, Pleasantville, Nova Scotia.

The Headmaster, St. Ambrose College, Altrincham, Cheshire.

Mr. Kevin Hickey, Church Accrington, Lancashire.

Fr. James B. Hurley, Wimbledon, London.

Professor Paul Jackson, University of Reading.

Mr. Neville McNally, Southsea, Hampshire.

Mr. Peter Molony, Great Elm, Somerset.

Miss Janet Boyd Moss, Edinburgh.

Mr. Daniel Moylan, London.

Mr. Christopher Newton, Ripe, East Sussex.

Mr. V.G. Osborn, Leicester.

Mr. J.V. Parker, Leicester.

Mr. Michael Parsons, Newton Abbott, Devon.

Mr. J.C. Petrie, Orrell, Wigan, Lancashire.

Mr. G.J. Pinsard, Saint Sampson's, Guernsey.

Mr. Michael Price, Manselton, Swansea.

Mr. Peter Pryer, Church Crookham, Fleet, Hampshire.

Rev. Roman Przetak, Lower Bullingham, Hereford.

Mr. Christopher K. Rance, Dulwich, London.

Rev. Scott M. P. Reid, Farnborough, Hampshire.

Mr. John A. Richards, Orton Wistow, Peterborough.

Mr. David J. Scorey, Cheadle, Staffordshire.

Mr. Anthony F. Schmitz, Aberdeen.

Dr. Margaret Sealey, Shirley, Solihull.

Miss I.H.S. Shaw, Port Navas, Falmouth, Cornwall.

Mr. G.V. Shugg, London.

Mr. J. Smiles, Brewood, Staffordshire.

Mr. P.A.H. Thomas, K.S., Eton College, Eton, Berkshire.

Mrs. Leslie von Goetz, Newport-on-Tay, Fife.

Fr. Eric Wright, Chelsea, London.

Fr. William Young, Barking, Essex.